Seeing Sociologically

Great Barrington Books

Bringing the old and new together
in the spirit of W. E. B. Du Bois

∾ An imprint edited by Charles Lemert ∾

Titles Available

Keeping Good Time: Reflections on Knowledge, Power, and People
by Avery F. Gordon (2004)

Going Down for Air: A Memoir in Search of a Subject
by Derek Sayer (2004)

The Souls of Black Folk
100th Anniversary Edition
by W. E. B. Du Bois, with commentaries by Manning Marable,
Charles Lemert, and Cheryl Townsend Gilkes (2004)

Sociology After the Crisis, Updated Edition
by Charles Lemert (2004)

*The Protestant Ethic Turns 100: Essays on the Centenary of the Weber
Thesis*
edited by William H. Swatos Jr., and Lutz Kaelber (2005)

Seeing Sociologically: The Routine Grounds of Social Action
by Harold Garfinkel, edited and introduced by Anne Warfield Rawls (2006)

Harold Garfinkel

Seeing Sociologically
The Routine Grounds of Social Action

Edited and introduced by
Anne Warfield Rawls

Foreword by Charles Lemert

Paradigm Publishers
Boulder • London

Copyright © 2006 by Paradigm Publishers

Published in the United States by Paradigm Publishers, 3360 Mitchell Lane, Suite E, Boulder, Colorado 80301 USA.

Paradigm Publishers is the trade name of Birkenkamp & Company, LLC, Dean Birkenkamp, President and Publisher.

Library of Congress Cataloging-in-Publication Data

Garfinkel, Harold.
    Seeing sociologically: the routine grounds of social action / Harold Garfinkel; edited and introduced by Anne Warfield Rawls; foreword by Charles Lemert.
        p. cm.
    ISBN 1-59451-092-X (hc) — ISBN 1-59451-093-8 (pbk)
    1. Ethnomethodology.   I. Rawls, Anne Warfield, 1950–   II. Title.
HM481.G375 2005
305.8'001—dc22

2005012522

Printed and bound in the United States of America on acid-free paper that meets the standards of the American National Standard for Permanence of Paper for Printed Library Materials.

Designed and Typeset by Straight Creek Bookmakers.

10 09 08 07 06
5 4 3 2 1

Contents

Foreword   *Charles Lemert*   *vii*

Respecifying the Study of Social Order—Garfinkel's Transition
from Theoretical Conceptualization to Practices in Details
  Anne Warfield Rawls   1

Introduction   Harold Garfinkel   99

Part I: Principal Theoretical Notions   101
  Action   101
  Actor   107
  Role and the Concept of the Finite Province of Meaning   117
  Noesis-Noema Structures   132
  Social Identity   145
  Identity Constancy and Identity Transformation   151
  Communication   179
  Style, Tactics, and Strategies of Communication   182
  Group   189

Part II: Specific Problems   205
  Statement of Thesis Problems   205

Notes to *Seeing Sociologically*   217

References   219

Index   227

About the Author and Editor   239

Foreword

The Indexical Properties of Sociological Time

Charles Lemert

The most common, if regressive, complaint about sociology as a sci-ence is that it fails to produce *cumulative* knowledge. The field may be properly divided into those who agree and those who don't care one way or the other. Those who care, however, care very much—to the point of dismissing the careless as a curse on their high scientific aspirations. In real life, the differences matter hardly at all. The scientific sociologists with an interest in cumulative knowledge do not read or talk with the others, although they may occasionally socialize with, if only because, as in all walks of life, the careless tend to be more fun.

Then every now and a while along comes someone like Harold Garfinkel who defies the established norms of the disciplinary game. I do not mean to suggest that Garfinkel is a defiant person. We have met only once. I found him kind and generous. I mean that such a one as this rarely comes along to think and work at odds with the prevailing norms. This Garfinkel has been doing since his graduate school days at Harvard. *Seeing Sociologically: The Routine Grounds of Social Action* was written, according to Anne Rawls, in 1948, after which it circulated wide and far to generate a considerable discussion among fellow students of the day, including Erving Goffman. To illustrate just how long ago 1948 was in real time, I suggest that most of the people alive today never tried to use something called a mimeograph, a technique for copying text only slightly more advanced, and surely less beautiful, than the medieval means of handing over the copying work to monks and scribes. We who once tried to use the process remember, first, of the ink that smeared our hands and running noses. Close after we remember how arduous the process was—requiring careful typing on a chemically treated page. The effect was to imprint words or characters into a gooey substance on the back of the page. One then attached the page to a roller, and turned a crank, to produce an impression on copy paper. The worst thing about mimeography is that there was no way to correct typos other than to start the page over. Hence another miraculous quality of Garfinkel's 1948 text is that it entailed 141 pages of mimeography. The mind boggles to think of the labor involved. Then too one is astonished that anyone could have begun a reflexive sociology of any kind on mimeograph which may be the least reflexive of all known methods for reproducing the written word. It is well known that the ancient scribes went back to their copy to correct in artful ways that surely changed the meaning of the originals.

Yet, there is another, more urgent, lesson to be learned from this work—a lesson more directly apt to sociology's understanding of its scientific vocation. If one had only one word to describe Garfinkel's contribution to the theory of social action, that word would be "indexicality," a concept behind the present text but one that did not emerge in its full technical meaning until twenty years later in *Studies in Ethnomethodology* (1967), where he gave his now famous, if to somewhat inscrutable, definition of ethnomethodology:

> I use the term "ethnomethodology" to refer to the investigation of the rational properties of indexical expressions and other practical actions as contingent ongoing accomplishments of organized artful practices of everyday life.

The genius of Harold Garfinkel's ethnomethodology lay in the way it accomplished, not just a theory of indexical process but achieved it under one of that age's least reflexive, though ironically indexical, writers: Talcott Parsons.

Parsons was once famous for what some readers consider his needlessly obscure writing style. He was one of my teachers. I had very little trouble understanding him—though this may have been due to prior training I had enjoyed in systematic theology—another notably abstract subject the referents of which are decidedly obscure and by definition beyond common-sense experience. For me the differences between Paul Tillich and Parsons—who lectured one year across the Harvard Yard from each other—was mostly a matter of vocabulary, not of method or purpose. For myself, I was taken in by both subjects. What separates Garfinkel from others is that, unlike me, he was not taken in and, unlike others, like C. Wright Mills, he was not obsessively critical of Parsons.

In fact, the wonder of *Seeing Sociologically,* apart from its enormous informative value, is the witness it offers (most especially to the young) as to how one can *both* work within the tradition as it is handed down by one's teachers *and* set off in a new, if not entirely new, direction—one that illuminates the tradition while moving it forward. This, precisely, is what one encounters in *Seeing Sociologically*—a thirty-one-year-old graduate student's thesis proposal that seizes the heart of his teacher's thinking and turns it on its ear to good and responsible effect.

The seed of the ethomethodological ideal, quoted just above, is found in that proposal's original title (which, truth be told, hints at the teacher's literary style without being bound thereto): "Prospectus for an exploratory study of communicative effort and the modes of understanding in selected types of dyadic relationships." In the retrospect of nearly sixty years it is stunning to read the key phrase in this mouthful: "communicative effort." In 1948, social theory's interest in communication theory and language was still a good quarter century in the future, as was sociology's appreciation of the fact that practical life is always an "effort" before, and if, it becomes an accomplishment. To write of "communicative effort" in that day was to transpose the concerns of Talcott Parsons to define and adumbrate a general theory of social action. This Parsons did, brilliantly I think, by setting forth an analytic scheme meant to systematize the distinctively social aspects of action in relation to the action systems with which the social actor must contend—namely, as Parsons often put it, against the limiting conditions of cultural meanings on the one hand and biological adaptations on the other. What Garfinkel did, already in 1948, and just as brilliantly, was to reformulate the idea of social action—as, in his words:

> ACTION. The problem of defining what is meant by this term is the problem of laying down the rules by which the observer goes about the business of idealizing phenomenal presentations which can be referred to for their origin to some person other than the observer. This means that the term, action, must be regarded for our purposes as a term peculiar to the investigative vocabulary of the scientific observer. This reservation is necessary because we shall see later that the agents being studied have their own notions as to what it is that they see, where they see it, what causes the appearance of the thing that's seen, how obviously the thing seen presents itself for treatment, and so on.

Another mouthful, this is. But not one that requires the reader to escape the realities of practical actions, which are, to be sure, a proper topic of scientific study, but only if the student accounts for what the actor must account for: "that the agents being studied have their own notions as what it is that they see," and so on. The "and so on," by the way, is more important than one might suppose. If, as Garfinkel's subsequent work went on to show in ever more alluring detail, a sociology must begin with the practical actor's methods for "seeing sociologically," then all sociologies, high or low, must take on the attitude necessary for life in the quotidian. In the course of daily life, action and meaning (that is to say: communicative effort) are always a matter of "and so on." Tasks are immediate and local, in the now and here. We focus, or bracket, our attentions on this or that one—calling the plumber, picking up the kids, closing the thoracic incision, or running the data, and so on. But always something enters to disturb the attention, if only one of those engaged in a parallel and similar task. "Honey, would you call the plumber after you pick up the kids at soccer?" Or: "He is bleeding out!" Or: "The server is down. We apologize for the inconvenience." These are the others to the others of the observer. Social action is, as some might want to say, engaged, but in the sense of embedded with on-going actors who are unrelentingly intrusive when they are not being helpful. As a result, as Garfinkel says in his original definition of action, the sociologist's "idealization of phenomenal presentations ... can be referred for their origin to some person other than the observer."

It is not just that the "some person other" is closer to the action at hand but that the "person other than the observer" is engaged in the same process of repair of the "and so on" character of the action at hand. And here precisely is the important difference Garfinkel took from Parsons. To see sociologically is not to look down upon the course of practical action, but to see from the complicating position of the method of the actors. Ethnomethodology is not so much a hermeneutic of the meaningful intentions of actors as it is, literally (if the word can be used), a method for investigating methods people use in the course of action. Ethnomethods do not conform to the sociologist's idealization—her analytic vocabulary even though, in the end, her "investigative vocabulary" is the one that must be used to study the routine grounds of practical action.

Put differently, sociology is neither an analytic nor an interpretative one, but a science, if I may say it this way, that cannot neglect the fact that the grounded theory is much more than an empirically tested or subjectively adequate one. Ethnomethodology, as it came to be after 1948, is the science that reasons as actors reason—a science of reasons that begin in the irregularities of practical life, which in turn are irregular because actors must constantly reflect on their own reasons for acting, reasons that are inherently practical (thus untidy) and never pure perfect logic. The initiated understand, more or less easily, that these actions are reflexive in that one must constantly, at the least, answer questions (many of them implicit) as to why one does what one must do. How then does a practical one "reflect" on the grounds of his routines? By, in the key word, indexically repairing them. To the degree that the term "reflexive" may be accessible to a first-time reader, the word "indexical" is likely to be inaccessible. Yet, if you have read this far with reasonable comprehension (or, at least, with the hope of comprehension), then you will note that the word "indexical" has been used several times without much accounting for its meaning. Most competent talkers and readers, while unaware of the rules, can inspect their talk and readily learn that this is the way the "communicative effort" works. One does not listen or read therein to capture the available meanings. Nor, in the language of this day, are the meanings "constructed." The meanings are in fact the reasons and rules whereby the actions are not so much intended as repaired. Strictly speaking, "to indicate" is to "point out" as in the index finger with which most English-language users point to stuff. Indexicality, thus, is the on-going, and so on, effort to lay down the rules of the daily round in which repair is made of the meaningful actions that scientists and dictionary writers attempt to stipulate. Social action goes forward, therefore, not because actors intend something or, even, because structures dictate a course of action, but because actors are somehow able to repair the uncertainties into which they throw themselves once their feet hit the floor at first light. The reader, thus, who has got this far on hope alone has got to this sentence by an unwarranted confidence in her ability eventually to point out in the due course of this *and so on* whatever will come into view. Seeing sociologically is to see the method by which practical actors see and account for the indexical properties of "practical actions as contingent ongoing accomplishments of organized artful practices of everyday life." Whether or not the reader *gets the point* is not nearly so important as the likelihood that she persists in the reading, as in the acting, to believe that reflecting back on the action will yield a *way of pointing out* its properties, the meanings of which are less to the point than the ability artfully to practice the "communication effort."

Sociology is slow to find its way. Those who want it to be a pure (or real) science are barking up just as wrong a tree as are those who don't care about the science of social things. Harold Garfinkel's work is as sure an evidence as one could hope for that seeing sociologically is a cumulative effort. What the accumulators neglect is that cumulative knowledge is never, or at least seldom, continuous and progressive. All sciences are corrupted by false starts and reversals. Remember cold fusion. Ponder intelligent design. The cumulative value of Garfinkel's *Seeing Sociologically* is that it provides a look at the foundations of the method by which he saw sociologically what came to pass. There is no tragedy, I think, in the fact that sociology proper has been slow to accept the lesson Garfinkel teaches:

If only one realizes that social action is reflexive, and that sociology is thus the science of the indexical work of the daily, then cumulative knowledge is a knowledge that moves not so much step-by-step, but back and forth over the time of social things which is a time that suits neither clock nor calendar. The time of the social is neither cyclical nor linear but the time of the assurance of things hoped for in the *and so on* of social life.

Respecifying the Study of Social Order—Garfinkel's Transition from Theoretical Conceptualization to Practices in Details

Anne Warfield Rawls

Harold Garfinkel's attempt to redirect attention toward the lived details of enacted practice through the study of "ethnomethods" (folk methods) for accomplishing practical activities has come increasingly to influence contemporary studies of situated social practice and is emerging as one of the more important arguments of the latter twentieth century. Indeed, studies of workplace practices, and communities of practice,[1] are increasingly influential in business, science and technology, computer science and AI (artificial intelligence), as well as in sociology and other academic disciplines.

While the insights generated by detailed Ethnomethodological research have grown in influence, however, students of practice have often felt compelled to reconstruct its theoretical foundations, citing the alleged failure of Garfinkel himself to do so, and frequently invoking pragmatist or phenomenological positions, rejected by Garfinkel, in the process. To further confuse the issue, those inspired by Garfinkel's teaching but who take a more technical methodological approach, or write in more conventional terms, have been better received by established disciplines and, as a consequence, have come to overshadow and define his position. Thus, ironically, Garfinkel's argument increases in influence at the same time that the understanding and appreciation of its theoretical foundations and implications have become more obscure and contradictory.

In this context of both increasing influence and increasing misinterpretation, the present book fills a void. *Seeing Sociologically: The Routine Grounds of Social Action,* written in 1948, represents Garfinkel's early elaboration of the relationship between his developing framework of ideas and mainstream sociology. The manuscript, published here for the first time, was written by Garfinkel as a proposal for a dissertation that was never written. He soon realized that the research proposed would be a life's work. It has been.

Originally titled "Prospectus for an Exploratory Study of Communicative Effort and the Modes of Understanding in Selected Types of Dyadic Relationship," the document has had an interesting history. Distributed in mimeograph form to a group of graduate students at Harvard, it fell into the hands of several key thinkers early on: Erving Goffman, Anselm Strauss, and Harvey Sacks among them. While its intersection with, and influence on, the work of these and other prominent scholars would be enough to make the manuscript important, in it Garfinkel takes up essential issues that he does not address theoretically anywhere else.

When I first saw this manuscript in Garfinkel's files in the summer of 2001 I was immediately struck by its importance. It represents a first attempt by Garfinkel to articulate his developing vision of sociology, addressing theoretical issues fundamental to his understanding of studies of situated practice in ways that shed light on the development of his thinking. It has the potential to clarify the relationship between his approach and other perspectives, particularly Pragmatism and Phenomenology, with which it is often conflated.[2] But it also highlights the degree to which Garfinkel was, from the first, focused on communicative interaction and situated reason broadly conceived. As such, the manuscript offers insights into the transition between his early and later work and has the potential to clarify misconceptions about both.

The manuscript represents Garfinkel's earliest attempt to bridge a gap that was emerging in American Sociology in the postwar 1940s, as sociologists began to turn their attention to the problem of morality and character in modern society, between a Parsonian paradigm emphasizing a scientific approach to sociological description through conceptual reduction and the concrete social phenomena from which that approach was increasingly distancing itself. By contrast, Garfinkel found in the work of the Phenomenologists Alfred Schütz and Aaron Gurwitsch a serious attempt to treat the details of social phenomena as essential to meaning, order, coherence, and understanding.

In sketching out the problem of an adequate scientific description of action, the manuscript raises issues that are of great contemporary concern and does so through a demonstration of the relative importance of practice in details versus conceptual reduction. In making this argument, however, Garfinkel did not simply adopt the positions of Schütz and Gurwitsch; rather, he used their insights as a jumping-off point for his own efforts. He also elaborated the differences between his position and the interactionism based on Mead and Pragmatism that was developing at the time.

What Garfinkel crafts is a novel perspective on situated action and situated actors, and in articulating these relationships in a context of what he calls "communicative effort," he elaborates a sequential relationship between actors in a vivid interactional present that provides a unique theoretical foundation for his later empirical studies of situated practice. In so doing he addresses issues of intentionality, reflexivity, motivation, conceptual typification, situated identity, role, social relations, and symbolic meaning—in each case criticizing accepted views and formulating a new approach.

Whereas Garfinkel in his later work increasingly refused to articulate the theoretical questions and implications of his work, this document attempted a thorough theoretical elaboration of the problems and conflicts in the work of those he was closest to—Gurwitsch, Schütz and Parsons—and those he distinguished himself from—James, Peirce, Mead, and Dewey—and did so as a way of staging the initial theoretical space for his own argument.

When, standing there with the manuscript in my hands for the first time, I asked Harold why he had not published it, he gave me two answers. First, he said that Goffman had repeatedly encouraged him to publish it. In fact, Goffman not only was enthusiastic about the manuscript (having read it sometime before 1953 when he reported his reading of it to Saul Mendlovitz) but had commented extensively on it. Garfinkel showed me a copy of the manuscript with Goffman's marginal notes all over it—still in his file drawer. Goffman's encouragement as a reason *not* to publish might seem odd. But, simply put, Goffman's continued emphasis in his own work on conceptual types, or typifications, concerned Garfinkel.

For Goffman the world of action was essentially messy and lacking order. It was the actor's job to create the *appearance* of order—a thin veneer of consensus. For Garfinkel, by contrast, the world of embodied practice—created and lived in by groups of actors working in cooperation with one another—was ordered in and through their efforts and had coherence and meaning only in and through—or as—recognizable orders of practice. This could not be a fictional, or messy, order; and the consensus, or "trust," underlying it needed to be real and substantial, not thin or only apparent. It was *necessarily* a visibly, hearably, recognizably just-so order, made in and through real reciprocities of trust. To view things otherwise was to allow conceptual reduction to hide the achieved coherence of events: to render social order *invisible,* as Garfinkel would repeatedly say.

If Goffman, who understood social order as a fiction, and was willing to reduce the actor and social action to types, liked the manuscript so much, then maybe Garfinkel's own argument—that the abstraction of *anything* from the actor or action rendered description *unintelligible* because recognizable order had actually to *be achieved* on the spot, in specifiable details of practice, and was *not a fiction,* was not clear enough in the manuscript. In this case he felt it would be a mistake to publish. Instead he concentrated on producing work that would exhibit his argument in its details.[3]

Garfinkel also expressed the worry that scholars would misinterpret the *apparent* heavy reliance on Schütz, the use of Schützian terminology, and of theoretical language in general, which he had moved away from as early as 1954, and arrive at the mistaken conclusion that Garfinkel's position was phenomenological and cognitive. I say *apparent* reliance because, even in this early manuscript, a careful reading shows that Garfinkel makes creative, unique, and transforming use of Schütz. The words are the same, but the meaning is very different—as Garfinkel's empirical descriptions of situated action make clear. Schütz's position remained essentially theoretical, while Garfinkel argues that the theoretical attitude is responsible for many of the problems with social research.[4] Nevertheless, the identification of Garfinkel with Schütz is something that has *indeed* happened repeatedly over the course of Garfinkel's career. His refusal to publish the manuscript at the time did nothing to curb this tendency—so the danger that this particular manuscript will *cause* the problem has passed.

Overall, however, I believe that Garfinkel has a larger and more substantial worry about the publication of this or, indeed, any other manuscript. The worry is that it might be *read*. This is not intended as an ironic comment. It sounds funny; after all it is a text—and are not texts meant to be read? It is a serious worry, nevertheless. Texts are comprised of markers for concepts. But what Garfinkel is trying to communicate about are practices: things done, said, heard, felt—and those recognizably. It is Garfinkel's position that the knowledge of practices he is trying to introduce is not a conceptual or cognitive knowledge but, rather, an embodied knowledge that comes only from engaging in practices in concerted co-presence with others. The details of these practices cannot be seen from within the theoretical attitude. Furthermore, they cannot be adequately specified with rules or descriptions, which are always incomplete. Unfortunately, actors themselves, while in the natural attitude, take these details for granted and thus are not aware of the details of the practices they enact. Consequently, in order to understand what Garfinkel is trying to convey, the reader would have to engage the world of action/practice and *embodiedly do* the things that Garfinkel is describing, while at the same time attending to them over their course.

The danger with any text by Garfinkel, then, is that it will be *merely read*. Garfinkel has worked hard in his later texts to present the reader with constant descriptions of tutorial problems that they could *do* in addition to the reading. Ironically, much of what is considered Garfinkel's difficult writing style results from his dedication to overcoming this limitation of texts, trying to make readers *do* the practices discussed. This early manuscript, by contrast, proceeds more conceptually and theoretically; therefore, he likely felt that it could only mislead. It has been with great misgivings, then, that Harold has agreed at my urging to publish this manuscript.

* * *

In spite of these potential drawbacks to an early, more theoretical reading of Garfinkel, ultimately the implications of his work for the way we think about social order, the actor, and social action, must speak to debates that have in practice been inherently theoretical. While his insights originate in empirical observations of practices and, as he would say, have been revealed through incongruities therein, they also speak to questions and issues—to the beliefs and preoccupations of scholars; and ultimately their great promise is that they might *shift the gestalt of theoretical perception* such that we could be enabled to ask new questions about the world if we can see the details of taken-for-granted practices through which that world is comprised, as Garfinkel hopes we will.

The great danger, according to Garfinkel (p. 172), is that "if we are not careful we may find ourselves assuming as given the very facet of the problem of order which we need to investigate. "The risk," he says, "is not indeterminacy," as most scholars have argued, "but the determinacy of ethnocentrism."

Seeing Sociologically, in Garfinkel's view, requires a focus on the routine details that comprise the coherence of activities, not a focus on the beliefs and motives of actors: seeing in new ways—seeing society anew—and in details. With the importance of this idea in mind, the original title of the manuscript has been replaced with a title that reflects a theme introduced in the first paragraph of Part I: that seeing things in new ways is essential to the sociological endeavor. This is not a trivial point, as Garfinkel's argument becomes heavily involved with the way in which "gestalts" seen, heard, felt, and embodied—"educated eyes" and "educated ears," as he says—are both enacted by and comprise the groundwork of social action. It has been Garfinkel's point from beginning to end that approaches which reduce the detail of social life to concepts, typifications, or models lose the phenomena altogether. They end up focusing on the self as a carrier of concepts, instead of on the situations in which they are given meaning. Learning to *see differently* sociologically means learning to see social orders *in* their details *as* they are achieved in real time *by* persons *through* the enactment *of* those details, instead of through conceptual glosses on those details after the fact.

By "communication," in the original title, Garfinkel meant "interaction"—a term he says he preferred, but avoided because it had direct connections to Stimulus Response theory at the time.[5] However, interaction has become an important focus of theory and research in the half-century since Garfinkel wrote the manuscript, and the word no longer bears the connotations of stimulus response, which had rather dramatically disappeared from the scene by the 1960s. The term "interaction," as we now use it, more accurately connotes what Garfinkel intended by "communication."

"Effort" invoked the idea that interaction involved "work" between actors to construct a mutually intelligible world—and that this work was a public, visible, and orderly passing back and forth of recognizable sounds and movements, and could therefore be profitably studied in details. But it was not the study of behavior; it was the study of how actions were given public and mutual meaning by actors working together within shared fields of practice to create witnessable orders. While it involved meaning, this interactional work was not carried by, or accomplished through, concepts, beliefs, ideas, or typifications. Nor was it embodied in projects as Schütz had proposed. Rather, the recognizability of projects and concepts was made possible in and through this work of ordering interaction in its material details.

Communicative work was accomplished in an interactional time frame that Garfinkel referred to as "sequential," which was situated entirely and completely within a context of situated action and was made on the spot. This conception of sequential time is essential to Garfinkel's project—inasmuch as all actions are situated actions in a sequence of actions, passed back and forth between actors, on a developing horizon of intelligible meaning, in a developing sequential time series, against which the recognizable boundaries of objects ("social things") become visible. Sequential time is embodied and consists of a series of interpretive acts, instructably reproduced, within recognizable mutually engaged fields of practice (Rawls 2005).

Since, as Garfinkel says, "any sign can signify anything," (p. 106) nothing has any particular meaning except insofar as its position in some ordered sequence of interaction establishes an understanding between the participants. Situated actors place their interpretations into this developing order of sequences for the others to see and comment on. The actors have methods for doing this—methods that allow them, among other things, to correct and elaborate on the interpretations made of the mutually developing line of action at any point.[6]

The subtitle, "The Routine Grounds of Social Action," reflects Garfinkel's argument that social action has "routine grounds" that are both a condition for and an outcome of this interactive effort—the methods involved, and the work of recognizably enacting practices with and for one another—as he would argue in a later paper, "The Routine Grounds of Practical Action"(1964).[7] The relationship between the problem of scientific description and various phenomenological and gestalt issues with regard to intelligible communication, on the one hand, and the actor as a situated accomplishment, on the other, is also given more detailed theoretical articulation here than in later writings. Thus, the manuscript has the potential to connect later, more empirical demonstrations with the original theoretical questions as Garfinkel saw them. The danger is that it will speak in terms too conventional and that the revolutionary position Garfinkel was already laying out here will get lost. But that is a danger for any argument that requires readers to make a gestalt shift in their thinking.

* * *

This introduction is intended to provide clarification that will help the reader avoid some of the more obvious pitfalls. As Garfinkel insists, this cannot be done entirely as a theoretical matter—one hopes that clarity might eventually be achieved through serious attention to studies of the details of practices, over time.

There are, then, several aims. The introduction will work to establish an overall sense of what Garfinkel was trying to accomplish in the manuscript, and to examine the historical and theoretical context in which the manuscript was written. The historical context is particularly important given that the manuscript was written at the onset of rapid changes in American Sociology in the postwar 1940s, just as the idea of character as a social construction and debates over the social organization of communication were first emerging.

David Reisman's *Lonely Crowd*—the first of many influential attempts to come to terms with the new situated quality of interaction, morality, and personal character in postwar society—was published by Harvard in 1950. Studies followed during that decade demonstrating the connection between the development of particular forms of character and social structure in prisons (Gresham Sykes's *The Society of*

Captives), mental institutions (Erving Goffman's *Asylums*), and mental health (Thomas Szasz's *The Manufacture of Madness*).[8]

In all of these studies the contrast between traditional ideas about morality and the moral demands of practices was a focus. However, for the most part, scholars tended to see the moral demands of practices as motivated by individual or institutional interests and, thus, to see their spread as something of a threat to morality in principle.

For Garfinkel, by contrast, the need for participants to maintain a commitment to the background expectations of situations, which he would refer to later as "trust," constitutes a moral dimension in its own right. While this morality does threaten traditional belief-based moral systems, by treating interactional reciprocity as more important than religious beliefs, traditional belief-based systems in turn conflict with the requirements of a public justice in a pluralistic society. The morality of situations, on the other hand, supports the practice of public justice. A public civil and secular morality thus emerges from the collective need to be mutually engaged in practices, and it has been a mistake to see the development of a secular morality as a threat to morality in principle.

This civil morality of practice—"trust"—is, for Garfinkel, not motivated by anything more than the mutual interest in producing those recognizable orders of practice on which intelligible social life depends. Thus it does not diminish morality overall but, on the contrary, introduces a very stringent requirement of interactional reciprocity, replacing traditional morality with something stronger that does not depend on shared beliefs—an argument that Durkheim suggested in *The Division of Labor* (Book III, chapters 1 and 2) in 1893, but to which Garfinkel gives shape and substance (see *Rawls* 2003).

* * *

The reader will be directed to places in the text where Garfinkel develops particular ideas that have become important in the decades since (such as conversational sequencing, the presentation of self, and frames and framing). There will be an effort to clarify the use of terms (such as "cognitive styles," "frames," and "reflexivity") that have been misconstrued in ways which have confused the understanding of his position. Contradictions between Ethnomethodology, Pragmatism, and Phenomenology, which Garfinkel begins to develop in the manuscript, will also be examined.

These issues will be taken up in the context of four thematic sections. A fifth section will take up Garfinkel's relationship to Pragmatism. While the original manuscript proceeds by defining terms, I have treated the manuscript as dealing with four themes that are important in light of later developments in Garfinkel's approach to society and situated action. These four themes are as follows: *first,* the problem of the scientific description of action; *second,* the treatment of actors as situated identities and action as situated fields of practice; *third,* the interactional time frame, and sequentiality in interaction and communication; and *fourth,* the group as a situated accomplishment through working acts. Numbered sections of this Introduction (some with subsections) will be devoted to each of these themes. The consideration of Garfinkel's criticisms of Pragmatism that follows in section 5 involves all of these issues. But viewing them through a focus on a sustained line of argument against Pragmatism throws some points into much sharper relief.

A brief note on the organization of the 1948 manuscript itself: Defining terms conceptually, and as an argument, is an exercise that Garfinkel would no longer engage in. The character of situated embodied action would now take center stage—and it would do so in details rather than in arguments. But in this early manuscript Garfinkel was engaged in trying to establish the argument that this focus on the detailed embodied character of action was necessary. Even this early on, however, Garfinkel's "definitions," are not really definitions, each covering many pages, involving extensive empirical examples, and constituting an argument in its own right.

After presenting various arguments regarding action, the actor, role, social identity, communication, style, tactics, and group, Garfinkel proceeds toward the end of the manuscript to make use of those arguments/definitions in a logical proof (pp. 166–167). The proof is complex and contains so many symbolic representations that it is very difficult to follow. But it is nevertheless a proof, that if any one of the characteristics of local embodied action are abstracted from, either the actor, the situation, or the embodied action itself, the action has been fundamentally changed. Thus, any research program that proceeds by reducing aspects of action to general terms (whether to render them available for statistical computation or for some other purpose) would change the social action studied such that the object would be *unrecognizable* and the research results would bear *no* relationship to what was studied.

Garfinkel ends the manuscript with an outline of proposed research. The section titled "Statement of Thesis Problems" develops the outlines of several research "cases" and explains how and why incongruities will be introduced, what types of outcomes will be expected, and why. The conception of incongruity and its relationship to Garfinkel's overall position is particularly well developed in this section. While in some respects the section appears to be constrained by the experimental requirements of the time (and should thus be taken with a grain of salt), in it Garfinkel sketches in broad outlines the research program that he will begin to pursue at the University of California after 1954, which he will call Ethnomethodology.

It is not clear whether Garfinkel realized at this early stage quite to what extent situated practices would turn out to exhibit recognizably witnessable orders in their own right. He reports that when he and Harvey Sacks began to look at tape-recorded conversations together, the degree of order exhibited was something of a surprise to both of them. Nevertheless, it is clear that even as a logical matter, in this early manuscript Garfinkel is sure that unless local orders of interaction exhibit a *recognizable* order, there is no shared meaning and cooperative social action is not possible. In Garfinkel's view, social order would not work if it were a conceptual fiction laid over an underlying mess.[9]

The difference between this early argument and later developments in Garfinkel's work is more a matter of degree—the change influenced by method of argument, increased access (or exposure) to empirical data, and changes in terminology developed as responses to misunderstandings—than of substance.

1. Garfinkel's Interest in the Problem of the Scientific Description of Action

The first and most obvious concern of the manuscript is with the problem of the scientific description of action. Although by 1948 changes in modern society after World War II were becoming obvious, and a host of writers were beginning to focus on the changing character of everyday life and the effects of increasing bureaucracy on feelings of emotional and moral disconnection, the way to best go about studying the problem was not at all settled. In fact, in an effort to be more scientific, a gap was widening in the 1940s between a developing and influential Parsonian paradigm, on the one hand, and Phenomenology and more traditional ethnographic approaches, on the other. This gap threatened to distance sociology from the actual social phenomena it needed to study. The statistical manipulation of interview and survey data that was becoming popular required a conceptual reduction that even practitioners realize distorts the subject. It was Garfinkel's position that these methods don't just distort but *lose the subject* altogether, and lose it in such a way that it cannot be recovered from the data collected.

Garfinkel proposed to bridge this gap through an innovative combination of Phenomenology and sociology that would address various issues with regard to the adequacy of scientific description. These issues included problems inherent in the position of the scientific observer and the adequacy of the sociological treatment of the actor and social action. But while working with elements of both Phenomenology and sociology, Garfinkel transformed both through his focus on situated interaction and situated actors in details.

While Garfinkel credited Parsons's action frame of reference with some important phenomenological insights, he felt there were essential flaws that, in his view, crippled the approach. Parsons, in trying to avoid individualism, had, ironically, built the individual into his social system. According to Garfinkel (p. 137): "Parsons went digging for the mole in the attempt to find out what in fact were the categories that were universal in the sense that any human being in reflecting on an action—that is to say, appraising the meaning of an action—would necessarily have to use." The problem was that in seeking a sociological counterpart to universal reason, Parsons had overbuilt the social components, resulting in ethnocentrism. There were several causes of this, according to Garfinkel, but primary among them was the effect of conceptual reduction on obscuring the actual processes from view. Thus, processes became naively imbedded in Parsons's categories. A thorough empirical study of reasoning as situated practice in details was needed to replace the detached speculation that was currently passing for the scientific description of action.

Throughout Garfinkel's career, this concern with the problems of scientific description and conceptual reduction would motivate the development of his work. He would eventually argue that no description of action could be adequate because all descriptions must in principle abstract something from the embodied experience of situated action. In later work he developed the idea of instructed action, recognizably enacted to instructable specifications, that nevertheless cannot be adequately described, or provided for by rules, or concepts. Thus, ultimately Garfinkel would argue that the adequacy of description depends on its praxeological validity: Does it work? Can it be used to do what it describes?[10] Combined with Ethnomethodological indifference, and unique adequacy, instructed action became the new way of addressing his concern with the problem of adequate description.[11]

In the 1948 manuscript, however, Garfinkel *begins* at least with the hope that adequate scientific description can be approximated by marrying a phenomenological attention to detail to a sociological focus on the "work" of persons engaged in communicative interaction with one another. It is also clear, however, that even this early on, Garfinkel realizes that the task will not be to remedy scientific description. The task will require a major gestalt shift of both theory and practice.

From Garfinkel's perspective, even Phenomenology and traditional ethnographic studies did not go into enough detail. And what they meant by detail was more conceptual and cognitive than empirical. A transformation was required. The task was to construct a sociology that would reveal the "more" detail there was to social order and meaning—not a sociology that would obscure that detail by burying it under conceptual reduction as Parsons did, or behind conceptual types as Schütz had.

Therefore, while invoking Phenomenology as a remedy for Parsons, Garfinkel also proposed a focus on the ongoing details of action and identity work—as a remedy for Schütz's preoccupation with actor's intended projects and conceptual typifications. The details of action and identity work would be the interpretive frame for understanding social action, not actor's projects. Communicative work, Garfinkel maintained, if examined in sufficient detail, would reveal those taken-for-granted features of the subtleties of practice that Schütz had treated as conceptual, but which Garfinkel had from the beginning recognized as both material and embodied (reflexively interpreted by situated embodied actors).

By 1948 Garfinkel's interest in Phenomenology and interaction was already of long-standing. He had arrived at Harvard in 1947, having read extensively in both Phenomenology and Chicago-style sociology at the University of North Carolina, where he took his M.A. degree in 1942. The sociology department there was focused on documenting the folk ways and social problems of the rural American South in ethnographic detail. North Carolina also had a philosophy department offering courses in Phenomenology, which was relatively unknown in the United States at the time. During his graduate career at North Carolina, Garfinkel had become familiar not only with Phenomenology (Husserl, Gurwitsch, and Schütz) but also with the theoretical work of Florian Znieneickei, W. I. Thomas, and the communication theories of Kenneth Burke.

In the midst of this oasis of serious thought, Garfinkel watched other graduate students at North Carolina longing for what they considered to be the more scientific sociology of Harvard and Columbia, winding out statistical correlations for their dissertations on a hand-wound calculator. Their idea that these statistical correlations were more scientific and more adequate as descriptions, or explanations, of what was going on in society than ethnographic description was something that struck Garfinkel as wrong from the beginning. He had a deep respect for the sociology he had learned at North Carolina, although he did not think it was going deeply enough into details. But the practice of reducing the details of social action to numbers moved sociology even farther away from detail, and would, he felt, simply lose what was important about social action.

Garfinkel had by 1940 already authored a study of accounting practices in conversation and interaction. [12] That article, titled "Color Trouble," explained how time—or lateness—could be accounted for in racial terms (persons of color refusing to move to the back of the bus, causing delay) on southern buses. A practice that would not be accepted elsewhere, and which could hardly be recovered by a statistical study of either race or bus routes, was nevertheless shown to be an organizing feature of locally situated action.[13] His M.A. thesis "A Research Note on Inter and Intra Racial Homicide" (*Garfinkel* 1942)—a shorter version was published as *Social Forces* in 1949—presented a careful analysis of how significant differences by race in the treatment of homicide cases were rendered invisible by statistical analysis. Statistics collected from courthouses in the ten counties where Garfinkel had done his research showed that there was no variation in treatment of cases by race.[14] But his observations of cases in court showed that there was great variation. His thesis explained the practices that created this illusion and allowed racial disparities to be buried statistically. In 1948, when he wrote this manuscript, Garfinkel (p. 161) referred to an article titled "The Social Personality of the 'Statistic' in Our Society," on which he says he was working at that time. This may be a reference to the 1949 article. Or he may have been working on a further development of this theme. Statistics have in fact often proved themselves to be a useful tool in the service of political manipulation, and Garfinkel knew this.

In spite of Garfinkel's misgivings about the "new" scientific sociology at Harvard, however, it was becoming clear that it was the place to be. If he wanted his consideration of the problem of scientific description to be taken seriously, it would do best coming from the new center of scientific sociology. So, after the war he went to Harvard to work with Parsons.

When he arrived at Harvard, Garfinkel was confronted, as he says, by the fact that the accountants and mathematicians had taken over. He reminisces about the many researchers set up all over campus after the war to count everything and produce models based on their computations. In the aftermath of World War II the government wanted to be sure that in the event of another war there would be better information about the basic needs of various types of community. How much food did they need? How would it be conveyed? What kind of cooperation between people was necessary? If the government needed to disrupt things again, it could do so more efficiently.

The growing love affair with statistics was not the only thing that disturbed Garfinkel about his experience at Harvard. While he had loved the idea of sociology from the beginning and had been moved by his first reading of Parsons's *Structure of Social Action*, he was disturbed by his first class in sociological theory at Harvard. He had been drawn to sociology as a bold and promising enterprise, but in this class, he says, on the first day they were told to just "make up" a theory. The idea was that any hypothesis could be tested statistically once it had been adequately formulated. The trick was to refine and operationalize the concepts. No understanding of social practices themselves was necessary. In fact, the less one knew about the social processes being studied, the more "scientific" and "objective" the research was considered to be. Absurd, of course—but an accepted practice in sociology then and now.[15]

The way Garfinkel understood things, by contrast, the details of how people did things with one another, the ways in which they used language, and the instructable order of things, had *everything* to do with social stability and mutual understanding. To ignore these details, or to reduce them to concepts and or theoretical glosses (which could be tested statistically), would be to remove society itself from the sociological equation—which in fact it has. What, then, would be left? Social order and meaning would become for conventional sociology what Garfinkel would refer to as the "missing what," missing because they had been eliminated in the first step—the step of formulating a scientific description of action.

What the conventional observer does, according to Garfinkel, is to take the perspective of scientific reflection, which reifies the actor. Therefore, taking the actor's point of view "means that the observer, after dealing with the Actor as a theoretical object within the cognitive style of scientific appraisal, brings under consideration another and different scientific object, namely, the model representative of the self-identified Actor" (p. 176).

What Garfinkel proposes the researcher do is very different. The actor is using procedures to accomplish their action. These procedures can be specified. A model of the actor is not necessary. By contrast with the specifiable and observable details of situated action, any model of the actor is like an object of fantasy.

Because the actor is absorbed in the details of "working acts," whereas the scientific observer is not, they are oriented toward different worlds—different realities. The questions that the scientific observer asks are based on reflection and deal with theoretical objects that they bring with them to the situation. The actor engaged in "working acts" does not have these theoretical objects/issues before them. When asked a question they can adopt the attitude of theoretical reflection and give an answer. But because they did not adopt this attitude when engaged in the action in question, their answer does not shed any light on what was actually going on.

Even though the observer is speaking to the same person who engaged in the action, they are now engaged with a different identity confronting a different reality. They have no privileged access to information the scientist wants, for two reasons: *First,* when an actor is engaged in working acts, meaning is a matter of sequential exchange between actor and other, and not the possession of any one actor (what happens, and why, bears little relationship to motives and intentions in any one actor's head); and *second,* because the actor was, at the time the scientist asks about, fully engaged in working acts, they had a different mode of attention to reality. To ask the actor to reflect on working acts is to ask them to adopt another mode of attention to reality. The modes of consciousness are so different that one might as well ask the question of two different persons, and assume that the one could answer for the other.

Attempts to solve this problem through a full disclosure of the observer's perspective and assumptions (autoethnography) further confuse the issue. The problem is not the assumptions and intentions of the observer, although insofar as they bring scientific assumptions with them those are all problematic. The point is that the social order of the situation has nothing to with intentions and motivations in the first place. Trying to clarify the "data" by clarifying the intentions and motivations of the observer only further obscures the actual situated details of action. The observer is not constructing the situation—the participants are. Focusing on the observer is a problem in itself.

Such problems have resulted partially from an attempt on the part of researchers to be more reflexive. There is an irony here. Garfinkel has greatly influenced our understanding of the fieldwork and interview process. It was Garfinkel who first insisted on the reflexive character of interaction. Researchers understood the point that there are all sorts of hidden assumptions involved in interaction. However, Garfinkel's injunctions that interaction is reflexive and must be approached as such have been taken to refer to a quality of reflexivity in the mind of the scientific observer. For Garfinkel, by contrast, reflexivity is a quality of interactional sequences themselves.

A focus on the observer's viewpoint, no matter how detailed, is irrelevant in any case, because it is retrospective and reflective. It takes the observer out of the action—and comments on their "state of mind" when they were not involved in the action. In order for observation to have any validity, the observer must remain embedded in the action and not ask either themselves or the parties observed to answer questions that would take them out of the action. Furthermore, observation must focus on the materials the actors have before them—that which can be observed—rather than focusing on ideas.

2. Situated Action and Situated Actors

What Garfinkel proposed in this manuscript was a new approach not only to the problem of the adequate scientific description of action. He also proposed new approaches to the sociological conception of action, the conception of the actor, the conception of time, and the conception of social order and meaning, or intelligibility. It was intended as a Grand Sociology in its own right, placing situated sequences of interaction at the center of the sociological question—not as a corrective to existing views, or a micro sociology acting as a tame companion to a dominant macro sociology.

While it was Garfinkel's idea at the time that phenomenological description, rendered in more empirical and socially interactive terms, might remedy shortcomings in the reigning Parsonian approach to scientific description, even this initial idea would not just have married a more conventional sociology to phenomenological methods of description. There would have been transforming results for both.

Garfinkel's years at Harvard were enriched by his relationships with Aaron Gurwitsch and Alfred Schütz, both of whom had come to the United States as a consequence of the war, Gurwitsch to Cambridge and Schütz to New York. The two German scholars were in a difficult position as Jewish immigrants after the war, and Garfinkel was ironically better placed. As a graduate student of Parsons at Harvard, he was connected; they were not. Garfinkel was able to maintain a close association with the two scholars while he completed his graduate studies, and his developing position during these early years was worked out in conversations with Gurwitsch and Schütz, whom he met with regularly between 1948 and 1952.

While often interpreted as having combined Phenomenology, and Schütz in particular, with Parsons, in order to remedy shortcomings in Parsons's approach, Garfinkel was in fact also concerned to remedy shortcomings in Schütz's approach that resulted from a focus on the individual—Schütz having treated both individual perception and individual interpretation as organized conceptually by a focus on projects. Garfinkel's actor and action, by contrast, were uniquely interactive and reflexive. Individuals and projects were inherently sequential and situated, and his view of the developing boundaries of fields of action and objects situated perception in what he would come to call a "phenomenal field" of situated practice.

In Garfinkel's view, action is not organized by the projects, or motives, of individuals. Rather, projects are organized, manifest, and made recognizable in and through the situated details of practices: through the concerted collaborative mutual engagement of persons in sequences of practice. In other words, actors can only come to recognize and understand the possibilities for their own projects in and as practices unfold sequentially. The possibilities of projects are seen emerging in the looks of things.[16]

At the beginning of the manuscript Garfinkel lays out two objectives. The *first*, which he calls the "leading aim of the project," is "to translate the concept of the social relationship into the terms of communicative effort between actors." The *second* is to study communicative effort "using the fact that the experience of incongruity can be experimentally induced as the means for teasing these various facets out of the closely woven fabric of social intercourse."

The first two sections of the manuscript, which are devoted to discussions of the actor and action, attempt this conceptual transformation from the idea of social relationships, as existing in historical time between whole historical persons and their values and beliefs, to a focus on interaction between embodied and engaged actors as participants in settings—situated identities—whose personal characteristics are of interest only insofar as they impact on their competence to produce the practices required/expected to enact their identity in the situation. Garfinkel develops a formulation of relationships and of group based on these ideas—one that posits a group as a set of interpretive procedures constituting a situated practice.

Discussions of the actor as a "dope" or "dummy"—which have been significantly misunderstood—relate to this transformation. If one works with a *model* of action and the actor, Garfinkel argues, that model will limit what the actor will be able to do. Garfinkel is attempting to move away from a model of the whole person—as motivated by a range of beliefs and values that intersect with the actor's personal goals and biography to produce motivations, or specific projects (a model that makes the actor a dummy of sorts)—to a view of a situated actor who has mastered a particular set of situated competencies, or procedural rules (as Garfinkel refers to them here), that can be observed and examined, for successfully bringing off particular situated forms of action, in particular situated contexts of action/practice.

Garfinkel is able to make this move, giving up the model and treating the actor as entirely situated in practice, because, unlike conventional sociologists, he does not need to know about the actor's motivations. For Garfinkel, motivations are sufficiently accounted for by the procedural expectations of groups and/or situations. In fact, he argues that if we do have recourse to actors' motivations, it does not get us very far. When action is approached as a result of actors' projects, the motivation question is usually considered to be the critical one. Garfinkel's point is that this is a huge mistake. In everyday practice, motivations are imputed to actors when actions fail to be recognizable or expected. But motives and/or projects do not organize action, and, consequently, motivation is not the important question.

In fact, Garfinkel argues, we know what the motivation to act in recognizable ways is. The person is essentially, in Garfinkel's view, a "symbol treater" or "animal symbolicum," and nothing makes sense unless they are able to treat symbols in recognizable ways in particular contexts. Intersubjectivity is an achievement that requires great attention to detail, without which we cannot engage in meaningful social relations with others. This is sufficient motivation to enact practices recognizably. According to Garfinkel (p. 113): "We are thus prepared to 'understand' [the actor], without, incidentally, needing to refer to a model full of needs and wishes or proclivities, cathexes, and predispositions in order to account for the regularities and sustained character of his actions."

Any actor's motivation can be sufficiently accounted for by saying that they are motivated by the need to produce recognizable practices in order to communicate with others. As Garfinkel argues (p. 104), "It is these [symbolic] expressions that we are seeking to set up, and it is in accounting for their sequences and changes in time that we come to grips with the 'motivation' problem." This not only answers the motivation question, however, but reveals it as an inherently uninteresting and unimportant question.

If one begins with the idea that social order results from aggregations of individuals, more or less orienting toward goals, an idea referred to by Garfinkel (2002) as "Parsons's Plenum," then the motivation question takes center stage. But if one understands that orderly recognizable practices are a necessary foundation for pursuing projects, then the need to enact practices recognizably, and the question of how this is done, supersedes the question of motivation. Given this transformation from actor as whole person to situated actor, it is no longer necessary to work with a model of the person that is limiting. Rather, researchers are free to concentrate on just how actors are able to produce recognizable and ordered practices for one another in just any particular situation. With this move, sociology becomes a discovery science.

In order to make this move, the actor, in Garfinkel's view, must be treated as entirely situated. The actor is not to be considered as a whole person but only as a situated identity in relation to a particular situation—and the specific identity work required of that actor in that situation. The *actor becomes a location for practices—instead of a container for motivations.* Changes in how identity work is done will change the actor's identity even within the same situation.

For the "symbol treater," the symbols treated have meaning only in and as they are embedded in recognizably patterned practices, related to the situated identities of actors in situations, and in relation to their placement in sequences of action.

Take, for example, the guard at Weidner Library on the Harvard campus. Garfinkel makes use of various scenarios drawn from the situated actions of this guard. Instead of making his points in the abstract, he paints word pictures of situated actors and action. In an extensive discussion of the guard (pp. 110–114), Garfinkel sketches in the situated character of both action and identity work. He describes identity and situated practices as being so much intertwined that there are "no norms without identity and no identity without norms" (p. 114). While he uses the conventional word "norms" in this passage, norms—in his description of the guard—have become situated features of the situated production of identities, not transcendent features of culture or social structure. The identity "guard" is so situated that he might have no other life. As Garfinkel puts it (p. 111): "We observe that he engages only in the most passing pleasantries 'during duty hours.' One might infer from the content of his conversations that he has no family, holds no political beliefs, cares not a whit for his own or for the personal lives of others."

The norms regarding the guard identity belong only to the location and circumstances of Weidner Library. The guard surely does have beliefs and feelings about family and politics—but they do not belong to this scene and so they do not appear there.[17] This is very different from Parsons's sense of norms. In Parsons's view, people choose courses of action with some broader goals and values in mind that they take with them from scene to scene, and share with others across many situations.

But norms as described by Garfinkel are not broad, and they do not furnish projects or goals that transcend situations. Rather, they are responsive to situated features of identity. Certainly, an identity can be invoked in other situations, but it still belongs to a specific situation. For instance, we could see the guard at home, or being stopped in the street on the way to work, invoking the guard identity in saying to someone, "Sorry I can't talk, I have to be at work by 8." The need to be at work by 8 is a part of the guard identity that organizes the guard's field of action even before he arrives. As Garfinkel says (p. 111):

> As we watch the guard the following things are seen. We observe that there is a regularity to his time of arrival and departure. He tells us later that "his hours" are eight til five, with an hour "off" for lunch. This we learn is not a private arrangement of his, but rather that there are others

who would be very indignant if he were in fact to come to regard them as his private arrangement.

This discussion of the situated orientation of the guard is not what Parsons meant by goals that people orient toward in making choices. Rather, it is a description of an observable order of situated practice. Parsons would have wanted a goal to furnish a motivation for wanting to be on time, or successful, or even for being a guard in the first place. The guard may indeed have such motivations. We might even call them goals if we liked. But Garfinkel's point is that those goals do not organize the guard's field of action. With regard to questions of how situations are ordered, these goals are inherently uninteresting.

By contrast with Parsons, what Garfinkel means by norms in the 1948 manuscript are elements of situated local orders of practice. They organize what the guard does and how he sees things: his phenomenal field. According to Garfinkel (p. 112):

> The world of the guard is not an object of his thought, but is a field of things to be manipulated, dominated, changed, examined, tested. It is a world of things whose reality and objective character are unquestionably taken for granted, and every action is such that his hypothesis of the world's ontological character is indubitably confirmed.

The guard has routines, practices, in which he and others regularly engage, and it is these practices, the way in which people engage in them, and the time frame they produce through these activities that construct for the guard an identity. The successful achievement of this identity allows the guard's work—his enactment of practice—to assume a *taken-for-granted* character. The guard does not *think* about the details of the practices he must engage in. In fact, Garfinkel will argue that, embedded as he is in the natural attitude (in the ongoing production of practice), he cannot *think* about them. Yet, it is only against this field of perception (the field of seeable possibilities that enacting practices recognizably makes visible) that he might even "see" opportunities for things like "advancement," which could be motivated by goals in Parsons's sense.

But while the details of practices emerge from this argument as the logical focus of any researcher's inquiry, the taken-for-granted character of any field of practice presents methodological problems. If the guard is not aware of these details and does not think about them—then he cannot tell the researcher about them. A researcher confronting the guard with interesting research questions might find that he appears to be curiously uninformed and uninterested. As Garfinkel says (p. 112):

> If you ask him who these people are that he is dealing with, he answers that they are library visitors who most often borrow books, but occasionally attempt to steal them. "Why would they steal them?" you ask "Who knows. But they get caught sooner or later." You try a shift of view to a world of theoretical objects. "Do you think there would be any more or less stealing if there were no guard?" He looks at you as if you were talking of things out of this world, which of course you are. "Books cost money" he says, "don't forget that." This, then, is what we have in mind by the concept "mode of consciousness" or "mode of attention to life."

The guard takes for granted the field of action in which he participates. This is his mode of attention to life. He is not thinking about it—and he takes no theoretical interest in his position. He is deeply embedded in the production of situated practice. For the time being this is who he is. For the interviewer, however, this is a huge problem. The interviewer has a different mode of attention to life. Actors experience their actions from a perspective—a situated identity, embedded in ongoing practice—which completely absorbs their view. The questioner stands back from practice, engaged in something quite different. The guard does not take the questioner's attitude toward things. Nor is he able to see it. His answers reflect his own embeddedness in his situated identity and practices.[18] This embeddedness in situated identity, and the practices that enact it, Garfinkel refers to as a mode of consciousness or "cognitive style"—a much misunderstood term.

Cognitive Styles versus Observable Situated Orders of Practice

While Garfinkel borrowed the term "cognitive styles" from Schütz, cognitive styles as Garfinkel elaborated them were more concrete, indicating observable qualities of social interaction rather than purposes or projects of individual actors. Here, as elsewhere, Garfinkel takes terms that are typically used to describe aspects of persons and/or minds (such as "cognitive" and "reflexive") and uses them to describe orderlinesses of interaction.

The way Garfinkel talked about the guard in this manuscript was essentially new—even though much of the language he used, including "cognitive style"—was familiar. Avoiding the loss of detail resulting from research methods that depended on asking the guard questions about his work and identity required a new way of seeing practices in details. Phenomenology promised a focus on detail with regard to individual thought and perception, and Schütz had used the idea of cognitive style to highlight particular conceptual configurations, or types, that actors oriented toward in particular social contexts. However, there was still a loss of interactional detail resulting from the focus on concepts (typifications) and individual projects. Schütz had tried to remedy this by situating the individual actor in social situations each of which required a different set of assumptions, ideas, beliefs, and values. But interactional detail was still lost through the treatment of those as conceptual typifications. Garfinkel wanted to bring the observable details of action *in situ* to center stage.

Although Garfinkel refers to the embedding of identities in practice as a "mode of consciousness," he does not treat it as conceptual or cognitive in the ordinary sense. He describes a mode of consciousness in details of action and not concepts. It is consciousness because it involves an attitude toward life and the active interpretation of ongoing affairs, not just responsive behavior. But it is not reflective consciousness; it is the active consciousness of working acts. The guard is so deeply absorbed in the practices—in doing things in just this way—that when he is asked whether they could have been done otherwise, he *instructs* the askers: He produces *accounts.* He responds as if the askers had posed the question only because they lack the most basic understanding of what he does (which is, of course, from his perspective true).[19]

It might be asked why, if Garfinkel differed so significantly from Schütz over the material versus conceptual character of situated orders of practice, he nevertheless adopted the Schützian term "cognitive style" to describe the patterned interactive work through which people constructed the ordered recognizability of their daily lives.

There are at least three reasons why Garfinkel might have used Schütz's term, even though what he meant was quite different. *First,* as a new Ph.D. student he would have been constrained to build on known ground as much as possible. In fact, it is the scope and vision of the argument at this early stage that is remarkable, not its indebtedness to mentors. But, *second,* he had also explicitly articulated his concern not to be confused with Stimulus Response theory, and, indeed, this whole section of his manuscript is framed to make it clear that they are not the same. This concern kept Garfinkel from referring to his work as the study of "interaction," when he preferred the term, and it would certainly have motivated the choice of cognitive versus behaviorist terminology; and *third,* Garfinkel refers in later work (e.g., 2002) to a practice of purposefully "misreading" authoritative texts as a way of forging new ground.[20]

Garfinkel was talking about a mutual work of creating meaning through a passing back and forth of interpretations to one another in public. He was talking about constructing meaning through observable aspects of behavior. Given the influence of Stimulus Response theory at the time, it would have been important in making an argument that social relations (the essence of meaning and communication) existed in the *heard and seen material constructions* of daily intercourse—to avoid the implication that one was talking about habitual behaviors and automatic responses. There have in fact been interpretations of Garfinkel of just this sort: that he means something more like Pierre Bourdieu's "habitus," and not intentional action, for instance, and that the methodology can be formalized to leave out the embodied individual—which it cannot.

Thus, the manuscript might appear from a current standpoint to have an overemphasis on the cognitive. But I think it only appears to be an overemphasis because we no longer read it with an understanding of Garfinkel's need at the time to distinguish himself from behaviorism, to build on known perspectives, and to purposefully misread them in an attempt to make clear his focus on the reflexive character of sequential communicative interaction.

The tension between the novelty of Garfinkel's approach and established terminologies can be seen in his examples. In explaining cognitive styles, as in the case of the library guard, Garfinkel focuses on very concrete matters rather than on discussions in the abstract. There are many similar examples throughout the manuscript.

In earlier passages Garfinkel works carefully against quotes from Schütz to show how basic sociological conceptions of action and actors, and the data that one would collect in studying them, could be enriched through the incorporation of a more phenomenological view. But intertwined throughout and becoming more prominent as the manuscript progresses is a critique of the phenomenological (and pragmatist) focus on the actor and their projects and values, which tended still to treat them as whole demographic persons. While Garfinkel does explain the importance of treating actors as situated identities, for the most part he relies on a subtle unveiling of situated actors and projects in terms of practices through the accumulation of examples.

The critique of Schütz is, characteristically, not specified conceptually. Instead, Garfinkel pairs Schütz's argument with examples that belong to a much more empirically focused view. This way of responding to a theoretical issue empirically, and not always elaborating the implications theoretically, is characteristic of Garfinkel's approach. With each next example it becomes clearer to a careful reader that his focus is on practices and not projects. For example, in a quote, Schütz might be discussing what he refers to as an actor's project. Garfinkel will then give as an example a discussion with the guard that makes use of the word "project" but which shows that while the guard is very competent to produce practices, *he cannot talk about his project*. The project is completely taken for granted—not something the guard orients toward, or uses to organize his activities. It is instead the practices that organize the field of action.

Thus, while Garfinkel turned to Schütz as the best existing example of description, he also worked out deep dissatisfactions with Schütz's approach that he began to resolve through an appeal to *incongruities* and what they revealed—focusing on the guard at Weidner Library in particular as a concrete device or "tutorial." Garfinkel was introducing an idea of situatedness that he would continue to develop throughout his career: that the coherence of practices resided not in the intentions of the actors but in the coherent production of mutually oriented action appropriate to the situation.

This is the dissatisfaction with Schütz—that for Schütz the means of order remained conceptual, which for Garfinkel was not sufficiently sociological. It required that we be mind readers. For Garfinkel recognizability resides in the made-together instructable details of situated action. There are unique configurations of developing practice that are made possible by following a closely patterned, recognizably instructable order of action. Such situated orders have competent members. In this sense, Garfinkel's use of members and membership meant communities of practice—but not communities and actors in the old sense in which whole persons belonged to persisting communities. He meant communities in a new situated sense—communities that consist only of situated practices and situated identities.

The transformation that Garfinkel introduces is the idea that fields of action are not organized because actors are engaged in pursuing projects (even though he often follows Schütz in calling them projects). Rather, actors have practices that they "normally thoughtlessly" follow in achieving the situations and identities which make the envisioning of their projects possible. When situated practices are enacted recognizably, every competent member of the situated practice can see what is being done. But the developing contours of a project (as moves/tactics/strategies) can be seen only against a recognizable field of practice.

Because both actor and observer are so deeply embedded in the taken-for-granted attitude toward ongoing practices, the task of revealing that such detailed practices even exist, at least initially, required something that would bring those processes to consciousness: Garfinkel was inspired to focus on the potential of incongruity.

Because each situation and situated identity (or cognitive style) has its own corresponding practices, this understanding of how conversation and interaction are organized also provides a way of introducing incongruities as a way of revealing the background expectations. Garfinkel says (p. 188), "We shall expect to find that various cognitive styles have their appropriate tactics.... Hence we have at least one set of considerations here by which it should be possible to induce incongruities." Wherever a practice, or tactic, is an expected feature of a situated practice, substituting a tactic that is unexpected—or having nothing occur—will constitute an incongruity. Such incongruities present themselves as moments of confusion or ambiguity, and they can be produced only against a background of finely articulated expectations.

3. Communicative Interaction and Conversational Sequencing

Communication, according to Garfinkel, "is a temporal process." In saying this, Garfinkel does not just mean that communication takes place over time, or that time can be used to separate, or measure, different occasions of interaction.[21] For Garfinkel, time is an essential part of the process of ordering bits of interaction. The resulting orderliness of sequences is what makes it possible for persons to achieve mutual understanding.

Why should mutual understanding depend on there being a witnessable orderliness to the ongoing production of interaction? *First,* symbols have many meanings. They also convey different ideas to different individuals. Some ordering process is required to indicate the meaning that symbols are intended to convey on any given occasion (grammar as an abstracted ordering system is insufficient to pin down meaning). *Second,* Garfinkel points out that, while thoughts may occur to an individual all at once, they cannot be spoken all at once. "If one will reflect on his own experience," he says (p. 185), they "will find that the succession of thought as it occurs 'internally' undergoes a selective ordering process in which form it is presented 'piece by piece' to the other fellow." This requires communication to have a sequential back-and-forth character.

For these two reasons, conversation requires an ordering of symbols that is social, shared, and public. For Garfinkel this ordering process is also sequential and reflexive. Conversation proceeds bit by bit. First one person speaks, then the other. The signs produced are meaningless (or too meaningful) unless and until they can be seen to exhibit an order. Then they are interpreted in light of that order. One person speaks, the other interprets. Then they change positions. The listener "treats" the symbols produced by the speaker as exhibiting an order, and the interpretation of that order, produced by the listener when they speak, is designed to display for the other the order the listener has seen exhibited in the sequence of interaction. If the interpretation is "off," the speaker can then add bits to the order that clarify its developing contours.

The importance of sequential placement in allowing conversationalists to convey their interpretations to one another explains why, even though interpretation stands at the center of Garfinkel's position, he places his emphasis not on interpretation but, rather, on "methods" for producing orderly sequences of interaction. For one person to "see" the meaning of a bit of interaction, Garfinkel argues (p. 184), is the same thing as being able to see the order that the other is producing:

> A acts towards B as if the signs that B provides are not haphazardly given. When we say that A understands B we mean *only this:* that A detects an orderliness in these signs both with regard to sequence and meanings. The orderliness is assigned to B's activities by A. The "validity" of A's conception of the signs generated by B are given in accordance with some regulative principle established for A when his return action evokes a counter action that somehow "fits" A's anticipations.

The interpretation by the listener confirms or disconfirms the validity of the speaker's conception of the sequential order they are building. Understanding is not achieved until the listener has detected an order, produced an interpretation in response, and the speaker has detected an orderliness in that response and either (a) recognized that interpretation as fitting their anticipations for what an interpretation of what they said should look like, and how it should be ordered if the listener understood them, or (b) recognized that it does not fit. If it does not fit the sequential order the speaker intended to produce, the speaker can then do something else to make that order more evident to the listener, or they can accept the listener's version and give an interpretation of that.[22]

Because, for Garfinkel, mutual understanding is the same thing as the mutual recognition of an orderliness in interaction, all parties to an interaction must use the same strategies and tactics for producing order. Furthermore, they must "trust" that this is so in order for the interaction to move forward. But even in a context of mutual trust, unless they are *actually using* the same methods for producing ordered interaction, the resulting actions will not exhibit a mutually observable order, the expected order of things will not be confirmed, and confusion and ambiguity will result.[23] This is what Garfinkel means by incongruity.

It is the job of the listener to detect the orderliness of the speech they hear, bit by bit, and to prepare responses that confirm the order they detect. It is the obligation of the speaker to produce speech that displays a recognizable order and to respond to the interpretations that the listener provides in recognizable ways that either confirm or disconfirm the listener's interpretations. While the speaker is speaking they cannot be focused on the job of detecting order. But as soon as they have finished producing an order of speech they become a listener. Then their job is detecting an order in the other's response and producing a response to it that displays an order. And so on.

Despite the complexity of these sequential orders of interaction, participants are able to constantly know whether the other understands what has happened in the way they expected them to, because each next bit of conversation is built to display each next participant's interpretation of the order that is being built.

An interpretation of symbols alone, or of symbols plus rules (as in a grammar), would always generate multiple meanings. That sequences exhibit the orderliness of conversation *as its meaning* is much more complicated than a set of definitions, rules, or a grammar of interaction, because unlike a grammar that order cannot be specified by a simple relationship between parts. Orders of interaction involve matters of sequentiality, situated identity, cognitive style, situated background expectancies, symbolic meaning, strategy, and tactics and always require a mutual reciprocity with regard to the interpretation of these.

As a process of interpretation, the treatment of signs as an exhibit of order is distinguished by the fact that it does not go on in the individual consciousness. The meaning of symbols, and the interpretive acts that express this, is to be located in observable sequential orders of events. The placement of one bit of speech after the other is produced in the visible hearable world as an ordered social process. The "symbol treater," Garfinkel says (p. 179), "in treating these signs [of the other] generates further arrays of signs for treatment." This back and forth, speaking and interpreting, between speaker and listener, is made mutually intelligible, according to Garfinkel, through a complex series of interpretive acts and mutual obligations that are organized through the use of various "strategies and tactics," appropriate to the cognitive style, identities, and background expectancies of any given situation of interaction.

Because it is not possible to routinely produce social, or symbolic, objects with no ambiguity, this mechanism for checking and correcting understandings as an ongoing part of communicative interaction must be built in. If the interpretation offered by B does not "fit," A can indicate this when they speak again. Either party can elect to try again. Given this mechanism, the sheer fact that any conversation continues without problems confirms for both speaker and listener that they are proceeding on the basis of mutual understanding and not ambiguity.

According to Garfinkel (p. 184): "Understanding means a mode of treatment of B by A that operates, as far as A sees it, under constant confirmation of A's anticipations of treatment from B." This rather neatly solves the philosophical problem of ambiguity. Paul Grice is the best-known representative of the argument that there can be no mechanism in conversation for signaling understanding as an ongoing matter. Clarification will not work because each clarification would require its own clarification—an infinite regress. But with the procedure outlined by Garfinkel, detecting and confirming order does not require clarification. Confirmation is displayed in the *configuration of order* produced next. The task of confirming the understanding of conversation occurs within the framework of a mutually experienced developing sequence of talk.[24]

This not only results in a high degree of mutual obligatedness and confirmation of understanding, required of all participants, but also involves parties to a conversation in a shared sequential time dimension. This mutual engagement in sequential orders of interaction, Garfinkel says (p. 181), results in a sequence built by the parties to a conversation which they experience simultaneously: "The communicator does not experience only what he actually utters. A complicated mechanism of retentions and anticipations serves to connect one element of his speech with whatever preceded and what will follow until the unity of what he wants to convey has been grasped." All the moments of a sequence form a unity as each next thing said conveys something about how the listener has understood the last thing said, and the next thing said is organized to display that understanding. The whole series goes into making up what the communication will finally have meant.

In introducing this argument, Garfinkel explicitly addresses the possibility that his position will be confused with Stimulus Response theory. This possibility leads Garfinkel to avoid the term "interaction." He starts off the section on "communication" by saying: "Except that the term 'interaction' seems to set men off to the task of tracing stimulus-response patterns in the vain hope of giving that term practical meaning, we would use it in place of communication. And excepting entirely the meaning of S-R patterns, the two will be used synonymously" (p. 179). In fact, Garfinkel is writing about what we would now call interaction, or communicative interaction—and not communication proper as it has developed.

Readers today would be unlikely to make the mistake of confusing Garfinkel's argument with S-R theory. But in 1948, because of the popularity of S-R theory, the problem must have loomed large. Like Garfinkel, S-R theory, quite strikingly, builds on the idea that interaction consists of a string of acts that bear some intrinsic relationship to one another: leading to a response in the other as the chain progresses.

There is a huge difference between the two positions, however. The relationship between elements of a conversational series for S-R theory is causal, each causing the next, and the participants are passive, caused to respond in predetermined ways rather than interpreting. For Garfinkel, by contrast, the relationship is intentional, interpretive, and reflexive—each next bit of conversation reflecting backward on the mutual understanding of the one that came before—and, only by virtue of the resulting change—or confirmation—in interpretive reflection, projecting an order of next possibilities. In contrast to S-R theory, each bit of conversation displays an active interpretive process, is not causal, and the actors are never passive. Furthermore, action has no mutually intelligible effect—even in reverse—except insofar as it either does or does not exhibit a recognizable orderliness.

A note on reflexivity is necessary here. Garfinkel referred to interaction as involving "reflexivity." But reflexivity is usually taken to refer to aspects of individual consciousness—for instance, to mean that a person can reflect on their action as they act, or that there are layers of interpretation available to introspection. Sometimes the word is used to refer to the fact that individuals can use a current sign, or document, to reinterpret a past action, or that they can have self-awareness while and/or after they act.

But for Garfinkel the words "reflexivity" and "reflection" do not refer to a process of consciousness. One rather striking thing about Garfinkel's position is that although he focuses on intentionality and interpretation he is always talking about mutually witnessable acts and never about consciousness. By "reflexivity" Garfinkel means that the next thing said reflects back on the last thing said and has the potential to show it in a new light—the light in which it has been understood by the listener. Thus, reflection, for Garfinkel, is a feature of the witnessable order of the conversation itself, not something happening in the minds of the speakers.

The single most distinguishing feature of Garfinkel's position is that, while he insisted that the embodied actor be always kept in view, he also insisted that the process of achieving mutual intelligibility was public and social and, therefore, did not concern himself with individual consciousness *per se*. For Garfinkel, the actor's point of view is not a private matter. From his perspective, intersubjective meaning could be achieved only through some witnessable, public, seeable-hearable process. Therefore, reflexivity, in Garfinkel's sense, refers to a characteristic of interaction as a witnessable social object, not to a characteristic of individual consciousness.

For each next bit of talk to be built to exhibit a coherent and developing order requires a constant mutual attentiveness by participants, and Garfinkel refers to ongoing conversation as a context in which the actors are constantly interpreting the order they see being built and testing their hypothesis with regard to the orders they think they have seen. In this way, he says (p. 180): "Every working act is an experiment in miniature; man is forever testing, accepting, and revising his universe."[25]

Sequential interaction has the characteristic of reflexivity because each next bit of conversation reflects back on the last bit in ways that confirm or disconfirm, alter, or add to the sequential order (and hence meaning) being built. As such, interpretive acts work backward, as well as projecting forward, and there is a complex reflexive sequentiality to conversation in which each next thing said both moves the conversation forward and works to confirm, add to, and/or change the meaning of what went before.

In attempting to highlight the sequential and interpretive character of communication between actors, Garfinkel considers the difference between two or more actors communicating, or interacting, with one another and an interaction between an actor and a chair. According to Garfinkel (p. 179): "Communication (or interaction) can take place between an actor and a chair, between the actor and himself, or between two or more actors." But there is a difference between these. Other actors can do things that change what the actor is doing, or the meaning of what they have done. The chair can be interacted with, but it does not do anything unexpected in return. It cannot either confirm or disconfirm the success with which the speaker has produced a publicly witnessable conversational order. The interaction with the chair may involve interpretation, but that interaction is not reflexive in character (in Garfinkel's sense—because the chair does not respond) and the interpretation is purely individual.

It is in this respect only, according to Garfinkel (p. 180), that interaction with a chair differs from interaction with another actor:

> The actor generates an array of signs which the other in turn treats, and thereby in turn generates another array which are unique to every exchange, are far less predictable and constant than the signs of "material" objects, do not depend on the effort of the actor for their *realization* as signs, are constantly changing or being replaced by others without the intervention of the actor, and always afford the actor more than he "asks" for.

It is the other who, in responding to, or treating the signs of, the actor gives them back more meanings than the actor "asks" for. The chair, of course, does not do this. Both interaction with a chair and interaction with a person involve an interpretive process. But in the case of two actors, the interpretive process involves both and is mutual. With the chair it is a purely subjective process. Because of this difference, the treatment of signs by actors together, which results in an orderly sequence of interaction, needs to be carefully distinguished from what interpretation is usually taken to mean as an individual act.[26]

In elaborating what he means by the interpretive nature of conversational sequences, Garfinkel also contrasts what he calls "signposts," or "culture," with the practice of building meaning sequentially through conversational exchange. Signposts, because they are artifacts of a sort, act more like chairs than actors. There are, he says (p. 180), "at least two types of signs." The *first* is "the ready made outcome of the other's communicating acts, as, for example, a signpost." These he calls "culture." The *second* type of sign is one to which the actor attends as it is being produced, where that production is an integral part of the understanding—as for instance, two persons engrossed in conversation. According to Garfinkel (p. 181): "In this latter type the signs are conveyed piece-meal, portion by portion and within a framework of space and time [sequentially]. While the one actor conveys his thought through this sequential order of actions, the interpreter follows with interpreting actions."

The first type—the "signpost," or "culture," like chairs—have some kind of independent existence and stand as artifacts of interactions that are already accomplished. They do not give back more meaning than the actor "asks" for and hence, ironically, involve more ambiguity and subjectivity than conversation.

By contrast, conversational meanings must always be established over their course, and the response is almost always "more" and transforming of what was said. Garfinkel (p. 181) says of the latter that

> the actor may attend in simultaneity to the communicating actions as they proceed, found for example, in two persons engrossed in conversation. In this latter type the signs are conveyed piece-meal, portion by portion and within a framework of space and time. While the one actor conveys his thought through this sequential order of actions, the interpreter follows with interpreting actions.

Garfinkel describes the process whereby the placement of one interpretation after another creates a sequential time for interaction that is different from what he calls "cosmic time" and the "inner duree." The ongoing process of communicating is experienced as the "vivid present" of the actor's working acts.

This vivid present consists of a mutually constructed sequential order of interactional bits—an interactional time dimension that all participants experience. This vivid present is a characteristic of conversation that is also missing in the case of signposts, culture, and chairs, which exist in both anticipation and reflection. According to Garfinkel (p. 181): "The communicator's speech, while it goes on, is an element common to his as well as the listener's vivid present. Both vivid presents occur simultaneously. A new time dimension is therefore established, namely, that of a common vivid present. Both can say later, 'We experienced this occurrence together.'"

The first type of sign, the signpost as artifact, is what most people mean by sign or symbol. It is the second type, carrying meaning only in the vivid present of working acts, that is most important for Garfinkel. He refers to the developing horizon of communicative utterances of the second type as a "performance" in which selves, confronting one another in a face-to-face situation, construct both the intelligibility of the situation and the situated identity of their respective selves within it:

> Like a working action it is a performance for it embodies an intention to realization. The listener experiences the occurrences of the other's action as events occurring in outer time and space, while at the same time he experiences his interpretive actions as a series of retentions and antici-pations happening in his inner time and connected by the intention to understand the other's "message" as a meaningful unit. (p. 181)

Working performances are witnessable displays of intended mean-ings, achieved through the mutual construction of recognizable orders, which occur in a shared dimension of space and time.

The elements of practice that comprise recognizable elements of ordering, placement, and sequencing Garfinkel refers to as "tactics" and "strategies." He says (p. 184), "It is the progressions of signs produced by B and interpreted by A that we are referring to when we speak of tactics and strategies. On the basis of the 'order of action' and of observing the orderly presentation of cues, the observer arrives at a 'reconstructed' plan which he imputes to the agent."

These tactics and strategies belong not to actors but, rather, to situations. Furthermore, the temporal ordering of conversation that requires tactics and strategies is not optional. For Garfinkel (p. 185), "The tactic and the strategy arise from the fact that the agent can not present his 'stream of thought' at one instant," combined with the need for constant confirmation and interpretation of the developing order. Not only does communication require a temporal ordering, but the tactics and strategies involved in this temporal ordering will vary from situated practice to situated practice and from situated identity to situated identity.[27]

Mutual intelligibility—the possibility of communication between persons—requires a mutual engagement between persons in a sequential production in which persons must make use of tactics and strategies (the ones expected for the situation they are in and the identities they claim) as methods for presenting their "thoughts" in a form that will be recognizable to others and thus convey meaning to them. Each situation has different practices and situated identities that are relevant to it. The actor—as a "symbol treater," who is enacting a particular situated identity—must produce speech that is recognized as appropriate to both the situated identity and the situation in which that situated identity enacts itself in order to be "effective."

In signaling the relevance of a bit of action to the situated order, *style* is also important. According to Garfinkel (p. 183): "Style is a cue in the communicative process." As such, Garfinkel argues, style should be a focus of research: "All that is meant by expressional aspects of behavior—tone, tics, posture, physical gesture, inflection, and so on—is meant by style. Our great need is for a vocabulary of style." He goes on to say that

> [i]nsofar as a style furthers the intentions of the agent, we might say that the style is effective. Where the style is not effective, the agent will experience the fact in that the action does not go "according to plan;" it changes direction, the agent "loses control" of it, and the terms of communication may consequently be at such variance with each other that the course of action, as far as the agent is concerned, becomes unpredictable. (p. 182)

What does Garfinkel mean by a "vocabulary of style"? Style involves the elements of cognitive style and communicative tactics—by which Garfinkel means the recognizably produced orderly sequential features of situated identity and practice—that effect the plan of presentation shared by participants to any given situation (not the utilitarian objectives of individuals). Of course, the plan of presentation must always take into account the background expectations relevant to the situation. Within this plan, what Garfinkel calls strategies and tactics must be evident, and recognizably so. The emphasis on strategies and tactics here is an early attempt to get a fix on the "members methods" that Ethnomethodology will focus on later.

Tactics and Strategies Versus Projects

This emphasis on tactics, as elements in a situated temporal sequential, mutually built, and developing horizon of order, distinguishes Garfinkel's position from the usual treatment of tactics and strategies as elements of plans for accomplishing an actor's "projects."[28] Garfinkel does sometimes talk about plans and projects—but by contrast with the usual treatment, he is clear that plans are imputed by the observer to the actor and are not the actor's actual plans, and, furthermore, that any actor's situated plans must first orient toward the ongoing practice and need have no objective beyond producing a recognizable order in the working act. According to Garfinkel (p. 184):

> He [the observer] calls this "plan" a strategy, referring to the fact that the communicator in organizing his cues for presentation *in effect* leads the communicant, *through* the acceptance of meanings, *to* an end state of action, whether that end be the purchase of a commodity or an acknowledgment that he has been understood, and including, as far as the observer sees things, unanticipated end states. (Any given point in a train of action may be considered as an end state. The designation depends upon the purposes of the observer. To fail to bear this in mind results in the search for the "natural" or "obvious" beginning and end of an "act.")

The pitfall in the conventional treatment of plans and projects is twofold. *First,* the actor's project stands at center stage as an explanatory mechanism. But the designation of the actor's project depends on the purposes of the observer, whereas the formulation of the project from the actor's perspective would evolve through their mutual engagement in an ongoing situated order. *Second,* the conventional view leads to the idea that individual acts, or projects, and thus "acts" have natural beginnings and ends.

For Garfinkel, it is situated action and sequences that have natural beginnings and ends—and any actor's plan or purpose needs first and foremost to intend to produce the coherence of that sequence. From Garfinkel's perspective, Parsons's notion of the "Unit Act" makes an artificial distinction between parts of action based on the idea of an individual's motivated project, considered in terms of any whole person's motives—whereas actual sequences of action have natural beginnings and ends in terms of the achievement of recognizable orders by situated identities working together: the real motivation of actors.

In considering the sequential aspects of situated practice Garfinkel makes a further distinction between "strategy"—which involves a situated orientation to the whole of the ongoing interaction over its course, and what he calls "sub-strategies," which operate across shorter sequences of turns—or what Garfinkel calls an "extended series." "If strategy be considered to designate the communicative 'plan' as it appears to the 'auditor' [hearer]," he says (p. 184), "then tactics refer to the sub-strategies which operate in extended series."

Whereas Schütz had focused on "projects," and Parsons had focused on action in relation to broader life goals and values, Garfinkel situates strategies and tactics in particular locations of the sequential production of interaction within which persons have involvement obligations because of the need for reciprocity (to provide interpretations of one another) with regard to the use of tactics and strategies. That all parties to an interaction must orient toward the same tactics and strategies in recognizably the same ways, in order to produce recognizable sequences of order together, becomes the primary motivation in situated interaction.

The importance of this distinction between projects, as they figure in more conventional approaches to social order, and Garfinkel's treatment of tactics and strategies as oriented toward the orderly production of situated sequences of practice, cannot be overemphasized. Garfinkel is proposing "strategies" and "sub-strategies" that operate sequentially and exhibit an order over their course and distinguishing those from plans that operate as valued social norms and goals, which are held conceptually "above," so to speak, the contingencies of interaction. For

Garfinkel, strategies and tactics are for *bringing order in and through the contingencies* of the situation. This is only possible if the strategies are themselves situated. Transcendent symbols and values are of no use for this purpose—as their meaning requires contexting.

Garfinkel's notion of "strategies" might seem to have more in common with the conventional view than "sub-strategies," in that strategies are said to take something beyond themselves as an end; but even so, they are closely bounded by the background expectancies of situations and are primarily driven to achieve internal coherence rather than either individual or transcendent ends.

There is something essentially "in its own right," however, about the orientation toward sequences of action that Garfinkel calls sub-strategies. Unlike "projects" more conventionally conceived, they take their own coherence as an end. They may have an objective in the situation beyond themselves. But they cannot accomplish anything unless they exhibit a coherent order—so they demand a great deal of attention in their own right as developing orderly coherent sequences.

Such strategies and sub-strategies, or a mutual orientation toward them, are in this sense examples of something rather pure—ends in themselves in Kant's terms—and, as Garfinkel (1963) will argue later, in the "Trust" paper, they demand a rather pure reciprocity on their own behalf. They have coherence as sequences, and they make demands on reciprocity and attentiveness just in their own right, as orderly sequences of action, regardless of intended outcomes. As such, they offer a very different answer to the motivation question, as Garfinkel points out. Any person with the intention of being understood must attend to the careful building of such sequences and their sub-strategies. This is their primary motivation in any interaction, regardless of other more individual motives the participants may have.

What all of this means is that the essence of situated order consists in the production of order using these strategies and tactics, in just the ways that are appropriate to the situations that actors find themselves in, with regard to just those identities they are trying to present. Changes in strategy and tactics may result in changes in identity. Unexpected strategies and tactics may even alter the situation itself. In order to be meaningful and coherent, interaction must display an expected order, and recognizably.

4. The Group as a Situated Order

In keeping with his treatment of the actor as a situated identity, and of mutual understanding in conversation as a situated sequential order, Garfinkel approaches the question of what constitutes a group as a situated production through working acts. He proposes that situated actors, engaged in constructing a sequential order of meaning, constitute a group only when, and only for as long as, the sequential character of the interaction in which they are currently engaged requires of them collectively a mutual commitment to the situation. The group—as a set of interpretive procedures—is, as Garfinkel will later say, "there before the actor gets there and continues after they leave: like a standing crap game."

The current situation, or group, would include the enactment of identity and commitment to background expectancies that are constitutive of its developing properties of order. Given this understanding of what a group is, Garfinkel argues, the idea that a single individual takes on multiple roles at the same time is a fallacy (an idea that will be developed further in section 5 of this Introduction, on Garfinkel and Pragmatism). Furthermore, the idea of an individual person as a unity of different roles is, for Garfinkel, as much an abstraction as the idea of an institution. In laying out his approach to groups, Garfinkel also addresses the issues of power and force (features of social action he is generally considered to have ignored), arguing that when the actions of one actor place limits on the actions of another, within a particular order of sequential action, the situation involves force or power.

Groups are typically considered to consist of whole persons with demographic characteristics, each of whom has other identities and relations with other groups, but who for the moment stand in a primary role or identity relationship with some collection of persons. Groups, in this sense, can be more or less enduring—as in a family, or a professional group—-or relatively momentary, as in a co-present, but temporary, aggregation of some sort, as for instance in "the group of us going to the movies." If a group were thought to be comprised of whole persons, each of whom belong to more than one group and have more than one identity—at least one identity for each group—then it would also follow that persons can be members of more than one group at the same time and, consequently, that matters of allegiance and identity could be divided and sometimes in direct conflict. For a sociology that sees order as resulting from aggregations of motivation, this has appeared to pose interesting problems.

Because this way of conceiving of groups as composed of whole demographic persons has predominated in social and political thought, the whole person, or individual—as a collection of identities and as a container for motives and values—has always seemed from a theoretical perspective to be more "real" than the group. Consequently, the history of Western academic argument has been dominated by individualism. Within sociology itself, this has taken the form of a preoccupation with the demographic character of social orders, rather than with the characteristics of social action *per se*.

One of the essential steps in overcoming individualism and embracing a genuine sociology, for Garfinkel, is to recast the conception of the group in terms that do not depend on demographic whole persons, or individuals. Because the Group, for Garfinkel, is a situated matter, as are the situated actors that populate it, the group demands immediate and constant attention to its constitution—regardless of what "individuals" may think they are up to. This provides an object for sociological study consisting of those practices that constitute the context of working acts, mutual participation in which, for Garfinkel, constitutes a set of actors as a group.

According to Garfinkel (p. 189): "Within a theory of communication the term *Group* means an aggregate of cognitive styles which are definitive of finite provinces of meaning which, while they may or may not be the same, are communicatively related to each other by working acts." Rather than seeing a group as composed of persons who stand in some relationship of proximity, kinship, or belief to one another, Garfinkel presents groups as configurations of expectations regarding situated practices and identities.

It is not enough for persons to be co-present for them to comprise a group. For Garfinkel a group is not an aggregation of physical bodies in space. Nor is it a collection of demographic whole persons (related by kinship, religion, community, etc.) over time. Nor is a group comprised of persons as collections of roles and containers for motivations. A group is, rather, a collection of practices and background expectations—cognitive styles, as he sometimes calls them here—that place constraints on the methods that situated actors can use to make sense and construct meaning in any given situation. A group would be those persons in any given situation who are committed to using the practices and observing the particular background expectancies that comprise the recognizability of that situation. Seen in this way, groups are collections of practices and their background expectancies, ordered through working acts. Participants in groups have commitment obligations to those practices and are thus not just participants but "members." Later Garfinkel will come to call the methods for constituting groups in and through working acts "members methods."

For Garfinkel, a person is a member of a group only when, and only as long as, they are committed to a shared set of methods for producing a situation, and are recognized by others as being so committed. In other words, when the coherence and meaning of what actors do depend on methods shared among a collection of persons, and cannot be explained on the basis of individual characteristics and interests alone, then they are a group. Furthermore, this commitment, according to Garfinkel, is assessed by other members of the group—and cannot be decided by scientific criteria. The question of membership is settled if the others are satisfied that commitment to the situated practices is ongoing (regardless of the "facts" of demographic, or other, characteristics).

This idea, that a group has nothing to do with the characteristics of the individuals who comprise it, is the kind of definition of society that Durkheim was trying to articulate when he said that society is more than the sum of its parts. That a group is *more* than the sum of its parts implies that what makes it a group does not come from *any* of the parts. True, it is largely the inability of individual humans to engage in mind-reading—and, as Durkheim would say, to think rationally without experiencing social forms—that makes mutual commitment to the situated practices that comprise the working acts of groups necessary in the first place. But this need for orderly practice is not a characteristic of any individual human being; rather, it is a general truth about the human condition.

The inability to read minds, combined with the potential for any sign to mean anything, means that mutual intelligibility can only be achieved if a social order is present and mutually recognizable in the *form* of interaction. In this way, Garfinkel gives concreteness to Durkheim's claim that social order cannot be explained as a sum of its parts. Just as words do not constitute the meaning of utterances (which get their meaning from their witnessable order), so the practices through which persons construct recognizable meaning must constitute an order in their own right—responsive to the demands of communicable orders—and not derivable from the individual.

Groups, then, rather than resulting from the actions of aggregations of individuals, or collections of values and beliefs, are configurations of working acts (situated practice, situated identity, and background expectancies) that have consequences for the premises of action for actors. According to Garfinkel (p. 202), "we have a *social group* when the communicative efforts of the actors, which is to say, when the conduct of the actors results in some order of consequences for the cognitive style of at least one of the actors. This is the same as saying that the action of *A* has consequences for the premises of action of actor *B*."

Whenever two or more actors are engaged with one another in such a way that the working acts of one have consequences for the "premises of action" of the others, they constitute a group. The idea of "premises of action" is the critical point here. It isn't that the action of *A* has consequences for the action of *B* (that might involve direct power or force) but, rather, that a group involves a particular set of premises for action that other members of the group must then use (if they want to be treated as members). If one actor invokes these premises and they have consequences for others, then they are a group.

The idea that a single working act can create a group, or change a group from one sort to another, and/or change its membership, is also different from the typical meaning of "group." In that it is reflexive (in Garfinkel's sense of changing what went before), this idea of swift change bears some similarity to the idea that when the person, who has been the listener, speaks, they can change what the former speaker comes to have meant. But in the case of a group, it is the premises of action that are changed, not just the meaning. The relationship of the persons to each other, through the configuration of working acts, changes not only the meaning of particular bits of speech but also the premises upon which interaction is sequentially ordered and subsequently recognized (interpreted). In other words, any actor's plan—or possible plans—are changed and/or affected by the mutual commitment of the others to held-in-common situated methods. The possibility of even conceiving of a plan is effected when the situated practices necessary for a plan to be conceived of have changed.

As a configuration of orders of meaning, not composed of persons but comprised of interpretive rules of procedure, a group, like an identity, does not "exist"; it is "meant." This way of approaching the constitution of groups has important implications for the way the individual actor and their motives and projects are conceptualized. According to Garfinkel (p. 199):

> We are in a position now to expand on what we meant when we gave a general definition of group at the beginning of this section. The following considerations need to be underlined: (1) The term, *group,* does not refer to persons; it refers to Actors. (2) It does not mean an empirical reality; a group does not "exist": it is an analytical construct, and is thereby a scheme of interpretation; a group is meant. (3) As a term it is a designator of certain interpretive rules of procedure.

In the decades since Garfinkel wrote this manuscript, with the development of Symbolic Interactionism, Labeling Theory, and the idea of the "social construction of reality," it has become a commonplace for interactionists to argue that formal institutions and groups are not real—that is, that they are comprised of something like rules and/or regularities of behavior, which cannot be located in space and time as material objects but, rather, exist only in particular social spaces as social productions.

For those who make this argument, however, the individual self has generally continued to appear, by contrast with institutions, to be eminently real. Social construction, for instance, has been conceived of as a work of individuals negotiating reality (even if their identities are sometimes pictured as socially or institutionally constrained). And the problem of multiple selves, and of conflicts within an individual person between selves, continues to be a focus of research. Thus, the idea of the individual as a unifying container of roles, values, and projects not only remains but has become stronger.

As a consequence, many interactionists have come to focus on the individual perspective, or individual consciousness, as a research object. Unfortunately, Garfinkel himself has often been interpreted as focusing on the individual and individual consciousness.

What Garfinkel argues quite explicitly in the 1948 manuscript, however, is that the individual (whole person) is *no more real than a formal institution.* Both are social constructs that do not have any material existence in actual situations of social action. It is only the enacted situated identity that acts (and only the situated identity who chooses "effective" courses of action who is mutually recognized). Both the "person over time" and the "institution," or "corporation," are in fact comprised of many occasions of situated practice and identity enactment, which can only be amalgamated conceptually. To identify the aggregate of these as a unity is, in either case, according to Garfinkel, an ideal construct.

The Scientific or Theoretical Attitude and Reification

For Garfinkel, the common objection to the idea of a group mind, by scholars who treat the idea of an individual mind as unproblematic, is a result of the fallacy of unifying conceptually moments of identity in action that are experienced separately. In this connection he argues that "[i]t is also the source of error of those who would allow that 'there is such a thing as an individual mind' while talk of a group mind only invites their wrath. Within the scientific attitude the rules by which they [individual and group mind] are constituted as existent entities apply in exactly the same manner to one as to the other" (pp. 195–196).

Garfinkel points out that only in the natural attitude, in which people take for granted the work of constructing the appearances of things, does the individual as an identity appear to be an unproblematically given reality, while the corporation does not. It is only within the natural attitude, he says (p. 196), that the question is possible: "But you can see a person; who ever saw a corporation?" What is seen, however, is in reality the actor, in the vivid present of working acts, engaged in producing one and only one identity at a time—not an individual as a unity of identities. In the natural attitude it does not cause a problem that the individual appears to be real, while the work of performing identities is taken for granted. In fact, it is necessary.

For Garfinkel the problem arises when scientists (social scientists in this case) improperly take ideas from the natural attitude and bring them into scientific discourse. In this case it creates the impression that persons as unities of identities are real while corporations are not. As a scientific matter, he says (p. 195), both are the same type of construct:

> We have repeated almost *ad nauseum* that "actor" does not mean "concrete person." In fact, one should make the case that the term "concrete person" is entirely misleading in the finite province of meaning of the scientific attitude in which the scientist lives. It is a concept employed in the finite province of meaning of the natural attitude, where the modes of treating the signs of the presence of the other are such as to render the hypothesis of the tangible objectivity of the other self irrefutable. As the child knows, what else can that gesticulating figure on the porch *be* than his mother. But for the scientist the reality of "a person" is the reality of a unity of meaning, with tangibility being one feature of this unity of meaning.... In other words, "person," like "actor," designates for the scientist an *ideal object*. As an ideal object it is refutable; its meaning can be challenged and changed. The only things that are irrefutable are the signs which pure intuition (as this term is defined by Husserl) presents.

Whereas "person" designates an ideal object for the scientist, for the actor in the vivid present of their ongoing working acts the other is given in their concreteness as detailed looks, sounds, gestures, and so on, and not as an ideal object, or unity of roles and meanings. As a situated identity, the experienced concreteness of the person in interaction is never a unity in the context of their working acts. It is the scientific attitude that mistakenly couples the idea of an ideal unity with the experienced concreteness of the person.

One of the consequences of treating the person as an ideal construct, according to Garfinkel, is that the scientist cannot lose. One of the defining characteristics of a discovering science, which Garfinkel elaborates in his later research, is that the scientist must be able to lose their phenomena (see Garfinkel 2002, ch. 9). If they cannot lose the phenomena, they also cannot discover anything—because not being able to lose it means that they are working within a circularity of ideal constructs. It is in this sense that the conventional social scientist cannot lose, because they have, as Garfinkel says (p. 196), "bumped off" the real person and replaced them with a conceptual dummy. They are guaranteed that this dummy will be what they propose them to be, because the dummy is of their own making. The problem comes with real people—who continue to act in what appear, to the scientist working with a dummy, to be unpredictable ways. The scientist's continued struggle to gain a purchase on predictability ironically leads to more elaborate ideal constructs, which further deflect attention from the actual interactional work of situated actors creating order in details.

Garfinkel challenges the scientist's view that the conceptual reduction of situated persons to whole persons is necessary. Identifying one body with the aggregate of many occasions of situated practice and identity obscures the actual situated identity and makes it appear ideal. For Garfinkel (p. 196):

> The scientist deals in a world of theoretical scientific objects where the only claim to reality that a concept can make must rest entirely on the test of utility. Compared to the world of the natural attitude, the scientist's world is indeed a strange and misshapen one, a veritable Alice in Wonderland world, where if a "man" is of no use to the game in progress he is ruthlessly bumped off; where a table is not a thing to eat on, but is a whirling dance of sub-microscopic particles. Viewed through the eyes of the natural attitude the objects of the scientific world are fantastic in a way that puts to shame the wildest offerings of the comic books.

In saying that scientists "bump off" the person if they have no utility, Garfinkel means that the way people *really* figure into the world of working acts, as situated actors, is of no utility to the scientist who views the world reflectively and takes no interest in the ongoing processes of working acts—so the scientist replaces them with concepts: whole demographic persons motivated by goals, projects, and beliefs.[29] As a consequence, the concrete actions of actors, and the way they go about constructing social order and meaning through working acts, are eliminated from social science as well—"bumped off," if you will, along with the concrete situated actor.

This causes serious problems for the way sociology approaches the problem of social order and social structure because it has replaced its object with concepts.[30] Groups, in Garfinkel's terms, are relationships not between persons in this ideal sense but, rather, between collections of situated actors/identities who are committed to performing situated practices. Relationships exist between members of situated practices, as situated identities, and not between persons as "unities of meaning." Interactions continually enact and display this membership as situated actors, working through trust relationships with others, bringing both practices and situated identities to life.

Garfinkel's actor does have a single body, with which different situated identities are enacted, and the embodied character of action remains important to them. But each identity is part of a configuration of situated action that the actor finds themselves in, not a quality of the actor as a whole person. Each identity has its own motivations, which come not from the collection of identities over time but, rather, from the demands of particular occasions of situated practice that the actor is currently engaged in. Instead of posing the actor as an ideal construct that comprises an aggregate of all the situated identities engaged in by a single physical body over time, and treating this unity of identities as the source of motives for action, the actor in Garfinkel's case inhabits situated moments of action as "identified action."

This way of approaching the actor is only an artificial construct, according to Garfinkel, insofar as situated moments of interaction can be said to have been artificially separated from others in order to produce this singularity of focus. In other words, to the extent that there are real separations between moments of interaction—moments organized differently from prior moments, with different configurations of identified action—then there are real differences for the actor who must orient toward ordering those differences. The consequence of this way of thinking is that persons, as unities of roles, are no more real than institutions.

Roles and Motives

One of the consequences of the conventional view of the actor, as a unity of roles and motives, is the attempt to measure involvement in a role, or membership in a group, in terms of an individual's attention to a situation. Garfinkel compares the attempt to define a group by the frequency with which actors exhibit a certain mode of attention to life with the attempt to define a group as a synthesis of individual egos. Neither preserves a view of the process through which group synthesis is actually achieved.

As Garfinkel (p. 197) puts it: "The 'synthesis' is effected within this principle *in the working act*. If Y *treats* X as a group member, then X *is* a group member." It does not matter how often the actor appears to move in and out of a group through lack of attention. According to Garfinkel:

> Let us assume two empirical persons, X and Y. Let us suppose that we have an intimate knowledge of X such that we know that he is "in" and "out" of a group 100 times a day as he gives up working on the pile of insurance forms on his desk in order to indulge in a day dream about his coming vacation. Now, is this the direction we follow in portraying group structure? That is to say, will we have eyes out for the frequency with which alternate states of attention to life come into evidence for the multitude of actors that make up "the office"? The answer is, no. X is a group member, not on the basis of the portrayal of his mode of "internal activity," *but rather is a group member on the basis of the treatment that is paid to him by Y.* (p. 197)

What matters is what the situation and its background expectancies require and how others in the situation regard the actor.

In making this argument, Garfinkel (p. 198) considers the case of an office worker paring his nails on the job and not being reprimanded by the office manager. If one used a "truth" analysis based on the idea of whole persons and a correspondence between something and reality—that is, whether the worker is actually doing their job when pairing their nails—then one might say that when they are not working they are not part of the group right then but taking on another identity. This would be the more conventional view, and the idea would be that sustaining an identity requires a truth correspondence between individual thoughts (and or behavior, or characteristics) and the identity they are enacting (with some "objectively" measurable consistency—that is, measurable by the scientist).

But Garfinkel insists that the test of identity, or group membership, is not a correspondence to some criteria (a truth test) but, rather, whether or not the others treat the actor as a member of the group. If the others treat the actor as a member of the group, then, for as long as they are treated as a member of the group, they really are a member of the group.

In the particular case of Garfinkel's example of the office worker, the office manager and the others do treat the worker as a member of the group. In attempting to show the sense of this from the perspective of situated practice, Garfinkel considers various attitudes that the others may take. If you ask the office manager whether the worker is getting paid to pare his nails, he says, the manager produces accounts. According to Garfinkel (p. 198–99):

> If the office manager be asked by the observer, "Is he being paid to indulge in reverie while the office papers go unattended?" and the office manager answers, "It's very boring work, those insurance forms," then we have isolated an interpretive tactic, an element of office ideology by which actions of the "others" are invested with reasonableness; are understood; a tactic by which group membership is retained and the system continues to operate without reorganization. It is one of a multitude of acts of understanding which comprise the dynamic background of the phenomenon of regularity in social relationships.

These accounts are oriented toward managing daily affairs so that things like personal reverie can be normalized and the appearance of the group maintained. When the others decide the worker is no longer a member of the group, that will become evident in their treatment of the actor, and only then could we say that the actor is no longer a member of the group.

Again, Garfinkel's point is that any appeal to a correspondence with "facts" to get at the truth of an identity, or membership issue belonging to the situation, is misplaced. Whether or not one is a member of a group is a situated matter, inhabits a closely circumscribed moment in time, and within that moment is wholly and entirely a matter of whether or not the others treat them as a member (reflexivity again—treatment by the other makes a thing true or not).

Power and Force

Finally, Garfinkel specifies four relationships—influence, power, force, and advice—which may operate within groups. These, he says, are only examples of types of relationships; he could generate as many as we had time for. Nevertheless, power and force are particularly interesting as they are important relationships that are usually considered in terms of either macro structures or wealth and status relations. When they are focused on as interactional matters, they are usually treated as relations between whole persons, as matters of status inequality or violence, and not as relations between situated identities in the context of situated groups, understood as interpretive rules of procedure.

Power and force are also relationships that Garfinkel is usually thought to have taken no interest in. He would not take an interest in them as demographic relations between whole persons. But here, Garfinkel sketches these relationships out entirely as matters internal to the dynamics of situated action.[31]

Regardless of the demographic characteristics of persons, there are features of situated action, both in terms of identities and practice, that can be mobilized by actors in ways that are consequential for the opportunities of others. Power relations in this regard, according to Garfinkel (p. 203), involve the ability of one actor to limit the elements of cognitive style for another actor or actors: "We shall speak of a relationship of Power when actor *A* is so regarded by actor *B* that *A*'s treatment effects a change in some element or elements of *B*'s cognitive style, the changes being of such a character as to limit *B*'s alternatives of action to those or that which *A* desires."

Force, by contrast, involves relations in which *A* limits *B*'s alternatives without intending any particular result, and without *B* standing in any necessary relationship of regard to *A*. According to Garfinkel (p. 203): "We shall speak of a relationship of force when regardless of how *B* regards *A*, the premises of action of actor *A* eventuate in a course of action by *A* the effect of which is to limit *B*'s alternatives of action without A intending a change of *B*'s cognitive style and regardless of *B*'s cognitive style."

Garfinkel's idea of the group as comprised of situated actors and working acts stands as a direct challenge to conventional ways of thinking about the group. One of the things he does with this idea in the 1948 manuscript is to use it as the basis for directly challenging conventional conceptions of the self, including the conceptions of Pragmatism and Symbolic Interaction. He argues that the self has been reified, positing the unified person as a container of motives, resulting in the idea that situated actors can have more than one identity and that these can conflict. Treating the resulting motivations as primary and focusing the energy of social science on trying to pin down the motivations of actors through demographic considerations has entirely obscured from view the primary motivation of any actor, to produce orderly interaction and identity in the context of working acts, so as to render meaning through order.

This notion of the group as an order of expectations, not derivable from the characteristics of individuals, involves Garfinkel (as it did Durkheim) in explicit criticisms of Pragmatism in the manuscript.

5. Garfinkel and Pragmatism: Situated Actors, Groups, and Objects

The view that Garfinkel's position is consistent with Pragmatism is becoming popular as a way to supply the "missing" theoretical context for his studies. This tendency is encouraged by the current popularity of Pragmatism as a way of framing the study of practices. However, because Garfinkel repudiates the questions of role, motivation, perspective, and project that are at the heart of the pragmatist (and symbolic interactionist) perspectives, treating his position as pragmatist has the unfortunate effect of making him appear to be a failed Pragmatist (or failed Symbolic Interactionist). The theoretical perspective that Garfinkel outlines stands in direct conflict with both.

As Pragmatism has regained popularity over the past two decades, and the tendency to treat Pragmatism as the theoretical context for studies of practice has increased, most of its shortcomings have been chalked up to the way the perspective was articulated by William James. By contrast, John Dewey and George Herbert Mead have been credited with enriching the approach sufficiently, by invoking a social dimension of self, to avoid the limitations of individualism. For sociologists who embrace Pragmatism, therefore, Mead and Dewey are key.

Garfinkel, on the other hand, challenges not only James but offers compelling criticisms of the formulations of self and social action in the work of all four founding pragmatist philosophers: William James, Charles Sanders Peirce, George Herbert Mead, and John Dewey. From Garfinkel's perspective, Mead and Dewey do not avoid the problems attributed to James. All they do is introduce those same problems into sociology in the guise of an interactive self, which he argues is not really interactive. That Garfinkel finds serious elements of individualism and the reification of the person and social roles in both Mead and Dewey, and argues that these ideas have obscured the understanding of social identity and social order, is of particular importance.

A single thread of argument runs through Garfinkel's discussion of all four thinkers. Broadly speaking, what he objects to is the idea, common to all, that the projects individuals pursue, and the roles they have mastered, provide the basic elements around which a mutuality of perspective, allowing for the successful completion of projects, is constructed. That projects and roles, which are conceptual constructions (by either individuals or social groups), are considered to be elements of "interaction" he finds particularly troubling. Interaction, for Garfinkel, consists of action in observable details, not invisible things like roles, or projects in people's heads.

In developing his line of argument, Garfinkel takes key ideas from each thinker, contrasts them with his own, and subjects the contrast to an extended analysis. His critique of James develops the idea that interaction is a matter of a finely ordered mutual engagement, in the course of which social orders of action in details configure individual perception, reflection, and motivation, and not the reverse, as James had assumed.[32] The critique of Peirce develops the distinction between identity as object, in which the accent of reality falls on identity as it does naively on other objects in perception, and identity as what Garfinkel calls a "symbolic object," which involves complex dimensions of social ordering. The idea that identity consists of orders of action that are specifiable in details, but not as roles, and the consequence of this view for an understanding of motivation, are developed through a consideration of Mead.

In considering Mead, Garfinkel also elaborates a reformulation of "taking the role of the other." Garfinkel rejects the idea of roles, and maintains that even if an exchange of perspectives between actors could occur as an act of imagination it would be insufficient to the task. What Garfinkel proposes is a real exchange in details.

Finally, the argument that the actor, engaged in working acts, is a situated identity, not a whole person, or a mosaic of roles, which runs through the discussion of all four, culminates in a consideration of Dewey's notion of the "segmental self." It is Garfinkel's view that the ideas of role conflict, role distance, and competing motives within one individual result from treating the actor as a container of roles, instead of as a single fully engaged situated identity. The consequences of Dewey's position, for Garfinkel, not only involve problems with the formulation of the self, but, as with Mead, the motivation question gets formulated in a way that sets sociologists off looking in the wrong place for social order.

Throughout everything, for Garfinkel, runs the idea that, with regard to identity, as with social order generally, the state of being in action is the relevant one. The actor is engaged in working acts in the natural attitude. The unified self or person contemplates projects in the reflective mode of attention to life, but does not act. Situated identity, as the immediate focus of actors engaged in working acts, is the relevant entity with regard to a study of social order, according to Garfinkel (p. 193), not unified self, or person: "Persons, then, do not act; nor is a group made up of persons. *Actors* act, and a group is made up of *actors.*" Because it is the actor and not the whole person who acts, it is the motivations that engaged actors take on in particular situations of action which need to be understood, not the idealized motivations of reified whole persons.

Actors enact identities through working acts and the background expectations of the situations they are engaged in. Treating actors as unities of roles, Garfinkel argues, has obscured the qualities of the actor and action that are relevant to understanding social order. For Garfinkel (p. 193), "an actor is not a 'concrete individual'; an actor is a series of propositions which incorporate and relate the six concepts of cognitive style."[33] The motivation to create social orders does not come from the individual, either as a reified mosaic of roles or as the possessor of a role, but, rather, from the need for the engaged actor to create recognizable orders, including their own identity, in specific situations of action in order to communicate with others. The primary motivation must be to produce orderliness, which is the same thing in Garfinkel's view as creating meaning (order = meaning).

All of this challenges Pragmatism at its core. The idea that individual persons, either as active consciousnesses or as collections of roles, go into interactions with motives and projects—and that those motives and projects, in some kind of intersection with the local definition of the situation, are the means through which persons negotiate to produce sufficient order and meaning to go on with—is at the heart of the pragmatist project. It is also at the heart of much Symbolic Interactionism.

Many will object that Mead and Dewey avoid individualism and offer a more sociological view. The individual constructed through interaction is, after all, not the purposeful individual of James or the rational individual of more conventional philosophy. But Garfinkel's point is that Mead's conception of taking the role of the other still involves an inherent reification of both the person and social action. He offers an alternative to Mead's formulation that locates the exchange of perspective outside of the actors in the witnessable details of interactional sequences—in the midst of working acts and not in the reflective mode of attention. Garfinkel argues that Dewey's idea of the segmental self also involves both a reification of the person and false assumptions about the actor engaged in working acts as a mosaic of roles.

Garfinkel's criticisms of Mead, in particular, may come as a surprise. It has become commonplace to think there is an essential compatibility between Garfinkel's position and Mead's Symbolic Interactionism, Dewey's Pragmatism, Erving Goffman, and what is called "micro" sociology in general. In fact, the identification of Garfinkel and most other "interactionists" with some form of focus on the individual is at the heart of the micro/macro distinction as currently conceived.[34]

The micro/macro distinction has never had any relevance to Ethnomethodology. Garfinkel works hard, in this early manuscript, to distinguish his position from what he sees as the individualism in these other developing forms of interactionism. If anything, he can be seen arguing against the early development of individualistic tendencies in interactionism. The actor, for Garfinkel, is not a concrete person, or a container for motivations, or roles. The actor is a series of propositions, or rules, for enacting identity and producing recognizable situated action. As such, an actor or identity belongs to a location or situation, not to a person.

While Garfinkel would no longer refer to these background expectancies as "rules," because of inherent problems in the concept of a rule, he would still insist on their instructably reproducible character in details. The essential point of his criticism is that the details of these propositions or rules are not available to Dewey and Mead, because they work conceptually, and in an attitude of theoretical reflection. Therefore, the processes of order are not available to them.

Whereas all four Pragmatists begin with some form of the individual and individual psychology, Garfinkel treats what others would call individual, or social, psychology—including the attribution of cognitive and affective states—as a matter of rules (instructably reproducible practices in details) of social transformation, maintaining that any conception of the whole individual is a reification. According to Garfinkel (p. 144):

> The point of all this is that whatever we mean by affective and cognitive as terms is defined in terms of the structural make-up and the structural transformations of actual experiences. A further point: these transformations proceed according to certain logics or rules. Thus we have the logic of rational discourse; the logic of expressional action; of the action of various pathological states, of free association; and so on. The problems ramify in their complexity if we extend our concerns to the logics of action of the various orders of social relationships.

It is the logics of social situations that explain the situated psychology of actors, for Garfinkel, not the character of persons, as collections of roles and motives—however socially determined. Garfinkel's focus is on the structure of social action, conceived of as situated action, not on the individual. In this respect he is the student of Parsons, not James. As we saw in the discussion of groups, Garfinkel argues that persons, just like institutions and the idea of group mind, are ideal constructions/objects.

Garfinkel's comments on the four Pragmatists will be taken up in the order in which they appear in the text: James first, then Peirce, Mead, and Dewey. James receives the most involved treatment, because the consideration of James is tied up with considerations of Schütz (who was writing about James) as well as Husserl and Parsons. Tracing the way Garfinkel's argument builds through his critique of the four Pragmatists lends a different emphasis to the various themes that have already been considered.

Garfinkel and William James: Consciousness versus Social Aspects of Modes of Attention

In the section titled "Role and the Concept of the Finite Province of Meaning," Garfinkel weaves his argument about perception, reality, self, and meaning through criticisms of the arguments of William James, Alfred Schütz, Edmund Husserl, and Talcott Parsons. Essentially Garfinkel uses the discussions of James and Phenomenology to set up his evaluation of Parsons and his own proposal for what a radical empiricism would need to consist of. Therefore, this section will also consider the relevance of the critique of James for Garfinkel's consideration of Parsons.

Garfinkel explicitly accepts "radical empiricism" as an objective in this manuscript. But he argues that James's own conception of radical empiricism lacks the social elements that would make it work. Schütz he considers to have improved on James in having seen that "reality" is dependent, not on a simple relationship between objects and the purposeful perceiver, but that the meaning of objects and the orientation of the perceiver is socially determined in specifiable ways. Husserl adds an additional dimension of complexity to the relationship between perception and reality, but retains an emphasis on the individual.

It is important not to take Garfinkel's acceptance of the goal of radical empiricism for an acceptance of radical empiricism as James articulated it. Like Durkheim before him, Garfinkel accepts the objective, while rejecting the pragmatist approach to it. Both argue that the solution is to locate the ordering principles in social practices, rather than in individual reason, or individual projects, motives, and desires.[35]

What a true radical empiricism required, for Garfinkel, was to get the researcher out of the theoretical attitude and into the situation, or, as Marx would say, to have them remain in "history"; to replace logic, as the explanation of associations in meaning, with situated procedures for interpretation, cognitive styles, and situated background expectancies; and, finally, to replace the idea of the whole person and their motivations (which is conceptual) with concrete situated actors and identities, and the production of situated order in details, as a primary motivation.[36]

Subjectivity and Objectivity

While Garfinkel follows James in inverting objectivity and subjectivity—arguing that what originates with the actor (subjectivity) is objective and that what originates with the observer (objectivity) is subjective—and references William James explicitly to this effect, what Garfinkel means by subjectivity and objectivity is something quite different. For Garfinkel, the objectivity of subjectivity is given by the response of the other.

"According to William James," Garfinkel says (p. 125), "the origin of all reality is subjective; whatever excites and stimulates our interest is real. To call a thing real means that this thing stands in a certain relation to ourselves." For James, subjectivity originates with the individual, and perception and interest are matters of individual consciousness. As Garfinkel says, for James "there are multiple numbers of such orders of reality, each with its own special and separate style of existence," all having origins in the individual. For James the difference between realities lies in the relationship between something and the self or perceiver. The difference lies in the manner of individual consciousness.

For Garfinkel, by contrast, subjectivity is given both by the response of the other and by the orientation of the actor toward that response. The way in which objects are given in perception and the way in which the perceiver orients toward those objects are themselves anchored in situated orders of expectation (cognitive styles, background expectancies, identities, procedural rules for interpretation, etc.) that are structured through reciprocating sequences of practice.

Garfinkel treats the subjectivity and objectivity of identity claims as a situated matter in just this way. Identity depends on the response of the other—not on membership in a demographic group but, rather, on the situated identity construction of group membership. Garfinkel gives an example of prejudice (anti-Semitism) as an illustration of the fact that one is an outsider, a minority, in the case in which the other treats one as a minority, whether or not one is "really" a minority in terms of some correspondence theory of truth. Similarly, one may be what others would call "really" a minority, and it may be irrelevant to the situation and therefore does not come up and does not become a situated identity. On the other hand, if a minority identity is imputed to the actor, then the question of whether or not the actor is "really" a minority is not relevant to the identity the actor finds themselves stuck with in the situated interaction.

The point, with regard to "objectivity," is important. The truth criteria that most scholars would treat as "objective" are in fact *completely irrelevant* in Garfinkel's view. So is what the individual perceiver believes about themselves. If we go with the so-called "objective" view, we encounter absurdities such as persons who are being discriminated against, who are told that it is not happening because they do not "objectively" fit some category of persons who can be discriminated against. On the "subjective" view we might have a person objecting that they are not "really" a member of the category in question, or don't view themselves in this way. According to Garfinkel, these "facts" don't matter (except insofar as they can be invoked in the situation in concrete actions to change the orientation of others toward one's identity). It is the treatment of the actor by other parties to the interaction—which would typically be considered subjective, variable, or even arbitrary—that in reality constitutes the facts of the case.

While Garfinkel's treatment of identity does result in different modes of consciousness, as does James's, the source of these differences lies outside of the individual in specifiable orders of practices in detail, and, therefore, "subjectivity" is rendered as an observable social matter. Thus, treating the relationship between a perceiver and an object of perception as a primary reality, as James did, is from Garfinkel's perspective a mistake. The possibility of perceiving objects as "objects of a sort" depends on the actor's location in a social organization and their commitment to the situated expectations belonging to that location. It depends on the response of the "other." It is the practices in which actors are mutually engaged that organize perception such that objects can be given to it as objects of a sort.

Schütz and Parsons

To begin to articulate what a social organization that would organize perception in this way might consist of, Garfinkel first turns to Schütz. Whereas for James any object that stimulates an individual's interest is real, for Schütz the relationship between an object and a perceiving consciousness depends on the *mode of attention* of the perceiver to that object, and these modes of attention have *social* components.

Schütz makes distinctions between several social modes of attention, which, according to Garfinkel (p. 125), are "the world of daily life; the world of phantasms; the world of dreams; and the world of scientific theory." Only while the perceiver is actively engaged in a mode of attention to life will the objects which appear to be real in that mode of attention continue to appear real. If there is a switch in the mode of attention, according to James, as quoted by Schütz (Garfinkel p. 125), the "reality lapses with the attention." Thus, it is the mode of attention to life, as *a social structure of attention,* that determines perception and gives objects within it the accent of reality and not individual consciousness.

This argument not only constitutes a critique of James but also sets up Garfinkel's discussion of Parsons. It is a critique of James because now (1) objects are real only while being attended to in a socially defined mode of consciousness; and (2) their reality is given not by their relationship to the perceiver but, rather, by their relationship to the particular mode of attention, cognitive style, and so on, in which they present themselves, which is a socially structured situated matter.

The argument also lays the foundation for a critique of Parsons, because while Parsons focused on the social, he remained within the theoretical attitude in trying to work out a radical empiricism (a challenge that in Garfinkel's view Parsons did accept). The problem is that in the theoretical attitude the accent of reality is given to concepts (like the person) and not to practices. Concepts would not receive the accent of reality in the mode of attention of everyday life; practices would.

Surprisingly, Garfinkel argues that Parsons's approach was phenomenological in essential respects, and that, in trying to specify social conditions for meaning, Parsons was after the same thing as Schütz. But just as Garfinkel argues that Schütz didn't go quite far enough in treating the conditions of understanding as social, he will argue that

Parsons overbuilt the social elements, reifying practices into transcendental structures, with the result that what needed to be examined was obscured. Thus, what Garfinkel refers to as Parsons's "phenomenology" focused on idealized objects and used the reasoning processes of reflection and scientific theorizing, rather than that of working acts.

Therefore, while Garfinkel will say that the form of Parsons's argument is phenomenological, it is embedded in assumptions about the perceiver and objects that belong only to the scientific mode of attention to life and therefore have no application to the world of actual working acts and, in fact, obscure their details from view. According to Garfinkel (p. 137):

> One can say, then, that while Parsons had been radical about the problem, he hadn't been radical enough in that he sought these apodictic structures without challenging some very important naturalistic constructions not the least of which are the idealistic conceptions of primal categories and the concomitant correspondence theory of reality. This would mean that there are still ontological elements in the meanings of the structures he proposed—in this case a scientific ontology—which would mean in turn that the break with ethnocentrism had been incomplete.

Since the appearance of not only persons/identities, but also of objects, depends on particular socially configured modes of attention to them (and ways of producing the appearance of them), to treat these objects as given is to allow everything about how one's world is socially structured into one's so-called impartial and objective "universally applicable" criteria.

Specifically, the two main consequences of remaining in the scientific attitude toward life mentioned by Garfinkel are, *first,* that the individual appears as a whole. This is because the scientific attitude is a contemplative attitude. The actor is not actively involved in working acts and so is engaged in reflecting back over a number of working acts. In this mode of attention, the stream of consciousness appears as a unity and creates the impression that the person as an actor engaged in working acts is also such a unity.

Second, the idea that there are not only multiple realities but also multiple roles, interests, and motivations, competing for attention in the person at each point, emerges from this reification of the person in both Pragmatism and Parsons's sociology. When an aggregation of motives are taken to be a source of order, problems are created. However, this problem of multiple roles, in Garfinkel's view, is the direct result of seeing the person as a unity. He will take up the idea of the individual as a container for motives, roles, and competing motivations in more detail in his considerations of Peirce, Mead, and Dewey.

For Garfinkel, Schütz is an improvement over James in that the accent of reality is seen to depend on something social outside the individual perceiver. But with regard to both Schütz and Parsons, Garfinkel argues that the social considerations invoked have a universal, logical, and ideal character that is unsuited to the actual situated and detailed character of working acts. While he applauds their initial insight, both Parsons and Schütz have remained in the scientific/theoretical attitude, and, as a consequence, aspects of the mode of theoretical attention that reify the details of working acts have been transposed into their perspectives.

A theoretical mode of attention is antithetical to discovering the details of social practices, in Garfinkel's view, because the theoretical mode of attention reifies separate things into wholes and concrete details into concepts. Furthermore, not only are the details of working acts taken for granted from within a theoretical mode of attention, but because work is necessary in order to render objects visible, and the theoretical mode of attention does not involve the work that would make them visible, they cannot be made visible from within this mode of attention.

This, of course, is in large part why Garfinkel has been so insistent on avoiding theory. The objects Garfinkel has discovered through his research conflict with the objects one would expect to find if one began from a theoretical mode of attention. Therefore, those with conventional theoretical training cannot fit his argument into a recognizable conventional framework of argument: It does not fit.

Garfinkel argues that the conventional framework for theorizing, and the objects that it apprehends, are not those which we need to know something about to explain social order, meaning, reason, morality, and so on. The answers to the large human questions are not available from within the theoretical mode of attention to life. Unfortunately, that is where we usually look for them.[37]

The way in which this theoretical attitude approaches the problem of social order is, according to Garfinkel, by building models and constructing "dummies." He says (p. 128): "The dimensions of the vivid present are inaccessible to the theorizing self. Consequently, the theorizing self is solitary; it has no social environment; it stands outside social relationships." As a consequence, it is the model and the dummy, and not the engaged actor, that receives the accent of reality within the scientific attitude. This characterizes Parsons, as well as conventional social science and philosophy. "The accent," according to Garfinkel (p. 128), "is not that of the natural attitude," in which this "dummy" would not be oriented toward as real.

It might seem that the difference between modes of reality would make translation between modes of attention to reality impossible. But Garfinkel argues that the distance between modes of attention is not total because the same person passes through many in a day. This is how it is possible to transpose the theoretical onto working acts. Otherwise, according to Garfinkel (p. 128), theoretical thought could not even be communicated intersubjectively.[38]

The relationship between meaningful acts in the natural attitude is governed by background expectations, identities, and so forth; but in the theoretical attitude, according to Garfinkel (p. 129), that relationship appears to be governed by "canons of rational discourse." So, another consequence of remaining in the scientific mode of attention, and of failing to distinguish between different modes of situated social organization, is that reason and logic appear to govern associations between perceptions. For Garfinkel, reason and logic can be invoked only in reflection. The original relations between perceptions that we attribute to reason and logic are constructed through the detailed social structures of working acts, a public reasoning process that is ignored.

In talking about the way in which clusterings of meaningful associations result from situated orders of expectation, rules of procedure, sequences, and so on, and not from reason, as a transcendent characteristic of consciousness, Garfinkel (p. 130) argues that "[o]nce the prejudice has been set aside that such combinations are little better than interesting and transitory aberrancies of man's basic rational or irrational endowment (one can take a choice or hold both with the same consequence) the questions of what these clusterings do in fact look like … are free to emerge." The essential issue is not the rational or irrational makeup of the person but the orderly character of reciprocal sequential practice that makes reasoning as a mutually engaged process possible.

From Garfinkel's perspective, individual thought, reason, perception, and so forth, are organized through specifiable configurations of social expectations from what he calls the logics of social situations. To begin with reason and individual perception is to mistake the result of social orders for the origin point in the process. "Thinking, willing, and feeling," which are so basic for James, have for Garfinkel (pp. 144–145) "no better than 'If … then' status, and," Garfinkel says, "much research is needed into the experience structures which these terms supposedly designate. Once we get behind the barriers that Kant set for us, we find a field that is practically unexplored."[39]

Garfinkel and Charles Sanders Peirce: Identity as Object versus Identity as Symbolic Object

In the section titled "Social Identity," Garfinkel contrasts his view with Peirce. He argues that identity is a symbolic object that is constructed in situations according to procedural rules and so on, and not a possession of individual selves. The conventional conception of identity as an object, according to Garfinkel (p. 145–146), accords "with C. S. Peirce's formula [Garfinkel citing Peirce]: 'Consider what effects that might conceivably have practical bearings you conceive the object of your conception to have. Then your conception of those effects is the whole of your conception of the object.'" With the modification that the object status of conceptions is given by social considerations and not by the perceiving consciousness, Garfinkel admits to a partial acceptance of this formula. "Like any object," Garfinkel says (p. 146), the meaning of identity "as an object is found in the mode of action taken with reference to it." Like other objects, Garfinkel says (p. 145), "[t]he social identity is seen by the actor as a real object, and is experienced directly as a real object."

However, for Garfinkel, by contrast with Peirce, it is the practices and their background expectancies that invest objects (including the self) with the accent of reality. According to Garfinkel (p. 145):

> [T]he identity is social in the sense that it is an element of a cognitive style which cognitive style is dialectically relevant to a series of transformations of social relationships occasioned by working acts performed with reference to another actor. As an object, its mode of reality, like any other object, is found with reference to a specific finite province of meaning.

It is only within situations and their expectations (and cognitive styles), in mutual engagement with others, that identities can be enacted and apprehended.

Furthermore, identity is a symbolic object and its meaning requires attention to social practices, not to the scientific laws of cause and effect. But for Garfinkel (p. 147), the meaningfulness of terms of identity and their rules of manipulation "are not constituted by the actor according to the guiding rules of scientific actions. That they exhibit their own lawfulness goes without saying. But what that lawfulness consists of still remains to be investigated." What Garfinkel means by "lawfulness" here is that identities are made in and through the situated details of practices. These practices have their own laws, which reside in the orderliness of their details, and could not be formulated by the individual by reference to their projects, scientific laws, or abstract principles.

Therefore, while Garfinkel appears to treat the self, or identity, as an object in a way that is superficially consistent with Peirce, there are two important differences. *First,* that object, real as it may be, is nevertheless constructed from symbolic procedures and interpretive processes that have their basis in situated social structures; and, *second,* according to Garfinkel (p. 146), identity for the observer is "a *symbolic* object, and always and only a symbolic object." It does not belong to any person but, rather, to situated practices, and its being symbolic distinguishes identity from other objects that are not symbolic.

Being symbolic means that identity has meaning, not existence. According to Garfinkel (p. 148): "When we are in the area of social persons, we do not say that identities exist; rather we say that they are *meant*." For the Pragmatists, identity is an object; it exists, has the accent of reality, and is a property of persons. For Garfinkel, identity has meaning, is meant, and, as such, is a property not of persons but of situated enacted practices in details: Only as such does it receive the accent of reality.

This symbolic character of identity makes it different from other objects for Garfinkel. In that it is a symbolic object constituted according to procedural rules of interpretation, background expectancies, cognitive styles, and so forth, there is a ritual aspect to identity. Like institutions and traditional social forms, identity takes on a more stable routinized character. This is achieved through a system of institutionalized accounts and accounting practices, and while the process is enacted over the course of sequences, it is also made with a view to accountable constraints. According to Garfinkel (p. 149), the actor confirms or disconfirms an identity by acting in ways that can be accounted for (or not) according to the relevant motivational accounts, which is not at all the same thing as having motivations.

This is what Garfinkel means by saying that identity has a ritual character. When actors construct identities, they not only have to observe the background expectancies relevant to sequences but must also keep ritualized aspects of identity, and the motivational accounts that violations will generate about them, in view ("If I do X what will people say about me?"). They are certainly not free to do whatever they "want." Actions that violate identity expectations generate motivational accounts that can have serious implications for both present and future action.

Labeling Sick Soldiers

During World War II Garfinkel was attached to the Gulfport Field Station Army Hospital. While there his observations of hospital practices led him to develop some observations about ways in which the possible identities for doctors and patients were tied to situated rules and regulations in specifiable ways. He observed that if you were a sick soldier there were very few "positions you could occupy as far as the army doctor was concerned" (p. 154). This had to do with, among other things, the doctor's accountability to army regulations. This meant that there was a labeling process for the sick soldiers, and that the assignment of different labels led to very different outcomes for the men. This section (pp. 154–158) sketches out something resembling what would develop later as labeling theory. It is also important as a precursor to studies in the 1950s, by Goffman, Szasz, Sykes, and others, of total institutions (hospital and prison) as settings in which special identities (often stigmatizing and not recognized elsewhere) are required.[40]

Garfinkel describes the relationship between doctors and patients, and the various identities that a wounded soldier could occupy at the hospital. He works out on several dimensions what it is about the institution, regulations, and social context of the hospital that require of patient and doctor alike that they take on closely circumscribed identities, unique to this setting. These identities then allow for the work of both doctoring and being sick, and ultimately provide parameters for deciding the fate of the soldiers. Examples are given of ways in which institutionalized expectations, with regard to accounts, and limitations on medical expertise, structure recognizable identities for the soldiers.

Whether a soldier is really sick or not, how sick, and how the case should be treated are matters decided on the basis of the soldier's presentation of self in one of four categories. Beginning with the designation "sick soldier" these were, according to Garfinkel (p. 154): "Sick soldier to cured soldier; sick soldier to malingerer; sick soldier to army dischargee; and sick soldier to very sick soldier." Garfinkel (p. 154) points out that "the latter four identities were logically derivable from the army regulations bearing on the treatment of sick soldiers." His point being that the doctors were accountable to these regulations, and, therefore, the identities they recognized needed also to be accountable to these regulations.

Once having assigned soldiers to identity categories, the doctors treated the motivations belonging to a given category as the *real* motivations of all soldiers who had been assigned to that category. In an interesting sense, the doctors are acting in the same way that social scientists act, in attributing motivation to the soldiers according to identity categories and then treating those motivations as originating with the soldiers. The thing is never seen from the soldier's point of view, and is not reciprocal. The soldier does not get to interpret the doctor's assignment of category; and as the soldiers found themselves constrained to working within a presentation of one of the existing four identities, they had few choices. Yet, the motivation assigned to the soldier by the doctor was supposed to be the soldier's own personal motivation.

Even though actors have a primary motivation to produce orderly sequences of action to create meaning, their primary motivation with regard to identities is to display behavior that confirms the identity they are trying to present. According to Garfinkel (p. 149):

> Regardless of the ways in which they are constructed, *identities furnish the premises* [emphasis added] for the treatment of the other person. Not only then are identities the source, so to speak, of the norms which govern social actions, but the terms of the motivational account point to the paths which lead directly to the operative values of a social system. We can hypothesize that as a social system changes, the motivational theories will change also.

In Garfinkel's view, identities generate norms, not the reverse. And the motivational accounts that can be imputed to identities lay out the values of a social system. Garfinkel is not arguing that the procedural rules for presenting and enacting identities will change as the social system changes. What he says is that the motivational accounts imputed to actors, and consequently the motivational theories about individual behavior, which are all retrospective and belong to the theoretical attitude, will change as the social system changes. It is in this sense that a scientific view of the actor, for Garfinkel, is inherently ethnocentric because it treats motivational accounts that belong to the system as belonging to the individual.

In Garfinkel's view, actors are not motivated by norms and values to pursue valued courses of action; rather, in trying to produce actions which accord with the motivational accounts that (in a particular configuration of social structures) go with their identities, actors can be seen in retrospect to have taken on the norms and values belonging to those identities and conferred on them the accent of reality. Conventional social science involves a circularity because it treats those norms and values as explaining the behavior (and the motivations behind the behavior) that norms and values are in fact *an exhibit of.* This is what Garfinkel means (p. 114) when he says that there can be no identity without norms: The ritual character of identity generates the appearance of norms and confers on them the accent of reality.

Actually, according to Garfinkel (p. 149), "the identity is nothing else than a scheme employed by the actor for interpreting the signs generated by the other persons—a scheme whereby the question of the other person's intentions is answered." However, the more the actor, or the observer (theorist), treats the identity as having an *ontological status,* the more norms and values will appear to be the real motivations for that identity. In other words, if the identity is seen as a construction, a scheme for interpretation, then *how* it is constructed and used for interpretation will obviously be important and become a research focus. But to the extent that the identity is treated as real, as an object, then values will also appear to be real and research will focus on values and motives.

So, we have returned to the initial point about Peirce. The social actor sees identity in reflection as a real object. But this obscures what is actually going on, because an identity is meant; it needs always to be seen in the context of the social practices that give it meaning. Therefore, researchers must avoid treating identity as a real object: It must be treated as a symbolic meaning/object, which has meaning, not existence, and whose construction takes constant care and must be explained as a configuration of interpretational and presentational procedures, not motivational values. The accent of reality is on meaning and not existence.

Garfinkel and Mead: Sequential Responses versus Taking the Role of the Other

Garfinkel turns to a consideration of Mead toward the end of the section on "Identity Constancy and Identity Transformation." There are several respects in which he challenges Mead's formulation of the self. *First,* Garfinkel takes Mead to task over his conception of the "I," arguing that it constitutes a reification of the person. *Second,* he argues that Mead's "taking the role of the other" locates the exchange of positions between persons in the imagination, or consciousness, rather than in the actual sequential exchange between actors in situations. *Third,* Garfinkel argues that the result of not grasping the importance of sequential orders in details, combined with treating actors as whole persons, leads to problems with the conception of motivation. Motivation comes to be treated as a property of actors and their roles, rather than as a property of the relationship *between* actors located in the background expectations of situated orders and identities.

The differences between Mead and Garfinkel are serious and consequential. Conceptions such as "taking the role of the other" are at the heart of Symbolic Interactionism as it developed—and much interactionism, including the work of Goffman, retains deep elements of what Garfinkel would criticize as reified conceptions of a whole self, considered from a scientific, or theoretical, perspective.[41]

The general view that Garfinkel should be understood as another interactionist in this regard is a problem. The reasons why begin to become clear in this section. Garfinkel's outline for sociology focuses on social order, in the form of situated practices, and refuses to accept any form of individualism. To take the perspective of the actor, for Garfinkel, is not to take the perspective of a person but, rather, to take a perspective embedded in "identified action."

Reification of the Self in Mead

The idea that Garfinkel focuses on the individual is directly contradicted by what he has to say about the self in Mead. Garfinkel (p. 167) argues that it is essential to avoid the idea that the self in its working acts is ever a "really-real-whole-full-blown-self." There is no "real" or "unified" self behind the identities performed by actors, in the natural attitude. Identity is a property of the actor engaged in working acts. The unified self is a property of the reflective mode of attention. In Mead's terms the experiences of separate identities are unified by the "I," which he posits as the source of creative action. But for Garfinkel (p. 168), "to take this course is to break with the attempt to account for action in its own terms and from the point of view of the actor."

In Garfinkel's view (p. 192), at any given point in working acts, the actor must be absorbed in producing the particular identified self with which they are currently engaged: The actor is always focused on only one situation when engaged in action: "Within the 'flow' of the actor's experience, at any given time he is acting with reference to one and only one system of action, and at any given time he is acting as a participant in one and only one group." Therefore, an actor can only orient toward one identity at a time.

There are only two ways that the self appears as a unity in Garfinkel's view, and neither is relevant to the perspective of the working acts in and through which identities are created and maintained. *First,* the actor, according to Garfinkel (p. 167), "experiences his own action as self-originated," and when they pause for reflection they attribute the action to an internal unified self; and, *second,* while the "identified self may designate a whole array of different identities," for Garfinkel (p. 167), "in one important respect they are alike: they all have reference to the actor; they represent the actor."

Garfinkel (p. 168) also dismisses the alternative of treating the "I" "as an unengaged Viewer—"found in the various vocabularies of motives which posit the mind (or its equivalents—ego, self, real person)...." This perspective is a problem because it treats something as "relevant or real to action" that is not subject to the rules of inquiry. Actors and observers have access to the details of practices, but the mind is beyond their view. The consequence of focusing on something that is not relevant to action, and could not be subject to the rules of procedure for action, according to Garfinkel (p. 168), is that "one courts properties of belief" instead of examining the details of practices.

For Garfinkel (p. 168) there is only one alternative that works: "The *I* in the language of things is a term used by an observer to designate a subject's actions. The concept of 'subject of action' designates not the vessel which 'contains' sources, or impellents, or motives (in the causal sense), of action, but designates only where the observer must look to observe conduct." As an observer's term, the "I" does not designate a quality of self-consciousness. It points toward a location where identified action is taking place.

For Garfinkel (p. 170), the self is not a container of motivation/action but a location, where you need to look to study action: "Self with the big *S* means action; self with the small s means an intended object ... identified Self means identified action."

The Motivation Problem in Mead versus Garfinkel

Garfinkel argues that the effect of Mead's position is to reify the person. He says (p. 168) that the person "is envisaged as the 'vessel of the motive,' resulting in a 'fuzziness of the motivation concepts.'"

Thinking of the person as a unity is a reification that results in losing sight of the social processes through which identities are engaged and enacted. The fact that the motive to engage in social processes in an orderly and expected manner resides in situations and their practices is obscured. The result is that we falsely come to think of persons as containers for motivations, and to think of the motivation problem as one of looking for the motives of individual actors—rather than looking for motives in the background expectancies, and so on, that constitute situations.

If the self is a location, where one looks to study "identified action," and not a container of motives, then where one should look for motivation is in the procedural rules of situated action, and not to individuals as collections of roles. This cannot be seen if the actor is treated as a given. Even though Mead argues that the self is a product of interaction, the existence of the actor as a person is confused with the existence of an identity as a meaning, and the idea that the individual provides the unifying function for identities is still treated as a given. According to Garfinkel, this is backward. He argues that "[a]ction and not the 'concrete individual' is the given" (p. 169). Because of this, he maintains that "what is needed as far as the motivation problem is concerned is (1) investigation into the structure of the various types of action …; (2) the scientific description of action sequences; (3) the 'discovery' of those ordering principles by which such phenomena as sequences, integration, etc. may be logically explained" (p. 169).

Garfinkel's focus would be on action as the location in which identities are created. This would require that action be taken as a given, not the actor. That in turn would locate motivations in situations and their procedural rules, not in persons. Garfinkel's argument that Mead's treatment of the self results in a misplacement of the motivation question is particularly interesting given Anthony Giddens's argument, in *The Constitution of Society* (1984), that Garfinkel's primary shortcoming is his failure to address the motivation problem. From Giddens's perspective Garfinkel is a failed Pragmatist or Symbolic Interactionist. But Giddens has attributed to Garfinkel a formulation of the motivation problem that Garfinkel argued resulted from reification of the self. Given Garfinkel's argument that the motivation to construct recognizable orders must be any actor's primary motivation, and that secondary motivations come from situated identities, it has always been clear that Garfinkel did not ignore the motivation problem. Furthermore, in Garfinkel's view, putting motivation front and center is a problem. The motivation question is *not* the important one when it comes to understanding social order.[42]

The order of situated action is the important question. For Garfinkel (p. 169), motives are properties of situations and situated identities, not properties of individual actors: "Every social relationship will have its peculiar order of motives that the actors assign to each other." But while the actors treat these motives as originating inside of the other, they actually belong to the situation, its background expectancies, and its cognitive styles. Furthermore, these motives are not assigned by the one who acts to themselves, but, rather, are assigned by one actor to the other.

Therefore, when social scientists look for the motives that impel actors, they are engaging in what Garfinkel (p. 169) calls "the will-of-the-wisp of subjectivism." Any research beginning from the perspective of the actor, as a whole person, or taking the "viewpoint" of a type of actor, would be a problem. Garfinkel focuses on the perspective of identified actors engaged in working acts—putting situated action first and treating identity as location for action. In view of his complete rejection of individualism, it is more than ironic that many people have seen Garfinkel as a subjectivist and have interpreted Ethnomethodology as focused on the individual.

Taking the Role of the Other

Garfinkel's reformulation of Mead's "taking the role of the other" begins well into the section on "communication" (pp. 169–195). Mead's formulation of this exchange of perspectives has been very influential. The idea that viewing oneself from the perspective of the other explains the possibility of self-reflection has become almost synonymous with social psychology. Given the influence of these ideas, and because it is necessary to give them up to some extent in order to grasp Garfinkel's position, his critique of Mead on this point is particularly important.

What Garfinkel argues is that Mead's conception of selves as containers for roles—who learn about themselves by putting themselves in the place of others, who are also containers of roles—both reifies the self and misses the point. Actors do something like this *in practice*—but not this thing in imagination, and not as a performance of unified selves. Not only does Mead's formulation miss the point, according to Garfinkel, but by positing the actor in these terms (as a unified container for roles, motives, and self-consciousness) it obscures what is really going on (the details and background expectancies of the situation) relative to identity as a *location* for the enactment of certain practices.

The direct result of Mead's conception, Garfinkel argues, is the effort to explain mutual understanding on the basis of individual perspectives and conceptual typifications. Because coherence is not produced through symbolic acts (typifications) but, rather, through the careful production of recognizable orders of practice (practices witnessable in details), it is impossible to explain coherence on the basis of typifications. Ambiguity appears to multiply and the postmodern "abyss" results.

In explaining the sequential production of mutual understanding in communication, Garfinkel describes a process of ordering interaction whereby hearers produce for speakers interpretations of what they have said as next sequences of interaction. In the description of this exchange we can see Garfinkel's answer to Mead.

In Garfinkel's formulation, the actor does not take the role of the other toward themselves—an act of imagination. The information about how the other sees—interprets—the actor is given in the other's sequential responses. According to Garfinkel (p. 170):

> [T]he actor's action with reference to the identified other takes place on the assumption by the actor of how he is given to the other. The other, by his actions, furnishes the actor with the material by which the actor discerns the intentions of the other, these intentions being the material by which the actor's assumptions with regard to his own self givenness are confirmed, threatened, etc.

The actor makes an assumption based on the procedural rules of the situation, and of the identified other. The other, by their response, either confirms or alters, but always gives back more. The response is incorporated into the premises of action of the next move, and so on. Motives are always imputed to the one by the other on the basis of the actual unfolding sequence of moves and its relationship to background expectations and situated identities.

The sequences proceed according to detailed expectations with regard to the order of interaction. Actors do not "choose" what meanings to present to the other just any way they want to. Rather, they must work within a framework of procedures and expectations in which achieving meaning is the same thing as achieving orderliness. Identity, like any other symbol, can mean anything. Giving identity a particular meaning is the same thing as rendering it in an orderly and recognizable manner, in a specific location of action, according to the procedures and expectations of that situation.

According to Garfinkel (p. 170), "the dialectic of the process is such that it is as if the actor says: 'By your actions you tell me who I am, and by my actions, I'll tell you who you are.'" It is not a matter of symbolic exchange of position, as in Mead's taking the role of the other, but of actual responses from others to one's actions. And it is not a response to the person as a role, or a collection of roles, but a response to a specific sequence of action (as identified action).

The actor is a *place* to look for the process of this mutual exchange— not a container of it. For Garfinkel (p. 171), "the library guard is a library guard because he treats another person as a book-borrower." Of course, the other must also treat him as a guard, and other things as well. Garfinkel also puts it another way (p. 171): "*[T]he stability of the actor's givenness as an identified self is directly dependent on whether it continues to be possible for the actor to treat the object according to the terms of the actor's definition of the object.*" Since the object in this case can be an identified other, the response of the other would need to be an expected response in order for the actor to continue with their original definition of the object.

Thus, for Garfinkel, it is not a sympathetic exchange in imagination that makes an understanding of the self from the perspective of the other possible; rather, it is the fact that the identities that they enact, and the relationship between them, are part of the situated expectations that any member of the situation has available to them. When they work within the framework of the situation to confirm and disconfirm one another's actions, they also give feedback about identity ("identified action") to one another. Treating the mutual exchange as having something to do with selves as containers, instead of being embedded in the reciprocating practices characteristic of the sequential practices of the situation, deflects attention from those sequential practices. It makes the self seem real, while at the same time it ironically renders the practices (which do exist and invest identity with meaning) invisible.

What we actually do in our working acts—what gives us the information about ourselves—is to see how the other treats *what* we do. This we actually see and hear. It is the other's treatment of *what* we do, interpreted in a way that is consistent with the cognitive styles and background expectations belonging to the situation, that tells us how they have interpreted our actions (what we look like from the other's perspective)—which is not an exercise of imagination.

The difference is not small. In contrast to Mead's formulation, Garfinkel describes a reciprocation through practice with an identified actor located in a situated place and sequence of time. As such, it does some of the same things that Mead claims for it. For instance, interpretation, intention, and self-reflection are involved. But it has some very different implications and, most important, would be studied in a very different way.

How coherence is made through practice would become a focus. Motivation would become much less important. Issues of identity, or membership categories such as race and gender, would be located in the background expectations of situated interactions (or collections of them over time) rather than in the life experiences of individual persons. "My perspective," which has become popular as a symbolic point of analysis—or anything else that involved a focus on the experience of the "whole person," as an expert informant on their category—would be out.

The details of interactions are not available to identified actors as details just because they stand in an identity. A woman, like any other researcher, would have to study the details of an interaction in order to discover the constraints on the production of her identity. Racial identities would involve similar productions of "identified action" at the level of "Interaction Orders," and would need to be studied in and as details.[43]

The mutual exchange of sequential confirmations of understanding is at the heart of Garfinkel's theory of communication. Each time the "other" speaks they are offering an interpretation of a prior action that tells the speaker how their "identified action" has been interpreted. The speaker then uses this information to understand not only the developing sequence of communication but also their relationship with the person they are speaking to in that situation. How that person sees them is given in how they treat what the speaker says. Since many interpretations can be given of most things, the interpretation that *is* given reveals much about how one is seen by the other.

Garfinkel's position is really a much stronger argument than Mead's because the exchange happens in a public and mutually verifiable way. It also explains why the presentation of self is so fragile and requires such a strong moral commitment. Goffman and Mead fall just short of this, the result being the idea of strategic and false presentations of self—with a "true" self and "true" motives hiding somewhere in the background. The process, as Garfinkel outlines it, can be studied in details, whereas Mead's cannot, and tends to devolve to discussions of particular perspectives, symbolic negotiation, and culture.

Garfinkel and Dewey: The Situated Actor Is Not a Mosaic of Roles

The critique of Dewey builds directly on the discussion of Mead. Garfinkel has argued that Mead's approach reifies persons and roles and results in the elevation of motivation to center stage. Now he argues that the result of this reification can be seen in conceptions such as the "role conflict" in Dewey's "segmental self":

> The fallacy [of role conflict] is an obvious one and stems from confounding (1) the relationship that exists between the identified self and the identity of the other, which refers to the form of sociality, one of the concepts by which the actor is defined, with (2) the relationship that exists between two actors. That is, the other actor is lost sight of entirely, with the result that group member becomes synonymous with group. (p. 194)

The relationship between two actors, which is situated in practices with procedural rules, background expectancies, and identities, is reduced to a mode of consciousness in one actor. The idea of a self as a collection of roles, and of conflict between these roles, is for Garfinkel purely an ideal construct, and involves the nonsense of a one-member group.

Garfinkel (p. 192) refers to John Dewey's "'segmental' representation of the 'public mind'" as an example of the conception of the person as a mosaic of roles and their corresponding motivations that results from treating the person as a whole.

For Garfinkel, the idea that a situated actor is a mosaic of roles and competing motivations is simply meaningless. He argues that "the statement that at any given time an actor participates in more than one system of action is neither true or false when it is proposed at the level of action depicted in terms of the premises of action: rather, the statement is nonsense" (p. 192). It is nonsense because it has nothing to do with what actually happens when an actor is engaged in working acts. In each working act any actor is totally focused on enacting one and only one identity.

According to Garfinkel, there is some accuracy in the insight that the self is a configuration of roles with simultaneous *membership* in different groups. But only in the following sense: (p. 192) "[E]mpirically the actions of a person have never been exhaustively depicted when one and only one classification was employed, although theoretically a one class person is 'possible.'" The actions of a person may, he says (p. 192), "after analysis" be classified in ways that attribute various "membership characters" to the same person at the same time. But they cannot actually be enacting different identities and memberships in different groups at the same time.

The idea that motives belong to actors, according to Garfinkel, comes partially from the fact that motivations are imputed to individuals in working acts when they violate expectations. Therefore, motivational accounts, which social scientists typically treat as explanations of action going forward, are in actual interactions produced only retrospectively, when action has failed to achieve an expected and recognizable order.

Garfinkel looks at the actor as a set of procedural rules. This way of looking at the actor provides, according to Garfinkel (p. 192), "a means for avoiding the representation of the actor as a mosaic of roles, and avoids the otherwise practical necessity of representing a group in ideal-typical terms." Here Garfinkel reminds us not only that our conception of the actor impacts on questions of motivation, role conflict, and individualism, but also that if we have a reified ideal self—whose identity is removed from situated action—we will find it impossible to locate what it is about people that makes them a group. We will end up with an ideal-typical conception of a group.

What this does, in turn, is to make it impossible to give any substance to the argument that society is more than the sum of its parts. Its parts on this conception would be reified whole persons and their motives and values. If we make this move, then the group is only more than the sum of its parts insofar as it involves routine and habit, the conventional view.

But if we take Garfinkel's view toward the actor as "identified action," then a group is more than the sum of its (reified) parts because a group—as a set of procedural rules for action and interpretation—makes it possible for the parts to exist (be meant) in the first place. The group makes it possible for there to be any shared meaning, identified action, actors, oriented objects, and so forth. The group is more than the sum of its parts because it makes it possible for any of the objects that appear within it (human or otherwise) to be meant, to exist in a intersubjective sense, to appear as objects of a sort.

According to Garfinkel (p. 179), once we start working with models of the actor we have entered the realm of fantasy: "All this is to be compared with the object of theoretical science, which like the fantastic object, can be anything the theoretician chooses *within a set of socially sanctioned and rational rules of action.*"

Conclusion

What Garfinkel outlines in this manuscript is a theory of social order that treats order as the foundation for mutual understanding—rather than maintaining that mutual understanding (or shared concepts) is the foundation for achieving social order. In fact, he argues that the process of making orderliness *is* the process of making mutual understanding. Furthermore, reciprocity and trust are necessary constituent parts of this order. So, it is not an arbitrary order—but one centered in egalitarian principles. Hence, according to Garfinkel, those who would engage in and produce mutually understood sequences of talk and action need to adhere to principles of moral reciprocity (or more accurately produce moral reciprocity as an observable order of practice in and through their actions). Of course, situated orders almost always take place in a context of institutionally accountable order, and hence reciprocity in practices often takes place under conditions of accountable structure that put one party at a disadvantage. Therefore, an understanding of the whole picture requires a distinction between and a focus on both situated orders of practice and the accountable orders they are usually embedded in.

The key to grasping social order as a working accomplishment in the way Garfinkel proposes is to remove the actor and their motives and values from center stage and replace them with a focus on the achievement of social orders in and through the recognizable and accountable details of working acts. Instead of treating the actor as the given and then trying to explain how and why they create the order of situations (which involves making up a model of the actor and a social structure they hypothetically orient toward), Garfinkel treats situated action as the given, the thing that has existence, and proposes that we try explaining how and why it produces the actors, orders, and motivations that it does.

Instead of treating logic and reason as the starting points for a theory of social order, theory of knowledge, or conception of justice, beginning with the individual mind, or shared conceptual structures (culture), Garfinkel argues that logic and reason are characteristics of situated orders and depend entirely on the details of these orders for their production. On this view, the mutual commitment to constitutive orders of practice is at the heart of everything that is considered essential to the human being: reason, self, and sociality. Garfinkel offers the study of social interaction as the key to unlocking the great philosophical questions. As he says, "once we get beyond Kant," reason, will, and moral reciprocity are revealed as questions of social order. They are not characteristics of the mind, however transcendental, and they are not values.

While Garfinkel's proposal remains a novel idea today, to appreciate just how revolutionary the argument is, it helps to put it in the context of the time in which it was written. Several streams of argument focusing on practices had been developing in the 1930s and 1940s. These were later eclipsed by Parsons and by more conservative mathematical belief and motive–based models in the 1950s. But in the mid-1930s Ludwig Wittgenstein and C. Wright Mills had both begun to argue that the way questions of social order and meaning had previously been formulated—as a correspondence between meanings and either rules or reality—were inherently misleading. According to Wittgenstein, meaning must be sought in the practices of use, while for Mills, the orderliness of institutions was to be sought in the "vocabularies of motive" constituting institutional practice. Asking for a correspondence either with reality or with rules, because they were not part of the process through which meaning and order are achieved, they argued, made the actual processes of meaning and order invisible, and, as a consequence, the essential questions seem impossible to answer.

This developing focus on practice was picked up in a serious way in the immediate aftermath of World War II, as a number of scholars began to focus on the great changes that were being experienced by the person in modern society: a disconnect that seemed to leave the individual without either a social or moral anchor. This disconnect also seemed to many to leave the institutions of capitalism without any moral constraints.

As the focus on practice developed, however, the focus on the individual also increased, until the social self, its perspectives, and its motives stood at the heart of the enterprise. As Garfinkel argues, because identity depends on practices for its achievement, and individual motives do not explain how and why situations are ordered, the focus on the self had the ironic effect of neutralizing the focus on practice itself. The growing influence of Phenomenology and Mead's interactionism at this time, both of which focused on the individual, underscored this effect.

In this context of increasing focus on the individual, Garfinkel took seriously the task of demonstrating the negative consequences of setting the individual (no matter how socially constructed) at the center of the argument. His extensive criticisms of Pragmatism, and of Mead in particular, in this manuscript (elaborated in section 5 of this Introduction) were intended to make this clear. Unfortunately, the point was missed and Garfinkel himself has often been classified as just another interactionist focusing on the individual.

The status of the individual in the crowd, or mass society, became a particular focus of the developing view. The crowd was a social formation in which individuals were now—really for the first time—seemingly pursuing individual, and uncoordinated, ends. Scholars worried that this created a scattered and fragmented social milieu in which the fulfillment of human potential was very much in jeopardy. Would human beings simply become detached, marginalized, and lose their bearings in such a context?

An early draft for a Foreword, written by Wittgenstein in 1930, well before the war, reflects this growing mood:

> A culture is like a big organization which assigns each of its members a place where he can work in the spirit of the whole; and it is perfectly fair for his power to be measured by the contribution he succeeds in making to the whole enterprise. In an age without culture on the other hand forces become fragmented and the power of an individual man is used up in overcoming opposing forces and frictional resistances ... so much as the unimpressive spectacle of a crowd whose best members work for purely private ends, still we must not forget that the spectacle is not what matters.[44]

These worries, emerging during the Depression years, raised again, in a new way, a strain of debate running through the late nineteenth century. Durkheim, in particular, was a major figure championing the idea of practices at the time. But most thinkers were still decrying the end of the old society and trying to figure out how to keep something equally collective, or universal, in place. It was in the midst of that debate that ideas like "culture," representing a collective symbolism and ritual binding of people together, were first articulated as a replacement for the old conception of "society."

Durkheim found himself virtually alone, at the end of the nineteenth century, in arguing that the way forward was to give up the idea that a collective binding mechanism was necessary. What held things together in modern social forms were practices with a self-regulating character: practices that organized themselves without the need for external constraint. Because these practices operated in a modern context in which shared belief could not be relied on, they required instead a deep mutual commitment—and something that Durkheim called justice—to sustain them. This, he argued, in contrast to the conventional view produced a stronger, not a weaker, interdependence between parts in modern societies.

William James was in agreement with Durkheim that collective mechanisms were no longer necessary. But James argued that order was worked out by aggregations of individuals pursuing goals/projects as a function of utility. For Durkheim, as for Garfinkel, this focus on the individual was not only wrong, but caused a problem because any focus on the individual deflected from social practices where the action and, hence, the order occurred. Durkheim argued that we should focus on the new form of social order that was developing—an order based on practices that he called self-regulating and spontaneous because they are no longer driven by a narrative of beliefs. His argument in this regard has still to be appreciated.

When the issue came up again after World War II, the debate took a new form. Scholars had pretty much given up on the idea that something comprehensive like general culture would develop to replace the older social forms. But, in general, they did not recognize the development of a new social form either, as Durkheim had suggested. What they found themselves doing was following James in describing the new circumstances in which *individuals* found themselves acting, and describing in great detail the constraints on such action—but without any broad theoretical formulation of the implications for social order.

In the hands of David Reisman, the modern individual—who was oriented toward pleasing others in their immediate situation—seemed to be something of a problem. Goffman's presentational self raised similar issues. If it was all performative, where did the motives come from? Where were the values? What about morality? If individuals were going to pursue their own ends, and the general system for coordinating those ends had eroded, then where was social order going to come from?

Reisman allowed that the "other-oriented" character, as he called it, might have some positive value, but he was not sure at the time what it was, and worried that something as essential as moral principles might have been lost. Goffman argued that a "working consensus" was necessary. But in his hands it was no more than a veneer covering questionable social arrangements. The idea that morality might have found a new location in the requirements of practices seemed to be counterbalanced by inherent inequalities in practices themselves.[45] By the 1970s some interactionists were turning to Pragmatism as a way of introducing a moral tone to studies of interaction.

* * *

What Garfinkel offered in 1948 was a novel way of approaching these problems. He pointed out that the worries about individualism, and the picture of individuals pursuing individual ends and performing selves in an uncoordinated and inherently amoral way was a result of looking at the problem of social order the wrong way around.

If we focus on individuals and their motives, then we believe that a "system" of values is required in order to coordinate the activities of individuals. Attempts to study social order will then focus on how those values are given order. But if we focus first on action, we can see that in order to get anything done, in order to have any mutually intelligible meaning in the first place, persons in situations must "play by the rules" of the situations they find themselves in: You can't score in baseball by throwing a pass. Situated action systems contain their own principles of coordination. They not only do not require overarching systems for their coordination, but, as Garfinkel argues, the idea of such systems can get in the way in several respects—not the least of which being that the belief in their necessity prevents anyone from focusing on the action.

Once the central position of situated action is recognized, the belief that order in modern society is in heightened jeopardy should dissolve. Persons in modern society are in no more danger of living in a disorganized social environment now than they ever were. In fact, they may be in even less danger. Meaning and action make demands on their own behalf—demands that do not need to be coordinated by culture. Therefore, threats to culture, or society, are not threats to meaning and order. In a form of social order coordinated through shared practices, there is less possibility of sustainable ambiguity—not more.[46] For Garfinkel, the orders of institutions and cultures are "accountable" orders, which are not as firm or absolute as the orders of situated action.[47]

Traditional societies require everyone to share something like cultural beliefs. These comprise traditional morality, and traditional societies can hang together only as long as the boundaries around these systems of belief are maintained. But Durkheim argued that, in modern societies (an ideal state not yet achieved), practices, which had always underlain the systems of belief, would be released—set free from beliefs—and come to the foreground. Freed from their narrative accounts, practices would be free to operate to produce order and meaning on their own account. This is particularly important in areas like science, but also essential for social change in general.

What people in modern societies are in danger of is damaging the foundations of the situated practices they depend on—because they do not see their value and in their attempt to create social cohesion they emphasize instead shared values that threaten, not strengthen, the situations that a diverse democratic context depends upon. A civil situated morality—which is necessary for stable and meaningful modern life—will remain in jeopardy as long as social problems continue to be approached in terms of a conflict between individual motivations and overarching structures of value, and as long as morality is equated with traditional beliefs rather than with reciprocities of practice.

Because practices are no longer sustained by narrative accounts, they require reciprocity and mutual engagement to produce recognizable meaning and order. This, Durkheim argued, would make justice a necessity in a modern practice based society.[48] Durkheim's students began to study the basis for practice-centered moral orders in detail, Marcel Mauss's *The Gift* being the most important example. Garfinkel, over the course of his career, has given a full elaboration to this idea of what it would mean to have a society based on reciprocities of practice in detail. What if we really got beyond individualism and focused on action? What would that look like? And what would researchers focusing on action in this way be looking for, and how would they talk about what they found? This is Ethnomethodology.

Many problems in contemporary interactionism (those associated with postmodernism, cultural studies, and Pragmatism) come from going only part way. Focusing on the details of interaction, while retaining the individual, for instance. Or, focusing on motives as something that individuals have, instead of realizing that situations make demands on their own behalf, and that these demands must become motives for any individual who will succeed in that situation.

Goffman saw much of this, and wrote about it eloquently. He nevertheless retained the "truth" of the unified self behind the scenes; retained a focus on conceptual typifications and frames; and, as a consequence, believed that order was only a surface veneer beneath which there was a very real chaos. Other influential modern interactionist thinkers have followed his view in this respect, with the result that interactionism has seemed to increase its focus on the individual over time—and to lose altogether any purchase on social order.

For Reisman, the advent of the "other-oriented" character signaled a loss of morality in modern society, because traditional moral principles no longer reigned. What he and others have failed to see is that traditional moral principles are precisely the obstacle to justice that must be overcome. The fact that traditional moral principles always exclude some people, while including others, and do not provide for a modern conception of justice for all, seems to have been overlooked in bemoaning the loss of the past.

We see this attitude often today in the wish to reestablish traditional communities of value. A truly open society requires a morality based in the public matters of daily life, not in the beliefs and values of demographic groups. Durkheim referred to this practice-based morality as "justice," and distinguished it from belief-based and exclusionary forms of morality. Justice as a principle of practices involves pure principles of reciprocity with no belief content: trust. What Garfinkel was able to show is that reciprocity is necessary in situated action. There is a real foundation for discussing issues of justice, social order, and modern personhood, to the degree that practices become entirely situated and, as Durkheim said, "self-regulating," running free of and ahead of beliefs.

It was Garfinkel's great genius to see this phenomenon in the interactions in which he participated. That this argument, as he elaborated it in 1948, runs ahead of what he would consider adequate empirical proofs worries him a great deal. It might be fair to argue that an argument that empirical details should drive theory must come before research—although Garfinkel would not accept the premise. But I think that Garfinkel has failed to appreciate the degree to which his own empirical insights, his sustained and detailed empirical observations of practice, have always been the foundation for his theoretical insights.

To that extent, even as preliminary as it is, none of the arguments in this manuscript are ungrounded. None are theory before research. All have emerged from the sustained "seeing" of practices in the world that is Garfinkel's great gift.

In fact, the 1948 manuscript is loaded with empirical observations. Enough to have inspired dozens of dissertations—as over the many years it did. Each point is given through empirical examples, and this to such an extent that it requires much theoretical elaboration to clarify the points. In my view, Garfinkel's insights are never merely those of theoretical reflection, which he is so critical of. They are, rather, a form of empirical theorizing. It is necessary to speak, after all, about the empirical matters we have seen, and the issues of meaning, order, and morality which they embody, or there can be no mutual understanding, no communication about these important matters.

* * *

Finally, there is a paradox concerning the reception of Garfinkel's work that should be considered. I think it would be fair to say that only a few people have even a partial grasp of his position. I myself am continually amazed by what I have not understood. Yet, his work has influenced most living sociologists in some way and has had a profound effect on many other disciplines as well. I would argue that the reason Garfinkel's work has been so influential, in spite of the fact that most people do not fully understand it, is because he turns our attention toward the practices that are really at the center of modern life. As such, his work stands as the only comprehensive statement of the social and moral condition of modern society. Consequently, it has played an important role in focusing research on practices in many areas.

The problem is that without a clear understanding of Garfinkel's overall insight, Ethnomethodology can be turned into a conventional research method. Researchers paying a great deal of attention to detail, who may have been inspired by Garfinkel in this regard, nevertheless continue to invoke the individual (or individual motives and/or perspectives as properties of individuals) as an organizing feature of interaction. There is a drive to make the work speak to conventional categories of person and institution and to treat practices as conceptual. This, of course, completely nullifies all the new attention to detail. It is necessary to give up the idea that properties of the individual are organizing features of social practice and to focus, instead, on the orders of practice themselves.

Durkheim argued that we needed to give up the individual and focus on social facts. Sociology as a discipline did not do this but, rather, has treated social facts as the social facts of individual beliefs and motivations—or of institutional constraints. These are the social facts of the way in which cultures would motivate people to act, not the social facts of a social order based on practices.

Garfinkel's injunctions to focus on detail have similarly found themselves married to motivational schemes. If we begin with the idea of a motivational scheme, no amount of detail is going to get us closer to answering questions about a social order created and sustained through practices. In fact, scholars "inspired by" Garfinkel often ask "What is all the detail for?"—one of the most frequently voiced complaints about Ethnomethodology. They can already, at a glance, see the typifications people are using—Why do they need more detail? And they will conclude, as Giddens (1984) did, that Garfinkel has, after all the attention to detail, in the end, failed to answer the essential questions of motivation and social constraint that are still the focus of most scholarship.

Of course, Garfinkel has not *failed* to address the motivation question. Nor has he ignored the problems of inequality and constraint. What he has done is to reformulate the whole conception of social order and where it comes from in such a way that the motivation question is no longer relevant. Typifications are also essentially irrelevant to an understanding of how practice-based structures work. And details, married to individual motivations and typifications, are worse than useless. What Garfinkel offers is a proof, of sorts, that because social order depends on mutual reciprocity with regard to the details of situated orders of action, we are not at the mercy of typifications and individual motives in the way we have assumed (since Hobbes). Social order does not require sharing beliefs, or belonging to demographic communities. Garfinkel has been addressing the essential question of modernity that everyone has been asking: What happens when "society" as we knew it is gone?

But an appreciation of the strengths of a practice-based view requires something of a gestalt shift in the way we see the world. It is necessary to stop seeing conceptual unities as "real"—they are, after all, only concepts—and begin to recognize that we are able to arrive at these conceptual unities in the first place only because of something else that we can truly see and hear—that we create for one another—and mutually participate in the building of right in front of our eyes and ears. With sufficient attention to practices in details we can learn to *see* what we have been doing all along, to see this in a *new* way, to see the details of situated practice, rather than performing conceptual reductions—a practice of *Seeing Sociologically.*

Notes

1. Garfinkel referred to members of situated practices, not to communities of practice. He avoided the word "communities," which has unfortunate connotations with regard to more traditional sociological views, and developed his own notion of a group as consisting of the procedural rules of interpretation of working acts. It is unfortunate that those who have been influenced by his work have not seen this point. Nevertheless, what it is being described as communities of practice are—in the ways that matter—situated practices, the members of which are identified by competency and not birth, belief, political association, and so forth.

2. Insofar as Symbolic Interaction can be said to have origins in Mead, the comments that Garfinkel makes about Mead and the conception of the self in this manuscript also distinguish his work from Symbolic Interactionism.

3. Additional objections that Garfinkel would have had to Goffman's work can be inferred from his criticisms of Mead. See section 5 in this Introduction and pages 151–179 in *Seeing Sociologically.* See also my Trevino paper (Rawls 2003).

4. For an elaboration of the consequences of the theoretical attitude for social research, see pages 47–50 in this Introduction as well as pages 126–129 in *Seeing Sociologically.*

5. It is interesting to think that the theory of communication articulated in *Seeing Sociologically* was intended as an alternative to the debate between Skinner and Chomsky. Chomsky had won the initial debate by the late 1950s. In a robotic way Skinner's theory was sequential. But there was no meaning or interpretation involved, and because responses were automatic he could not see the uses to which sequential positioning could be put in creating "just this" meaning. See pages 179–184 in *Seeing Sociologically,* as well as the discussion in section 3 on sequentiality in communication in this Introduction (pp. 29–41).

6. Conversation analysts have worked out in details some of the recognizable properties of turns that participants may use in building the conversational aspects of such sequences. There are some significant differences, however, between Garfinkel's original approach to conversation and the work of conversation analysis. For Garfinkel, there is more to the developing sequence than the turns taken by participants. While he

would agree that the ordering of turns is meaningful in its own right, he would argue that preferred orderings of practices that allow participants to display their understandings, or interpretations, of ongoing meaning, membership, and identity display have properties of sequence, cognitive style, background expectancies, and identity.

7. See *Garfinkel* (1964). A version of this article also appeared as Chapter 2 in *Studies in Ethnomethodology* (Garfinkel 1967). The original and longer statement of Garfinkel's "routine grounds" argument appears in *Seeing Sociologically.*

8. The theme of the relationship between character and society was taken up also in studies of the family by Talcott Parsons, Uri Bronfenbrenner, Beatrice and John Whiting, and others.

9. "Work" in this context means "facilitate mutual understanding"; it differs from "work" in the Pragmatist sense that because a project can be accomplished with a practice, it's true. In fact, Garfinkel is arguing the reverse. Shared practices are the criteria of truth and validity. They are the ultimate arbiters of meaning, identity, and social order. It is possible to get something done only if participants in a situation understand one another, which requires a high degree of trust and consensus on practices. For further discussion of these differences, see section 5 in this Introduction (on Garfinkel and Pragmatism) as well as the Conclusion.

10. The section on Garfinkel and Pragmatism explains why this approach to validity as praxeological is not Pragmatism. To oversimplify, it is because the test of validity is not whether a person or group can effect a project based on assumptions about reality. Rather, it is a test of intelligibility: Can the person or group approach practices in detail such that others interpret them in the same way they do? Mead would invoke the idea of significant symbols here. Garfinkel would argue that there is no such thing. Any symbol, he said, could be significant. But only if the work of achieving the same interpretation were accomplished.

11. See also *Garfinkel* (2002) for a discussion of instructed action and unique adequacy. There has been much misinterpretation of these ideas. The argument is not that researchers could come up with adequate scientific description by being disinterested, as some have argued, but, rather, that adequate scientific description is simply not possible either as description *per se* or from a detached scientific standpoint. It is the mutual interest of actors in the developing situation in which they participate as well as their use of shared methods that give social scenes order and meaning. Scientific observers do not share this orientation. The interests of formal scientific disciplines are in principle not those of actors in situations. Therefore, the observer's perspective will always be inadequate.

For Garfinkel, instructed action would replace description, and adequacy—instead of being a product of objective distance—requires complete submersion in practices. The desire to describe would itself disappear if the scientist adopted the perspective of the actor, because description—except for the purposes of instructing—is not a member's concern. Instructions, however, could never satisfy conventional science because their questions are different. The questions would therefore also have to change. Garfinkel came to talk of hybrid studies of work as those that satisfied both interests.

What the researcher needed was to be indifferent to the interests of academic sciences and, adopting the actor's perspective, to become competent in enacting a given practice (unique adequacy). This indifference does not make the data objective, as some have argued. But it does allow the researcher to take the perspective of an actor in a situation rather than taking the perspective of science and imposing problems on them from outside. A good researcher who achieved unique adequacy would then be able to instruct others on the reproducibility of those practices.

12. The work of Kenneth Burke on accounting and accounts was particularly influential. While Garfinkel was not at this point influenced by C. Wright Mills on accounts, Mills had been influenced by Burke, and there are significant parallels between the positions developed by Mills and Garfinkel on accounts. See my introduction to *Ethnomethodology's Program* (Rawls 2002) for a more detailed discussion.

13. Instead of worrying that he might get fired if he did not move the bus, the bus driver treated the persons of color as though their presence in the front seat literally prevented the bus from moving. It was a nuisance, yes. But he was not being called on to make any decisions. Anyone could see that, just as if it had a flat tire, the bus could not move until these persons had been removed

14. In this case, lenient prosecution of black-on-black homicide hid the severe prosecution of black-on-white crime. Furthermore, judgments about the civic standing and character of both victim and accused were allowed to influence outcomes in all types of cases that contributed to the effect.

15. The idea is that personal knowledge of social situations and/or practices introduces a subjective element of interpretation into the data. Of course, as Garfinkel would argue, without some personal knowledge and interpretation, nothing means anything (or anything means everything). Therefore, interpretation being necessary, it had better be informed interpretation. What Garfinkel says about Parsons and other advocates of scientific sociology is that they built the interpretation into the "categories" they used. What was supposed to be objective, then, was in actuality ethnocentric at its best and nonsense at its worst.

16. That is what is "emergent" about situated action—projects—not the background orders against which the possibilities of projects can be seen. Mistaking projects for the basis of order leads to the idea that order, as a matter of situated procedures, is itself emergent. Contemporary theories of "emergent" order tend to make this mistake. It is also important to understand what is meant by "situated." It is a word, like "context," that has often been used to mean "contingent," or "emergent." But, for Garfinkel, situated action is not just anything that happens in a particular place and time. It does not just "emerge" as a new form resulting from what people "choose" to do. In fact, Garfinkel's point is much the opposite—that in a given situation only certain forms of practice are expected and recognizable. Therefore, anything else will create incongruities that have to be handled. People can choose, yes; but in order to be understood, they must choose to produce practices that can be seen in the situation to mean what they need them to mean and they have to produce the sounds and movements, and place them just so, and attend carefully to what others are doing. Situated, then, refers to recurring patterned orderlinesses of action that constitute the recognizable boundaries of situations. These

practices, Garfinkel argues, are used to construct situated sequential frames for meaning, not the reverse.

17. This is why, according to David Reisman (1950), character becomes increasingly "other oriented" in modern society—in short, because traditional norms and values are increasingly less relevant to the recognizable production of situated practices in contexts that are increasingly civic and populated by persons with whom we do not share values. Persons must learn to orient toward the situated character of identity and practice in order to communicate at all in the modern civil/civic context.

18. See section 3 of this Introduction for a discussion of sequencing and its relationship to the researcher's perspective. The guard's answers might reflect a sensitivity to fulfilling interactional obligations to provide answers more than a sensitivity to representing the "truth" of things. The guard is making sense of the interviewer's questions from his—the guard's—perspective. There is also a deeper point elaborated in section 3: that it is the job of all actors to take things as they see them from the perspective of their situated identity and to put their understandings from that perspective on public view in front of others. In this way we achieve common understandings—made in common understandings. Furthermore, the researchers, to the extent that they participate in the event, will also be caught up in the natural attitude. Thus, their understanding, to the extent that it is mutual, will also be situated. To the extent that they retain the position of a detached observer, on the other hand, they will miss *everything*.

19. Practices cannot be questioned from within. They *are* how a particular thing is done—any particular thing. As such, practices have a circular logic that explains everything relevant to themselves that is similar to traditional religious beliefs. (See Edward Evan Evans-Pritchard's [1937] account of the Azande.) It is only by removing the explanation of action to the level of projects that action can be made to look logical; in actual practice, in the natural attitude, every action can be explained from within the circle of expectations of the practice. The only thing that escapes from this circularity is the observable orderliness of the practice itself, which is a logic in its own right; meaning is contained entirely within the circle of this order.

20. For a discussion of Garfinkel and S-R theory, see pages 44–45 in this Introduction. See also page 179 in *Seeing Sociologically*.

21. See Norbert Elias's *Time: An Essay* (Elias 1992) for a discussion of the importance of time as a comparative device.

22. This process of exchange is Garfinkel's alternative to Mead's taking the role of the other. Instead of performing an exchange in imagination based on roles, there is an actual sequential exchange based on much more detailed situated expectations than roles. For details on Garfinkel's critique of Mead, see the discussion of Mead in section 5 of this Introduction, on Garfinkel and Pragmatism.

23. Garfinkel elaborates on this point in the "Trust" paper (Garfinkel 1963). Unfortunately, most interpreters of that argument took him to be describing the rules for something like a game. From Garfinkel's perspective, conversation is not at all like a game. It does not have specifiable rules. The methods participants can use to produce witnessable orders of conversation are much more complicated than rules. Largely because of his disappointment at being misunderstood in this regard Garfinkel did not

publish his elaborations on the "trust" argument. However, for years he gave lectures on trust and on what was wrong with the way the argument had been interpreted as a conception of rules with regard to trust. Hopefully these lectures will someday find their way into print.

24. The problem of recognizing the boundaries of this developing order as a phenomenal field of speech became a focus of some of Garfinkel's later tutorial exercises.

25. It is tempting to wonder whether Garfinkel means to indicate a difference between situations in which the order is ritually prescribed and one has only to give the prescribed responses—thus requiring no experimental method—and situations in which the order is not specified in advance and participants have only their shared methods, identities, and background expectancies from which to build a mutually recognizable order. In the latter, the experimental method described by Garfinkel would predominate—and the differences between traditional and modern societies in this regard might explain the development of an experimental (or rational) approach to thought and communication over time. Garfinkel mentions ritual or cultural products in two contexts: in the discussion of signposts (p. 180–181) and in the discussion of identity as symbolic (pp. 167–191). See also the discussion of Mead and Dewey in section 5 of this Introduction.

26. Contemporary studies tend to treat interpretation as an individual matter, whether or not they treat identity as structurally determined. In this view interpretation introduces indeterminacy into interaction. For Garfinkel, the process works in the reverse and interpretation is a method for producing mutually intelligible orders.

27. While the distinction between signs that exist as the result of prior courses of action, and tactics for producing meaning sequentially, lays the groundwork for later empirical studies, the tactics that Garfinkel enumerates at this point are, unfortunately, not ones that deal with the turn by turn, or instant by instant, organization of interaction that his work will focus on later. The examples he gives are of "voting for an essence, casuistic stretching, devaluing the currency, ringeleveo with symbols, Ingesting the opposition, Consulting the dictionary, Do not handle the merchandise unless you intend to buy, being driven into a corner, transcendence, and so on" They are more like strategic interaction in Goffman's sense than like the fine details of practice in Garfinkel's later work. Of course, as Garfinkel would point out—not having done that research yet—he did not have the more detailed examples.

28. This distinction between Garfinkel's approach to plan and projects and the importance of the role they play in the work of Schütz, James, and Pragmatism in general will be taken up in section 5 of this Introduction.

29. Garfinkel argues that the scientist should change the model and not the actor. He writes: "In the face of it [that the subject does not act according to the tenets of the scientific method] the model and not the subject must be challenged and changed" (p. 105). This seems obvious, he says, but common practice is to change the actor (as if one could) instead of changing the model.

30. For a discussion of the way in which this creates problems for sociology as a discipline, by stripping sociology of its object in the context of modern society, see Rawls 2004.

31. This is the way Garfinkel approaches "race" in both "Color Trouble" (Garfinkel 1940) and in his M.A. thesis on "Inter- and Intra-Racial Homicide" (Garfinkel 1949).

32. Social action, for most people, conveys something conceptual or symbolic. It is essential to Garfinkel's point that social action be understood to refer to those details through which it is made manifest and not to the concepts that we usually associate it with.

33. An elaboration of the six concepts (epoche, sociality, attention, spontaneity, time, and experience of self) can be found on page 110. Garfinkel would no longer argue that something like six elements of cognitive style was sufficient for specifying the parameters of recognizability. As his work developed, so did his understanding of the highly complex character of local orders of action.

34. See my paper on the micro/macro distinction (Rawls 1987) for a discussion of why this distinction as a whole is a misconception.

35. See Rawls (1997) for an extended discussion of Durkheim's critique of James, which has in common with Garfinkel's a sustained critique of individualism. See also Rawls 2001, 2003, and 2004 for discussions of Durkheim's theory of practice.

36. It could be argued that "situated" is also the time dimension of action/praxis for Marx. Marx argued that the reifications leading to contradiction occurred only when one stepped outside of social relations: Consider, for instance, supply and demand, which are generally treated as independent constraints, but which Marx argued, in his 1844 manuscript, are in reality part of a single social relationship of production. The unity of such relationships could be seen from within history only as an ongoing set of material relationships. In this respect, his position is in accord with Garfinkel's. It was this understanding that led Marx to advocate a study of praxis.

37. Note the irony here. It is the theoretical mode that lacks intersubjectivity—while the apparent messiness of actual interaction is well designed to produce mutual understanding. There is a strong similarity to Wittgenstein's argument that the Augustinian picture theory of language prevented philosophers from seeing that language has meaning through use, not reference. In Garfinkel's case, the argument is that ways of approaching social reality that reify its objects, and render its essential processes invisible, prevent social theory and philosophy from comprehending human moral relations and social orders. What the researcher needs to understand is how social orders are made in details, and that requires leaving the theoretical mode of attention and entering into the details of working acts.

38. It is theoretical thought that has no basis in the natural attitude. The mutually oriented toward practices, which construct the reality of theoretical objects, are not only not available to the ordinary persons who supposedly act in the theoretical universe, but not inspected by theorists. Therefore, for Garfinkel, theory is, ironically, entirely dependent on the details of its own working acts, which it not only ignores but considers trivial, irrational, and contingent.

39. Among Garfinkel's later researches, reason and logic as wittnessable productions through social practices figure prominently. (See also Livingston 2003, on reasoning in checkers.)

40. This description bears a strong relationship to several very important later

studies, Erving Goffman's *Asylums* (1962), Thomas Szasz's *The Manufacture of Madness* (1970), and Gresham Sykes's *The Society of Captives* (1958) among them.

41. In this connection, see my paper on "Orders of Interaction and Intelligibility: Intersections Between Goffman and Garfinkel by Way of Durkheim" (Rawls 2003).

42. Garfinkel did not clarify this point theoretically in his later work because he hoped that his more empirical studies would make it clear that the creation of recognizable orders in practices in details was necessary for mutual intelligibility. For some reason, although the studies themselves have made a great impact, their relevance to the motivation question has been missed.

43. See my paper "Race as an Interaction Order Phenomenon" (Rawls 2000) for a discussion of the situated production of racial identities and their consequences for race relations in the United States.

44. See Wittgenstein (1953), p. 6.

45. One reason for this outcome was the "is/ought" problem: If situated action requires morality, then why is the world not moral? Of course, the argument is not that simple. The fact that practices require moral reciprocity does not eliminate the unequal social contexts in which practices take place. As Durkheim argued, practices will take place in contexts that fundamentally contradict them until justice becomes a reality. But this realization diminishes neither the moral requirements for practice nor the fact that, at present, practices do exist in this context of contradiction, and that the contradictions undermine our experience of morality.

46. This explains the experience of less freedom in a context where we apparently have more.

47. See my paper on "Interaction Order" (Rawls 2000) for an elaboration of this distinction between levels of social order.

48. See my paper on the relationship between Durkheim's focus on practice and Justice in *Critical Sociology* (Rawls 2003).

Introduction

Harold Garfinkel

THE ATTEMPT TO APPROXIMATE SOME SORT OF PRECISION IN THE study of human conduct is not unlike the task of swatting flies with a hammer. Apart from the fact that one must make the tenuous assumption that the fly will remain still, one must be willing to settle for a low batting average while facing the prospect of leaving the room in a shambles when the game is done. It surely takes an optimist to make the attempt for optimism stemming as it does from the state of the bowels is lost to the restraints that detached appraisal proposes. Within such a mood one can effect a meaning transformation of "obstacles-as-chances-against" into "obstacles-as-opportunities-for," then pick up the hammer, and get to it. An optimist, in any case, has no real choice in the matter.

The reader is asked to regard two notions as home plate to which we can return to renew our perspective whenever the going gets tough. First, the leading aim of this project is to translate the concept of the social relationship into the terms of communicative effort between actors. Second, our problem is to study this communicative endeavor with regard to contents, organizations of meanings, the processes and logics of communicative expressions, and the tactics of communication and understanding using the fact that the experience of incongruity can be experimentally induced as the means for teasing these various facets out of the closely woven fabric of social intercourse.

This paper is organized into two parts. Part I is devoted to an exposition of the principal theoretical notions we shall use in the attempt to lend our problems some systematic references. As these notions are constituted at this point in the program they provide no more than enough light to see by. The specific problems of the thesis are presented in Part II. The problem remains of working out the specific experimental settings within which to investigate the problems cited in Part II.

Part I

Principal Theoretical Notions

MUCH OF THE SUCCESS OF OUR RESEARCH PROGRAM WILL DEPEND upon seeing things anew. This we take as sufficient excuse for introducing many new words as well as introducing new meanings for old words. They will be important instruments with which the investigator would "see" the world. Since every instrument in a rational discipline is the embodiment in miniature of an underlying philosophy of inquiry, the course has been taken here of writing a very brief essay on several of the most crucial terms, this having been done by way of defining the principles of their application as well as conveying at the same time the philosophy and leading hypotheses of this inquiry.

The definition of one term often involves the usage of others. Thus, the essential overall outlines will be apparent after the terms have been gone over. Faced with a circle, then, one may as well break in at any point and begin.

Action

The problem of defining what is meant by this term is the problem of laying down the rules by which the observer goes about the business of idealizing phenomenal presentations which can be referred for their origin to some person other than the observer. This means that the term, *action*, must be regarded for our purposes as a term peculiar to

101

the investigative vocabulary of the scientific observer. This reservation is necessary because we shall see later that the agents being studied have their own notions as to what it is that they see, where they see it, what causes the appearance of the thing that's seen, how obviously the thing seen presents itself for treatment, and so on. It is of crucial importance for our purposes that the guiding interpretive principles employed by the agent, as well as the rules governing the combinations of meanings he works with, differ in a most remarkable fashion from the attitude and modes of idealization that the scientific observer employs with reference to the same naïve material. We propose this insight in order to set on record the problem of what is involved in "seeing sociologically." The problem is that of recognizing, at least, that the relationship of the sociological observer to his data is in need of more conceptualization than is provided by either of the two most widely employed epistemological premises that (1) the objects of scientific inquiry are given through naïve sensory encounter, or (2) the objects of inquiry are limited to those which "manifest themselves" as sense data apprehended "in terms of a conceptual scheme." If we would question the sensationist doctrines in this matter, we would also question the idealistic doctrines. For the record we would say that the world is a fact; how is it possible? We shall need to get into the meanings of such crucial scientific terms as existence, reality, and objectivity though we shall not do it here. We shall refer instead to the phenomenological researches of Edmund Husserl, and accept his views with regard to the considerations involved for the scientist who seeks a radical and rational empiricism.

Whatever else we may come to mean by the term *action* one thing stands: the term designates the data that we shall be dealing in at the empirical level. We shall use the term *action* to mean meaningful or *intentional experience*. We do not mean *action* in the sense of *actus*; we do not mean action in the sense of behavior, or even "psychical activity" in the sense of the "psychic functions" or operations about which the nineteenth century act psychologists spoke. Rather we are referring to the rules of procedure by which the manifestations of a person's "spontaneous life"—gestures, talk, movement, posture, facial contortions, and so on—are to be idealized by the observer;—are assigned their significances by the observer in *his* task of interpreting an "other." Our problem in recognizing our data does not lie in asking what occurs to man as a psychophysiological unit or his response to these occurrences,

> but does lie in seeking out what attitude he adopts toward these occurrences and his steering of his so-called responses—briefly, the subjective meaning man bestows upon certain experiences of his own spontaneous life. What appears to the observer to be objectively the same behavior may have for the behaving subject very different meanings or no meaning at all. (Schütz, 535)

> Meaning ... is not a quality inherent to certain experiences emerging within our stream of consciousness but is the result of an interpretation of a past experience looked at from the present Now with a reflective attitude. As long as I live *in* my acts, directed toward the objects of these acts, the acts do not have any meaning. They become meaningful if I grasp them as well-circumscribed experiences of the past, and therefore, in retrospection. Only experiences which can be recollected beyond their actuality and which can be questioned about their constitution are, therefore, subjectively meaningful.
>
> But if this characterization of meaning has been accepted, are there at all any experiences of my spontaneous life which are subjectively not meaningful? We think the answer is in the affirmative. There are the mere physiological reflexes ...; certain passive reactions provoked by ... the surf of indiscernible and confused small perceptions; my gait, my facial expressions, my mood ... characteristics of my handwriting, etc. all these forms of involuntary spontaneity are experienced while they occur, but without leaving any trace in memory ... Unstable and undetachable from surrounding experiences as they are, they can neither be delineated nor recollected. They belong to the category of *essentially actual experiences,* that is, they exist merely in the actuality of being experienced and cannot be grasped by a reflective attitude.
>
> Subjectively meaningful experience emanating from our spontaneous life shall be called *conduct.* (The term behavior is avoided because it includes in present use also subjectively non-meaningful manifestations of spontaneity such as reflexes.) The term conduct ... refers to all kinds of subjectively meaningful experiences of spontaneity, be they those of inner life or those gearing into the outer world." (Schütz)

Conduct can be overt or covert. The former will be known as "mere" doing, the latter "mere" thinking. The term *conduct* as used here will not imply any reference to intent. All kinds of so-called automatic activities of inner or outer life fall under this class.

Conduct which is devised in advance, that is, which is based upon a preconceived project, shall be called *action*, regardless of whether it is an overt or covert one. As covert, it is necessary to specify whether there is attached to the project an intention to realize it—to carry it through, to bring about a projected state of affairs. Such an intention transforms the mere forethought into an aim, and the project into a purpose. If an intention to realization is lacking, the projected covert action is to be regarded as a *day dream*, if the intention subsists, we shall speak of a purposive action or *performance.* The attempt to solve a scientific problem mentally is an example of a covert performance.

With regard to the so-called overt actions, that is actions *which gear into the outer world by bodily movements,* the distinction between actions without an intention to realization, and those with an intention is unnecessary. Any overt action in the sense just proposed is a performance within the meaning of the definition proposed above. Covert performances will be referred to as thinking; those performances requiring bodily movements will be called working. By the term *working* is meant action in the outer world, based upon a project and characterized by the intention to bring about the projected state of affairs by bodily movements.

The all of an empirically relevant datum within the view of action as intentional experience is obtained after we as observers have translated the manifesting signs of spontaneous life into more or less technical representations of the subject's experiences as they are meaningful for him. *Our data will consist then of symbolic expressions and the transformations of these expressions.* It is these expressions that we are seeking to set up, and it is in accounting for their sequences and changes in time that we come to grips with the "motivation" problem. That the expressions which the observer sets up are not recognizable by the subject as his own is of no importance, inasmuch as the two will coincide only where subject and observer employ the same attitude and the same tactics with references to the same purpose. To expect otherwise is to expect the subject to act according to the tenets of scientific investigation, a limitation which is methodologically unnecessary as well as practically very difficult. The scientist is always interested in interpreting the subject's action with reference to some analytical scheme, within the purpose of predicting the regularities of the subject's flow of experience. The scientist is faced constantly with the problem of testing his model against a batting average of successful predictions. This means he must take the subject as he finds him. That the subject does not act according to the tenets of scientific method and does not reflect on his "true motives" in the manner that he "should" *is problematical data.* In the face of it the model and not the subject must be challenged and changed. The point can hardly be overstressed, obvious though it may appear. It bears directly on what the scientist will regard as evidence for the acceptance or rejection of any hypothesis he sets up. The whole "heads I win, tails you lose" design of experimental procedure that is so widespread in our thinking today stems from the failure to state beforehand those conditions under which the subject's expression, "I felt bad," is to be regarded as evidence for or evidence against, or simply that boon in disguise of unassimilated data. It is important, if we are ever to get beyond the stage of sophisticated anecdotes, that in our interviewing (to take one very complex and as yet comparatively ill-conceptualized investigative setting), we know what it is that we are assuming whenever we say that the subject in responding in a particular manner was expressing whatever it was that we say he was expressing. (Later in the paper we shall list those things about which assumptions need to be made.)

We said that the empirical data is found in those symbolic expressions that the *observer* sets up on the basis of the manifestations of the subject's spontaneous life. The data then is found in the representations of the meanings involved in the subject's spontaneous life; that is what we need to search out. In many cases practical exigencies make it necessary to assume what the subject's meanings are that lie behind the gesture. This assumption, however, is a tricky one, and the further one gets from highly formalized and standardized discourse, the trickier the problem becomes. The Freudians have shown how even in such discourse, symbolic overtones are operative. At the other extreme, one need only listen to what is actually said between two close friends to realize that the heard speech conveys infinitely more than Webster would have allowed. The reductio ad absurdum is found in the verbalizations of schizophrenics—and students of the schizophrenic have admitted the confounding effect of his communicative efforts by scratching their heads and calling it "word salad." Thus, to take a few examples of the problems we face in rendering the symbolic expressions representative of the subject's meaningful spontaneous life, suppose that a person familiar to us enters the office and says, "May I examine your chairs?" Whipping out our record sheet we might record that he meant just that: a request for permission to examine the chairs, in which case we have data that might later be used in support of the hypothesis that the requester is a considerate kind of guy. But suppose we recall that he has always taken Fearless Fosdick as an ego ideal; we might run after him to find out if he has a Thompson gun hidden on him with which to destroy the Chippendale Chair in the office, in which case the expression we write down changes. Or suppose that we have arranged a secret set of meanings, such that any request he makes when he enters means, "There's a suspicious looking guy out here that looks like a summons server," then the expression we note as primary data changes again.

In principle, then, the things that the subject says, the gestures he makes, his posturing, his tics—whatever the signs he exhibits—are not to be regarded in their naïve givenness as the data to which our empirical propositions refer, *and this because of the principle that as far as the problems of communication are concerned, any sign can signify anything in the communicative universe. That such is not the case is problematical.* Hence the rule that as a matter of principle, the subject needs to be questioned to ascertain what it is that he means when he says or does *anything.* Actually, the rule can hardly be thoroughly applied without giving up the possibility of ever getting any research completed. We can make therefore certain assumptions that simplify our task—the assumption of the regularity of meanings; assumptions regarding the nature of the phenomenon of social order; the assumption that the method of understanding works. But where we are concerned with the phenomenon of communication and where we hold the method of understanding and the problem of order as problematical, it becomes necessary to keep these assumptions close at hand and accessible for examination. At any rate, the empirical data consists of that which the subject has *meant* in his expressions. What it is that he can possibly mean, which is to say, how complicated we'll allow the subject to get in the meanings he deals in, is dependent entirely upon how much stuff we invest our model of the subject with: that is, what kind of assumptions we make about what we'll "allow" the subject to be capable of. By holding in mind the fact that our model is a set of procedural rules rather than a faded reproduction of the "whole man," we allow evidence to test our rules rather than the other way around. Thus, we will know when our model needs to be changed, because it will be considered in need of revision whenever it proposes hypotheses that Intractable Nature will have nothing to do with.

A word now about the model of the actor that we intend to use.

Actor

We shall use the term *actor* in two senses. First, we shall use it as a shorthand generic designation of the agent to an action. The term is thus a differentiator that the observer uses to make the difference between himself and the referents of the action he is intent on studying.

There is a second sense of the term. Once the observer shifts his view so as to bring into focus the rules by which action is initiated and carried through, he needs a concept that will represent epithet like the body of concepts he uses to bring experience as it flows past the agent to static representation. These concepts are (1) *animal symbolicum,* (2) role or cognitive style, and (3) noesis-noema structures. To have described the contents of these concepts is to have represented the actor.

What is it that *we do not mean* by actor? The term will not mean a "concrete entity"; it will not mean "the whole man" or even the tiniest little part of the "part man"; it will not mean "person" as that term is so often and so loosely used to represent "actual blood and bones"—the thing "within the skin and within the environment." Nor will it mean "self," "ego," identity, organism, animal, role, functioner, or disfunctioner.

To the question, "What is man?" we would answer, man for our purpose is to be considered a dummy, a dope, a lifeless puppet, all of whose potentialities for activity we shall invest him with. His portrait will reveal a series of assumptions as to the kinds of experiences he is capable of experiencing under specified conditions. The dummy heart that beats beneath that dummy breast is made up not of nerve and muscle but the rules of hypothetic-deductive method.

We shall assume for our dummy—*the animal symbolicum*—that "seeing" is possible, though what it is that he "sees," how he "sees," and under what conditions he will "see" in any particular way is entirely problematical and needs to be investigated. Our animal symbolicum is an experiencer: this is our leading assumption. He is a "reader" of his world, and an interpreter, a "critic." When dealing with the things of his world, he deals with them in terms of their significances; and such treatment that he affords them, he affords in terms of their significances. He's the kind of dummy that always has something to "say"—he's engaged in a running conversation that never lets up, not even when he sleeps, and he tells us of all this by what he does, says, dreams, fantasizes, etc. He is a peculiar guy and he lives in a peculiar world. The world "exists" for him, which is to say that the objects he encounters and accounts as existent, real, objective, are existent, real, and objective *in particular ways.* It is a world of private and public objects. It is a world which, in the observer's notion, is to be conceived of as nothing else than reified possibilities of experience. What the actor's principles of reification consist of is the gist of the observer's concern. Given the fact that the "face" of the world looks the same for many actors, the observer's problem is to account for the conditions under which this will or will not be the case. (The observer, therefore, merely begs the question when he says that communication, for example, is possible where the communicants see something in common.) And this must be done without recourse to the common observer's assumption of a world of objects which, after all is said and done, really exist out there.

Some say the world the actor lives in is now physical, now social, now private, but we'll deny this and say instead that he lives once and for all in a symbolic world in which, for example, through the various forms of symbolism found in the activities of myth, poetry, language, art, religion, science, he comes to recognize signifying or intended objects. These symbolic forms present to him the various "physiognomies"—the faces—Husserl's *Wahrnehmungsabschattungen*—which in the dummy's experiences are accounted by him to be real in their particular ways. Thus for the military strategist, the mountain is the material representation of an obstacle; for the sheep herder, it is the material representation of grazing lands; for the tourist, it is an object to appreciate.

In our assumptions we make no provision for such things as basic needs, purposes, drives, basic motivations or basic purposes. Insofar as concepts such as these recommend themselves, they must be recommended on the basis of the evidence that we encounter with regard to the agent's various modes of experiencing. (Like the possibility of order, "basic" motivations for us must be demonstrated, not assumed.) We set as an aim the ideal that a full explanation of the agent's conduct must be rendered in terms of a description of the empirical conditions under which the conduct appears. By full explanation, then, we mean full description where "full" means description that exhausts the logical limits that our analytical conceptions specify at any particular time to be pertinent.

Having portrayed our actor as a dummy who deals in significances and only in significances, we need to say now who or what it is at the empirical level that we turn to for information and to whom our empirical statements have reference. This is provided by the empirical construct, *person.* "Person" means any subject of an interview or observation who is not illusory. Later we might want to fill out this picture by specifying such criteria as age, sex, marital status, literary, income, color, etc., but the selection of the specific criteria with which to specify the relevant empirical persons to which our generalizations will apply would seem to depend on further studies into the cruciality of such criteria in representing the presence of the data we hope to pick up. The intent at this point is to allow the empirical person to get as complicated as he will, and reserve the problem of boiling out the crucial signifiers to later correlational studies. It is hoped in this way to allow for an expanding vocabulary of empirical objects and thus prevent the choking off of new ranges of data and new combinations of data that a theoretical venture, if it is at all successful, soon points out.

So far we have provided that the statements we make about the person are based on the premise of the actor as a symbol treater. This has been done with the concept of the animal symbolicum. Now we need a set of conceptions that will specify *the conditions* of treatment. That is, we are going to say later what it is that is being treated and how it is being treated, but first we need to specify the ground of the experience; those conditions which must somehow be accounted for if we are to render an exhaustive description of the actor's experience. So we shall talk of a thing called role, by which we do not mean playing a part, nor do we mean expectancies of behavior, or "systems" of rights, duties, and obligations, etc. We shall say that a role or "cognitive style" has been defined when the empirical specifications of the following concepts have been provided: (1) epoche; (2) a specific form of sociality; (3) a specific mode of attention to life; (4) a specific form of spontaneity; (5) a specific mode of time consciousness; and (6) a specific way of experiencing the self. There are at least these six features of cognitive style. Further experience may reveal more.

This concept is taken from the article by Alfred Schütz, "On Multiple Realities," *Philosophy and Phenomenological Research*, June 1945, pp. 533–575. The concept is exceedingly important to this inquiry in that we shall rely heavily upon it in the task of representing social relationships at the "dynamic" level of the way in which the signs of the world are read by the animal symbolicum. It is with reference to a specific cognitive style that we shall say what an object means for the actor, how it is real, in what sense it is objective, what the terms of its existence are.

The task of setting out the operational rules by which these concepts are to be given their empirical referents remains as yet incompleted. For the present the following partial analysis of the cognitive style of the guard who works at the main entrance of Widener Library is offered by way of presenting definitions which are implicit in the way in which the concepts are used in the analysis.

Within the structure of "Widener Library" as a system of coordinated actions, one finds a class of social persons whose responsibility it is to prevent theft. This responsibility depends for its fulfillment upon a closely coordinated checking system, of which the guard as a social personality performs a final operation. It is his action by which the relevant participants are finally released from the system—the world of "library things"—passing his gate to enter the multitude of other potential worlds that may be accessible to them. In an extended, though literal sense, the actions which he is responsible for initiating and concluding are those of formal divorce, involving as they do a formal alienation from a definite order of obligations and rights, and the loss of an identity—a process that is altogether comparable to such spectacular rites of enstrangement and rebirth as dismissal from employment, conversion, excommunication, divorce, discharge from the army and similar social forms.

As we watch the guard the following things are seen. We observe that there is a regularity to his time of arrival and departure. He tells us later that "his hours" are eight till five, with an hour "off" for lunch. This we learn is not a private arrangement of his, but rather that there are others who would be very indignant if he were in fact to come to regard them as his private arrangement. We observe that he engages only in the most passing pleasantries "during duty hours." One might infer from the content of his conversations that he has no family, holds no political beliefs, cares not a whit for his own or for the personal lives of others. Occasionally he reads a newspaper or a book, but he puts them promptly aside when a person seeks to pass his desk. Faced with simultaneous prospects of a person seeking information and a person seeking to pass his desk, he turns his attention first to the book holder; or if already engaged with the request for information, he holds up his hand to the book holder, while watching him and finishing his remarks to the other. His back is turned to those who enter, and he scarcely turns from what he is doing at any time to regard them. He pays only perfunctory attention to those who seek to leave empty handed, while on those who are carrying something he turns an unswerving glance, often picking them up when they first come into sight from around the turn of the staircase. He requests persons leaving the library to stop while he makes a selection of their parcels, placing on the desk in front of him any books they might have been carrying. These he opens at the back cover, examines something inside and then either waves them past or detains them for some sort of conversational interchange.

Suppose we ask him the equivalent of the following questions: Who are you? What do you do here from 8 till 5? Who are these people you are dealing with? What criteria do you use in selecting those you will stop and those to whom you will pay no attention? What are you looking for in the backs of those books, and why and in what way do those things in the backs of the books concern you? What are the criteria by which you recognize that you have done a good job or a poor one? What mistakes are you allowed to make, and how do you know when one has been made? Why don't you go on reading your newspaper when these people appear? Do these people like you? Do you like them? Does it make any difference whether they like you or not? Look at that distinguished looking gentleman with the Van Dyke; look at that student who hugs that volume as if he were hungry and the book were bread; why do you stop them? Aren't they different? It must get lonely here; why don't you pass the time playing solitaire?

The operational rules will be derived from the rationale behind such questions as these. The material elicited by the questions give us the concrete characterization of the guard's cognitive style. What, in fact, does this cognitive style appear to be in the case of the *guard*?

The world of the guard is not an object of his thought, but is a field of things to be manipulated, dominated, changed, examined, tested. It is a world of things whose reality and objective character are unquestionably taken for granted, and every action is such that his hypothesis of the world's ontological character is indubitably confirmed. The guard's world—that is, the world of things recognized by this identity, "guard,"—is one in which his is *absorbed,* so to speak; he lives *in* his working acts; he deals pragmatically with the things that are meaningful in the "manipulatory area," to use Mead's phrase. He does not reformulate the world; he takes it literally at its face value for what it "*is.*" If you ask him who these people are that he is dealing with, he answers that they are library visitors who most often borrow books, but occasionally attempt to steal them. "Why would they steal them?" you ask. "Who knows? But they get caught sooner or later." You try a shift of view to a world of theoretical objects. "Do you think there would be any more or any less stealing if there were no guard?" He looks at you as if you were talking of things out of this world, which of course you are. "Books cost money," he says, "don't forget that." This, then, is what we have in mind by the concept, "mode of consciousness" or "mode of attention to life." It can be compared with the mode of attention to the life of an actor engaged in contemplating the mysteries of the term *God,* or a scientist engaged in scientific theorizing.

If in his specific epoche, or bracketing of the world, the scientific theorist suspends his belief in the outer world and its objects, the "guard" suspends his doubt that the world and its objects might be otherwise than as it appears to him. The epoche may be defined in terms of a particular set of principles which define the areas of the world as meaningfully relevant to the actor as an identity. In the case of the "guard" these principles are found in the criteria which define the "job well done." This statement states the problem rather than solves it. Nonetheless, the definition is useful inasmuch as it tells us where and how we are to find a body of statements that will enable us to account for the fact, for example, that the guard will be able to tell us at length about the number of books he checks out in a day, their sizes, their colors, the average number per person—in fact, everything that has to do with the book as it means an item to be checked out and practically nothing about titles, content, usefulness to the borrower, and so on. It also allows us to predict the typology of borrowers he will employ, and tells us as well the motivational theory he is likely to employ in predicting how the borrowers are going to act toward him as "guard" engaged in fulfilling the tasks he is charged with. In a word it tells us what the objects of his world as guard are, and in naming these objects as he does we see them "as he does"; we are thus prepared to "understand" him, without, incidentally, needing to refer to a model full of needs and wishes, of proclivities, cathexes, and predispositions, in order to account for the regularities and sustained character of his actions. The key problem that the investigator must lick is that of devising a method for tracing the extremely devious ways of the logic of symbolization. Where utilitarian criteria are solely involved the problem consists of no more than the effort required to consult the dictionary of occupational titles. But there are always overtones of meaning to these criteria, and these can only be searched out with the use of a theory of *symbolic* action. In this regard the work of the psychoanalysts in symbol analysis (disregarding their beliefs in the "laws of association of ideas") is monumental while it is still discouragingly insufficient. The logics of symbolization can be investigated and their modes of lawfulness defined without invoking a psychological representation of the symbol user. This investigation can be done in the same way that the logic of rational inquiry and discourse can be investigated without referring to those canons by which a world of objects is rationally constituted to the psychological make-up of the user.

Another characteristic of cognitive style is designated in the concept "specific form of sociality." Unlike the concept of group, which is defined as a relationship of actors, the specific form of sociality is a relationship of social identities. In the case we are analyzing, the form of sociality consists of the relationships that obtain between the "guard" as an identity, and the meaningfully relevant identities of those actors with whom the guard gets engaged in the course of treating the objects of his "guard" world. These various identities are objects to the guard in precisely the same sense that the books are objects. Within the mode of attention to life and the system of relevances effected by the epoche the long flow of persons past his desk are seen as "borrowers," "visitors," "information seekers." His relationship to them is defined by the way in which this array of objects is relevant to the way in which the self is identified—in this case to "guard." In the case of the guard we find that many more identities are related to "guard" than the three we have listed; for there are the relationships of "guard" to "guard," "guard" to "employer," "guard" to the host of other identifying concepts of library employees.

It is in tracing out the various forms of sociality that one can see the extent to, as well as the manner in which the actor participates in the various areas of the social system. It is at this level also that the norms which govern the social actions of the actor will be found. Indeed, it is here that the norms "originate"; *no norms without identities, and no identities without norms.*

A fourth characteristic of cognitive style is the "form of spontaneity." In the analytic sense this term refers to the fact that the observer attempts to "see" activity as orderly in the sense that a riot is orderly: that is, with reference to some ordering principle. Thus, the quiet moves made by the chess player, and thrashings of a temper tantrum "make sense" to the observer in terms of some organizing principle which the observer uses as an instrument for rendering in an atemporal, static formulation the host of phenomenal presentations which he encounters in unending temporal sequence. Thus the observer will say that the activity is organized with reference to the attainment of some preconceived end, the teleological principle; or that activity is organized with reference to the expressional principle, where the intention is not to realize a project but rather activity occurs "for its own sake." These two formulae are quite distinct in the experience structures and the transformations experience structures that they depict. Compare, for example, the representation of the salesman trying to effect a sale with that of the child grieving for a lost parent.

Now in speaking of action, conduct, and performance we have included in the definition of these terms a statement of the form of spontaneity. In a sense, these terms represent "predigested" phenomena. So we need now a set of terms which tell us not only *what* is being digested, but how to go about digesting. These rules we find represented by two terms, *tactics* and *style*. These terms are discussed in the section "Style, Tactics, and Strategies of Communication"(pp. 182–188).

Two concepts remain to be defined: time perspective, and the specific form of experiencing the self. The two are closely related and can best be treated together.

Suppose we distinguish first between acting as an ongoing process—action in progress—and action as a thing done. While the actor lives in the act in progress, he is directed toward the state of affairs to be brought about by his action. In order for him to bring into view his experiences of this ongoing process, he must abandon his living in the act, and adopt a reflective attitude toward his acting. But in adopting this reflective attitude, he does not grasp the on-going act but grasps only the performed act. Thus, to live in the on-going process of the action is to experience the acting in the present tense—the "vivid present." But the reflective glance at the action entails removal from the "ongoing flux," such that only the actions of the past tense or present perfect tense are discernible.

And what of projected action? To project action means that future action is rehearsed in imagination; that is, the anticipations are set up regarding the outcome of future action. In projecting the action, the action is viewed in the future perfect tense. The past or present perfect act shows no such thing as empty anticipations. What was empty in the project either has been fulfilled or has not been fulfilled. Nothing remains unsettled or undecided. The actor may remember the open anticipations, but they are remembered in terms of *past* anticipations which have either come true or not. Only the performed act, therefore, and never the act in progress, can turn out as a success or a failure. These insights apply to all actors and to all actions.

On the basis of these insights, we can now define what is meant by time perspective and the mode of consciousness of the self.

Husserl has emphasized the importance of bodily movements for the constitution of the outer world and its time perspective. The actor experiences his bodily movements on two planes simultaneously: (1) Insofar as they are movements in the outer world he regards them as events happening in space and spatial time; (2) but insofar as these events are experienced *within* as changes that are occurring, that is, as manifestations of his spontaneity pertaining to his stream of consciousness, these events partake of an "inner time" (duree). What occurs in the outer world belongs to the same time dimension in which events in inanimate nature occur. Our watches provide us with the measuring stick by which the idea of time in this sense is constituted in meaning. It is this spatialized time which is the universal form of objective time. On the other hand, it is the duree, within which our actual experiences are connected with the past by recollections and retentions, and with the future by protentions and anticipations. Now, the crux:

In and by our bodily movements we perform the transition from our duree to the spatial time, and our working acts partake of both. (Schütz)

In simultaneity we experience the working action as a series of events in outer and inner time, unifying both dimensions into a single flow which shall be called the vivid present. The vivid present originates therefore in an "intersection" of duree and objective time.

Living in the vivid present in its ongoing working acts, directed toward the objects and ends to be brought about, the working self experiences itself as the originator of the ongoing acts, and thus as an undivided total self. It experiences its bodily movements from within; it lives in the correlated, essentially actual experiences which are inaccessible to recollection and reflection. It is the world of open anticipations. It is the working self and only the working self that realizes itself as a unity. When the self in a reflective attitude turns back to the working acts performed, this unity disappears and is replaced by a form of experiencing in which the self which performed the past act is brought into view. It is the self that refers to the system of acts to which it belonged as a role taker, a "me," an identified self.

A qualifying note before going on to the next concepts. It will be noticed that the contents of these structures can and do change almost from one moment to the next, though they may also remain constant over a rather extended period. With each change we have a different configuration and hence a different role, as, for example, when the person engaged in a project pauses in his efforts to become lost in a daydream. *This means that when we come to define a role we must necessarily reify the concept: in effect we say that we shall allow the flux of life's possibilities, but for theoretical purposes we reify certain sets of them.* It is our task, then, to draw from our model those predictions of what the subject would experience within a role, relying on our interview procedures to find out what were in fact the experiences of the person.[1]

Role and the Concept of the Finite Province of Meaning

In discussing the animal *symbolicum* we emphasized that the actor's universe is a symbolic universe, an *experienced* universe. Hence to portray the actor's actions we need to know how things look to him; what significances he attaches to the things of his world or worlds. Hence we decided to reject any notions regarding how the world "really" is; that is, we chose to reject the possibility of an ontology, even a scientific ontology, with which to measure the actor's deviation from "true reality" and "true objectivity" and set for ourselves the empirical problem of determining what the actor's ontological assumptions consist of. That is, we say, all manner of things are real to him and are objects to him *in particular ways.* What are these ways?

The peculiarities of the objectivities and realities of his universes are to be sought in the meanings that all the possible objects of his experience "have" for him. Were we to say nothing more beyond this principle, (1) we should be left with a universe of disparate and unconnected meanings and (2) would have to look to an ego-principle to account for the phenomenon of continuity and organization in experience. Both courses must be rejected: the first, because reflection shows a very real relationship to exist between one experience and another; and the second, because invoking an ego-principle would mean that experience would have to be recapitulated and then attributed for its possibility to the acting ego, a position that is rejected not because it is erroneous but because it is unnecessary. (We may still talk of an empirical ego, however, but this is not the same thing since the empirical ego, according to our definition of the social identity, is an object of experience.)

If then we are to explain the continuity and organization of experience, we must look elsewhere. But where? If we are to avoid any "pre-given" explanatory principle, we must bypass such easy "outs" as instincts, basic wishes, needs, predispositions, tendencies, drives, "efforts after meaning," etc. But if we do this, we have only one thing left: experience itself. Accordingly, we propose to look to our representation of experience to furnish us with the terms of explanation. These terms we find in Husserl's theory of the noesis-noema structures.

We shall discuss the theory of the noesis-noema structures at a later point in this paper. For the present we shall indicate just enough of the conceptions involved to help us through the problem of talking meaningfully about the finite province of meaning.

We shall say that an action has been described when four elements of it have been specified. We shall speak first of the "quality" of an act, the noesis, by which we refer to the meaning element of judgment, feeling, desire, assertion, denial, hope, fear, affirmation, etc., and say that the quality of the act always has reference to the "material" or noema of the act, by which we mean that which is judged, felt, desired, asserted, denied, hoped for, etc. A third element is to be referred to as the "meaning-essense" of the act by which is meant that object which is meant in just the way that it is meant—that which the object means which contains the all of what it signifies. For example, I may make the statements that equiangular triangles exist, and equilateral triangles exist. In both cases the quality and matter of the act remains the same, but the essential meanings of the objects involved differs. A fourth factor is the vividness, the clarity or distinctness with which the content is "presented."

Now we shall accept the evidence of Husserl that these four factors are invariant elements in experience—that is, (1) that the description of an experience is elliptical to the extent that any of these four are omitted from the description—and that (2) the relations between them are such that any one of them may change in value while the others remain the same, and that (3) the fact that *this relationship* is invariant can be stated as a synthetic a priori statement. (We refer to Husserl's investigations for the descriptive investigations of consciousness for the truth of this statement.) When we speak of the *structures* of experience it is these factors that we are referring to as structures. Logically, they are equivalent to what Parsons has in mind when he refers to the actor, norms, means, and ends as the apodictic structures with reference to which we talk about experience. Without telling us a thing about the nature of an experience, they are the invariant terms in which we conceive of experience. (This is not to say that they mean the same as Parsons's categories. In a later paper we hope to show that Parsons's categories do not have the apodicity he claims for them.)

We are now prepared to talk about the first criterion of the finite province of meaning—where our problem is to cite the criteria by which we are able to talk about what is meant by the "organization of experience."

Our first criterion is continuity. We shall say that continuity of experience is possible by virtue of the invariant character of the relationships that are possible between the various parts of an intentional experience. Thus, a series of experiences may be spoken of as being continuous by virtue of an intended object (matter) which remains the same while the quality of the act varies. Thus I look at a cigarette, pick it up, light it, puff it, make statements about it, throw it away. Another example would be a conversation where one person after another contributes to "the topic."

A series of experiences may be continuous by virtue of the quality of the act which remains the same while the intended object varies. Thus, for example, the continuity of the euphoric state or the negativistic state, where one votes "aye" for all things, or "nay" for all things.

A series of experiences may be continuous by virtue of the fact that the quality and the matter of the act may remain the same while the meaning essence varies. For example, a friend of ours in the course of a political conversation repeats pensively, "I'll vote Truman." By questioning we learn that the first time he said it he meant, "I'll vote for Truman;" the second time he meant, "I'll vote for Papa." The third time, "I'll vote for any candidate of the Democratic Party."

One can have continuity where the meaning essence remains the same while the quality and matter vary. Or there can be continuity where any combination of these factors remains constant as long as one varies.

There is no continuity under any of the following conditions: (1) where one expression alone is given; (2) where, in a succession, all the factors remain constant as to their meaning values; (3) where, in a succession, all the factors vary in their meaning values.

Continuity is one criterion of organized experience. But there must be more criteria because, for example, saying that the actor has been speaking about his job is not enough. We need some rational "limiting principle" by which we would be able to say where the job as an object begins and ends. If we want to say what the actor meant by the term, we need to be able to say what he did not mean by the term. How are we to know what *in all* a term embraces as a concept. We need, metaphorically speaking, a "horizon." And this "horizon" will provide us with another criterion of organization.

Lying on the desk as I write is a package of cigarettes. I perceive a package of cigarettes. Now, we need to remember that we have rejected the notion that what the package of cigarettes means to me is to be regarded as entirely a function of the sensory impressions. Rather, whatever the object perceived, it is to be referred to for our purposes as a meaningful object, an intended object, *a noema*—and thus while it may be presented by hyletic elements, it *means* on the basis of the way in which the hyletic elements have been *idealized* by the subject. Thus, it is no "flight into metaphysics" to insist that the package of cigarettes as a meaningful object is an ideal object. We are not denying its material existence. Rather, we seek to embrace more closely than ever its empirical existence by insisting that we be able to say with reference to what rules of procedure its existence is to be confirmed. Thus we shall find that one crucial difference between display packages of cigarettes and the pack on my desk is found in the meaning element of availability of "smokes."

Now the visual image of the package of cigarettes is one thing while the perceived package of cigarettes is quite another. The two are not meaningfully congruent. As Kuhn writes, the second "protrudes" beyond the first. The visual object is presented in three planes, each plane being marked off by a configuration of print and color. Perceptually, however, the object I "see" has six sides. For me the tax stamp doesn't end at the plane of the table, but continues around the pack to the approximate distance of the stamp on the other side. I see the ends of two cigarettes in the torn opening, but I "see" many more inside. All these things I "see" in addition to what is visually presented, and these things are not adventitious with regard to the initial perceptual act. Each attaches to the perceived pack by a change in viewpoint, and each change in viewpoint develops the potentialities that were, so to speak, "predelineated" in the original percept (be sure to differentiate "predelineated" as used here from Aristotelian use). I do not see an aggregate of color impressions (though with a change in intentionality these may be what I bring to attention), but *really* I see the concrete thing, this package of cigarettes. The visual image presents one aspect of the thing "charged" with potentialities which may be actualized by coordinate perceptions revealing further aspects of the same thing.

"The initial aspect is one among countless others. It signifies something other than itself, conveying the more or less decipherable index of related views of the same thing." (Kuhn)

It remains for me to actualize these potentialities as I can or wish by further action such as examining the package, or performing in imagination, or recollection, such an examination. But in any case the possibility of this change of viewpoint exists as a *relevant possibility*. Knocking the package off the desk is a possibility and would constitute a specification of the possibility of handling the package, but we will limit our use of the term relevance by making it mean that the possibility or series of possibilities is *implied* in the percept. *A relevant possibility is one that forms a constitutive element of the appearance of the thing.*

The potentialities which we have in mind are clustered around the visual image. They can be eliminated only at the cost of destroying the unity of meaning of the thing perceived. "Horizon" is only another name for the totality of organized serial potentialities involved in the object as *a noema*—the intended object of the intentional act. Both the "nucleus" and the "horizon" compose the percept—the object in mind—the job, the topic, the thing about which we are talking, or toward which we aim our aggression, etc. Horizon in this sense means the same as Carnap's statement that an empirical construct is defined by a given totality of reduction sentences; e.g., this object is a package of cigarettes if and only if one can find a paper container labeled Chesterfield. This object is a package of cigarettes if and only if it is cellophane wrapped. This object is a package of cigarettes if and only if cigarettes are exposed when the tinfoil is torn away.

This characterization of horizon is incomplete. Only one of several dimensions of horizon have been marked out. The potentialities to which we have been referring constitute what Husserl has called the "inner horizon." The explication of these anticipated aspects we have noted leads to the "intrinsic" structure of the object; it is what we mean by the "intrinsic" structure of the object. Kuhn says it amounts to the "intensification" of the object—the making of it ever more concrete.

The object has its "outer horizon" as well. By this we mean that in meaning the object means more than this momentary appearance and multiplicity of its aspects. The relation of potentiality to actuality, comprehensive anticipation and gradual "unfolding" of anticipations occur *mutatis mutandis* in the make-up of the "outer horizon."

The concept of outer horizon arises out of the insight that there is no such thing in our experience as an *isolated object*. The perceived thing is related to other things, to its closer and wider "environment." As I view the object, I see also its relatedness to other things, though only by way of implication. To avoid misunderstanding we need to underline the fact that implication does not always mean rational logical implication. Consider, for example, the poem: Roses round the door, make me love mother more. We shall have more to say about this later. All these relations taken together form an organized whole. Even the patron of the Fun House at Coney Island who enters a room of miscellaneous and bizarre items—skeletons walking upside down on the ceiling, a living room set arranged on a vertical wall—brings them together under the term "Crazy Room." The package of cigarettes is an object within the world. This relatedness is not an incidental addition to the object taken by itself. Rather, seeing it, I see also the things to which it is related.

Further, both outer and inner horizons are interwoven with a temporal horizon. Kuhn writes,

"The present perception of the object before me is a link in a chain of successive perceptions each of which either had or will have a presence of its own. Accordingly, the apprehension of the thing points both ways: to the immediate and remote past on the one hand and to the immediate and distant future on the other."

The present apprehension is informed by the remembrance of the past as well as the expectancy of coming things. The actual percept at any given point in time is always touched by some temporal mode of apprehension and is concretely inseparable from a long series of former objectivating acts, or rather with their product, the well known, easily recognized thing. The present percept also points forward to its successors.

Though there may be discontinuities, there is no real break in the temporal background encircling the "here and now" of actuality. The absolutely new is inconceivable. Strangeness exists only with familiarity; novelty only with the ordinary. Every object then presents itself within the world and this world is the world of the percipient. Defined in terms of temporal experience, "world" is an organized body of expectations based on recollections. To perceive an object, means to locate it within this system of expectations, though compared with the fullness of perception the expectation is diagrammatic. Nonetheless, the perception is a fulfillment of the expectation, and may in turn furnish the foundation for new expectations. *Anticipations and continuance, the before and the hereafter, do not belong to separate acts in the succession of experiences. They are ingredients of the one act under consideration and compose the temporal horizon of the intended object, the noema.* Each previous or subsequent act has its own past and future. *Only because it fits into a preconceived pattern is any object perceivable.* Being acquainted with objects of a characteristic make-up, filling a certain sector of the total space, limited by other objects, impenetrable to touch—these are the features I expect things to bear. They constitute the basic lineament in which I build up my picture of the world. They are the component elements of my various "pieties"—to borrow a term from Kenneth Burke—my "feelings" of "proper relations," my convictions of what those things are that go together.

Wherever there is experience, rudimentary though it may be, there is already the horizon around the envisaged objects. It is of no use to search for a beginning of the anticipatory pattern of the world within experience. We may trace its differentiation and transformation but not its commencing in time.

To recapitulate briefly: we have designated three critical meanings of the concept, "organization of experience" and have indicated the structural terms of their definitions. These criteria of "organization" are (1) continuity of experience, (2) consistency of experience, and (3) compatibility of experiences with each other. The first was defined in terms of the act components, quality, matter, and meanings essence (there is a fourth, intensity or clarity, which we shall attend to later.) The second was defined in terms of the "inner horizon" and the third in terms of the "outer horizon." All three criteria are related to the concept of the temporal horizon because the concept of the finite province of meaning, in answering the question as to how a thing is real—in what *sense* a thing is real—refers back to the elements of the cognitive style or role, which in telling us about the actor finishes the statement to read "real for a percipient." Temporal horizon then ties meanings to the role element of "mode of time consciousness." In a similar manner, the noesis-noema structures are tied to role elements through the concept of meaning-essence, which is derived for any given object from the epoche, or way of "bracketing the world" of the actor. Thus, for example, the epoche of the dream differs from the epoche of the natural working attitude of everyday life. Hence, two noesis-noema structures that are identical with reference to quality and matter in the two states must necessarily involve objects whose meaning-essences differ, and conversely, if we encounter meaning-essences that are different with reference to the same intended object, then we must hypothesize that a change took place in the principles by which a sphere of relevance was defined. Thus, for example, the psychiatrist and my wife may both hear me say, "The prospect of a statistics examination gives me the willies." Both may nod their heads and say, "You have my sympathy," but one may mean by the identifier, "you," "neurotic" in which case he is likely to mean, "Neurotics have my sympathy," while the other may mean by "you," "dear husband" in which case she is likely to mean, "They have no business making you unhappy." The two are employing different epoches—different ways of bracketing the world.

Our big question at this point then is where do we get the principles by which a finite province of meaning is delineated. The principles are found in the terms that comprise the values of the cognitive style. Suppose we get a closer look at this.

According to William James the origin of all reality is subjective; whatever excites and stimulates our interest is real. To call a thing real means that this thing stands in a certain relation to ourselves. There are multiple numbers of such orders of reality, each with its own special and separate style of existence. Every object we think of is referable to one of these orders of reality. "Each world," Schütz quotes from James, "whilst it is attended to is real after its own fashion; *only* the reality lapses with the attention." In his article on "Multiple Realities" (*Philosophy and Phenomenological Research,* June 1945) Schütz marks out four such orders for examination: the world of daily life; the world of phantasms; the world of dreams; and the world of scientific theory. For its bearing on the problem of understanding we shall review here his view of the world of reality of scientific theory.

Schütz prefers to speak of many finite provinces of meaning upon each of which the accent of reality is bestowed by the actor. A certain set of experiences will be called a finite province of meaning if all of them show a specific cognitive style and are with respect to this style, not only consistent in themselves, but also compatible with one another.

The basic characteristics which constitute the specific cognitive style of the world of everyday life, the natural attitude, are full attention to life, the suspension of doubt, the intention to bring about a projected state of affairs by direct involvement with the outer world, the experiencing of the self as a totality, a specific form of sociality of the common intersubjective world of communication and social action, and a specific time perspective in which inner time or duree and social time intersect. As long as our experiences partake of this style we may consider this province of meaning as real; the accent of reality is bestowed upon it. With such a natural attitude our practical experiences prove the unity of the world as working as valid and the hypothesis of its reality as irrefutable.

All such provinces of meaning, such worlds—of dreams, phantasy, art, religious experience, scientific contemplation, the play world of the child, the world of the insane—have a peculiar cognitive style. All experiences within each of these worlds are with respect to the cognitive style consistent in themselves and compatible with one another, and each of these finite provinces may receive a specific accent of reality. Consistency and compatibility of experiences with respect to their peculiar cognitive style subsists merely *within* the borders of the particular province of meaning to which these experiences belong. That which is compatible within one province will not also be compatible within another province of meaning. Thus the provinces are said to be finite. This finiteness implies that there is no possibility of referring one of these provinces to the other by introducing a formula of transformation. The passing from one to the other can be performed only by a radical modification in the mode of attention to life. Thus, to each cognitive style peculiar to each of these different provinces of meaning belongs a specific mode of consciousness, a specific epoche or bracketing of the world, a prevalent form of spontaneity, a specific form of self experience, a specific form of sociality, and a specific time perspective. The world of working in daily life is the archetype of our experience of reality. All the other provinces of meaning may be considered as its modifications. One starts a typing of a particular province of meaning by analyzing those factors of the world of daily life from which the accent of reality has been withdrawn because they do not stand any longer within the focus of our attentional interest in life. What remains *outside* the brackets could be defined as the constituent elements of the cognitive style of experiences belonging to the province of meaning thus delimited.

What does the world as an object of scientific contemplation appear to be? Schütz rules out of this province contemplative thinking performed for practical purposes as well as pure meditation which is not based upon a project to be brought about by the application of operational rules. Scientific theorizing serves no practical purpose; its aim is not to master the world but to observe and possibly to understand it. It is thus to be differentiated from science within the world of working.

All theoretical cogitations are actions according to the noematic-noetic relationship described before. Theorizing has its own in-order-to motives. It is purposive thinking, the purposes being the intention to realize the solution of the particular problem in hand.

The attitude of the disinterested observer is based on a peculiar mode of consciousness. It consists in abandoning the system of relevances which prevail within the practical sphere of the natural attitude. Unlike the man in daily life he is interested merely in the question of whether his anticipations will stand the test of verification by supervening experiences. This involves a certain detachment of interest in life and a turning away from what Schütz calls the state of "wide-awakeness."

Because theoretical thought does not gear into the outer world it is subject to permanent revision, without creating any change in the outer world. Premises may be changed, judgments discarded, conclusions redrawn, and so on. The theoretical thinker does not look for solutions fitting his pragmatic personal and private problems which arise from his psychophysical existence. The province of theoretical thought involves the resolution of the individual to suspend his subjective point of view. Thus only a partial self, the role of theoretician acts within the province of scientific thought. Within this sphere other persons subsist as reality, but it is the reality of scientific contemplation and not practical interest The shift in relevances means also that terms referring to action within the world of working—motive, goal, needs, and so on—change their meaning and are placed in quotation marks.

The system of relevances that prevails within the province of scientific contemplation originates in the voluntary act of the scientist by which he states the problem at hand. The anticipated solution becomes the goal. The demarcation of elements that actually are or may become relevant is also served by the statement of the problem. In the statement of the problem the scientist enters a preconstituted world of scientific contemplation given to him by the historical tradition of his science. This theoretical universe is itself a finite province of meaning having its peculiar cognitive style and peculiar implications with regard to present and future problems. By the constitutive principle of this branch of his science his discretion in stating the problem is closely limited. Once the problem has been stated, however, no such latitude remains. The process of the inquiry must proceed according to the rules of scientific procedure.

With the theoretical attitude the objects of the natural attitude become theoretical objects, objects of posited being, in which the ego apprehends them as existent. This makes possible the comprehensive and systematic view of *all* objects. All objects are seen in the theoretical attitude as ideal objects. Within the natural attitude the distinction is drawn between ideal and "real objects." The dimensions of the vivid present are inaccessible to the theorizing self. Consequently, the theorizing self is solitary; it has no social environment; it stands outside social relationships.

How then does the solitary theorizing self find access to the world of working and make it an object of its theoretical contemplation? How is it possible that the solitary thinker who stands outside all social relations should find an approach to the world of everyday life in which men work among their fellow men with the natural attitude, the very natural attitude which the theoretician is compelled to abandon? That it is possible is the presupposition of all theoretical social science.

The theoretical thinker, while remaining in the theoretical attitude, cannot experience originally and grasp in immediacy the world of every day life. He has to build up an "artificial device"—the method of the social sciences—by which he substitutes a model of the life world for the intersubjective life world. This model is not peopled with human beings but is peopled with dummies, which are so constructed that they are endowed by the scientist with working actions and reactions. These actions and reactions are assigned by the grace of the scientist. Insofar as the puppets are constructed in such a way that their fictitious working acts are compatible with the scientist's data of the world of daily life, the model becomes a theoretical object. It receives the accent of reality although the accent is not that of the natural attitude. All such objects as representations of the objects of the natural attitude are never more and never less real than "if ... then." Thus their practicality is always limited to the scientific problems to which they have reference and their value as theoretically real objects is dependent only upon their relevance to the purposes of scientific theorizing.

But if the theorizing is carried on outside of social relationships, and since theories are subject to corroboration and criticism from the scientist's colleagues, how can theoretical thought be communicated and theorizing itself be performed in intersubjectivity? The "paradox" exists only as long as we take the finite provinces of meaning as ontological entities, objectively existing outside the stream of individual consciousness within which they originate. If this were the case, then the notions valid within one province would not only require a thorough modification within the others but would become entirely meaningless in another province of meaning. But this is not the case. The finite provinces of meaning are not separated states of mental life in the sense that passing from one to another requires the extinction of memory and consciousness. The various provinces of meaning merely designate different modes of one and the same consciousness in the same life *which is attended to in various modified forms.* Thus in a single day one passes through a range of such modes as one lives first in working acts, then indulges in a day dream, and then works out a conceptual scheme. All these different experiences are experiences of inner time, belonging to the stream of consciousness, and capable of being remembered and reproduced. Thus they can be reproduced in working acts.

There is another facet to the problem of the consistency and compatibility of experiences that we need to take note of. It will have been noted that while we have pointed to the relationship that obtains between the package of cigarettes and the meanings of smokes (re inner horizon) and match box (outer horizon), we have not specified what this relationship consists of. This relationship was referred to by the term *implication.* Unless we are to settle for the unsatisfactory term *associated,* we need to specify the rules that govern these linkages: in a word, the logics. By assuming that cigarettes implies smokes, or the presence of a pack implies that matches are near at hand, we may tend to settle by assumption the very problems that we are trying to drag out into the open for investigation. Such an assumption does no less than propose that the terms which an actor employs may exhibit very interesting twists, but the ways of going from one term to another are governed by the canons of rational discourse. But we have chosen to make no such assumption about the make-up of the actor. We assume only that he sees. What and how he sees is exactly our problem.

With this in mind, we would like at this point to call attention to a problem which we'll refer to as term clusters and their properties.

Term clusters and their properties

Philosophers have long been wont to talk of the "imminent dynamism" of meanings, by which was meant the simple but crucial insight that a term is said to signify only insofar as it signifies something other than itself. This is the basis for differentiating between a mark and a symbol, and furnishes the basis for linking meanings through such copulas as implication, equality, contrast, opposition, summativeness, contradiction, and so on. While the students of logic have mined hell out of this insight, the students of communication and conduct have contented themselves, as least as far as formal investigation of the phenomenon is concerned, with the single term, *association,* to cover in amalgam-like fashion the various kinds of linkages involved. To my present knowledge, Freud alone, in his analysis of dream work, presented any large body of evidence for such "non-logical" combinatorial phenomena as parts representing wholes and wholes representing parts, of repetition meaning summativeness, of a term meaning its opposite, etc. Kenneth Burke, in the *Philosophy of Literary Form* tried to analyze the "symbolic action" in similar terms. No doubt the field of literary criticism abounds with similar analyses. But except for scattered sources including Whorf and a few fugitive writings on the logic of questions and promises, the field is unworked—if one may depend on the assurances of Hanfmann and Quine and several anthropologists to whom the writer has spoken.

Once the prejudice has been put aside that such combinations are little better than interesting and transitory aberrancies of man's basic rational or irrational endowment (one can take a choice or hold to both with the same consequence) the questions of what these clusterings do in fact look like, how they are related to specific types of conduct, what their roles are in the various kinds of understanding processes, etc., are free to emerge. We find some introductory references to the phenomenon in the phenomenological concept of "horizon" and in the concept of "the pieties" as it is used by certain literary critics. The two terms, *horizon* and *piety,* do fine service in pointing up their complementary insights.

The first term designates the fact that an ordering principle is to be found with reference to any cluster of associated meanings, and that any given meaning, either in the general or specific case, is not associated to all the meanings in the communicative universe. An equally important postulate is that any term is capable of functioning as a designator of any meaning. That it does not is problematical. The ordering principle, or rather principles, set the limits both as to what meanings will enter into an organization as well as to the range that can be traveled from any given point in the system. Purpose, pragmatic considerations of time and effort, the principle of "mental economy" are three examples of such limiting principles. (A logical concomitant of the principle of limits is found in the problem of infinite accrual; granted that infinite accrual does not take place, the question, is, why, and under what logically possible conditions would it indeed occur?) They are found in full blown operation in the experiment where the subject is faced with a huge array of miscellaneous objects and is asked to select those objects he would use if he were a student. His selection would be compared in extent and significances of objects with those he would come up with if asked to view them as an expectant father.

With the concept of piety we come face to face with the problem of the logics which govern the combinations—the logic of social participation compared with the logic of free association, compared in turn with the logic of rational discourse. By "piety" is meant here the sense of what goes properly with what. One encounters the problem in a most dramatic fashion in grading examination papers. Let the name on the blue book be anonymous and one feels free to be arbitrary in the peculiar way that scientific objectivity and arbitrariness go together. But let the name ring the chord of familiarity—Jones, oh, yes, this was the student who told me he was applying for medical school—and one plus one starts adding up to three because one may lack faith in the ability of the test to discriminate accurately between B plus and A when the differences in grade can have very important and immediate consequences for the recipient of the grade.

Just what these logics are we would hesitate at this point to state specifically. That the clusterings are differently organized we would insist on, however, and point to the manner in which one makes sense of a blueprint as compared to the manner in which one reads poetry to furnish the empirical materials for making the difference. One finds it exemplified in its bearing on social identities in a story out of the lore of Yiddish humor. An old itinerant rabbi once came to a village where he had been many times before. He was old and feeble, but immensely loved and respected. When he read the prayers at the synagogue he faltered, erred, and could hardly be heard. The congregation said amongst themselves, "Blessed is the old one, he hardly knows what he is reading." A few weeks later a young rabbi came to town. He was strong as an ox, clever, but new to the populace. That evening he read the prayers and his prayers flowed "like water." The congregation judged him: "A curse on him; prayers and wisdom fall like pearls from his mouth." Is it enough to say that the two judgments were syllogistically constructed, but differed in being based on different sentiments? I think not. The promise seems to be far richer than one encounters by restricting himself to an accounting in such terms. We shall touch on this problem in other places in this paper when we speak of social identities and identity transformations.

Noesis-Noema Structures

All meaningful acts, according to Husserl, have the peculiarity of presenting the subject with an ideal object, whether the object be real or fictitious, existent or imaginary. This peculiarity is not to be considered a quality of acts as intensity—for example, it is held by psychologists to be a quality of sense data. The act does not transcend itself to seize an object belonging to a universe external to the sphere of consciousness. Rather the subject is aware of the object by the reference that the act bears in itself to the object. This conception Husserl developed in his investigation entitled "Expression and Meaning."[2] Taking the unanalyzed cognitive situation in which actual psychical processes and physical events are involved, Husserl began with the psychology of meaning with its dependence upon signs, and with their function of manifestation and communication, and sought to account for the sameness of meanings and their reference to an objectivity, whether real or fictitious. The theme of his analysis of meaning was the determination of the sameness of signs and meanings. He shows that in speaking of the same signs we are not describing what really occurs, but we are referring to an ideality. Ideal meanings are inexpungible features of our mental life. They don't "exist"; they are *meant*. Only the experiencing of them is said to be real. They are found within what Husserl calls a meaning-situation analyzable as Farber describes into:

1. meaning-endowing acts, together with the meaning-fulfilling acts which may blend with the former; the fulfillment may be accom-

plished by means of a real experience of intuition, or by means of a phantasy-image; (2) the "contents" of these acts, or their meanings; (3) the reference to an objectivity that is meant.[3]

In being aware of an object in the present experience, one may be aware that the object is the same as that which one was aware of in some past experience, and is the same as that which, generally speaking, one may be aware of in an indefinite number of presentative acts. This "repeatability" Husserl calls identity, and it is identity that is constitutive of objectivity.

But how may identical and identifiable objects exist for and stand before a consciousness whose acts succeed one another in an incessant stream of temporal variations? Husserl meets this problem with his theory of intentionality as it is found in his doctrine of *noesis-noema*.

When an object is perceived there is on the one hand the act as a real event of psychical life. This act is capable of description after the phenomenological reduction has been performed. Husserl demonstrates this in his series of six investigations. The act as an event occurs at a certain point in phenomenal time; it appears, lasts, and disappears never to return.[4] On the other hand, there is what in the concrete act stands before the perceiver's mind. This "what" presents itself in a well determined manner, whether this "what" be the house one sees during a walk or the house of memory. The object, exactly and only as the perceiving subject is aware of it, as he intends it in a concrete, experienced mental state, is the *noema* of perception. *Noesis* is the act. Gurwitsch writes:

> It is with respect to the noema that the given perception is not only a perception of this determined object, but also that it is such an awareness of this object rather than another; that is to say, that the subject experiencing the act in question, the *noesis,* finds himself confronted with a certain object appearing from such a side, in the orientation it has, in a certain aspect, and so on.[5]

Noema then may also be designated as the perceptual meaning or sense. Husserl uses the terms synonymously.

The noema is to be distinguished from the "real object." As a real object, a tree, for example, may appear now in one determined manner, and appear in another determined manner as one shifts his spatial position with reference to it. The tree may show itself in a multiplicity of perceptions, through all of which the same tree presents itself. The "perceived tree as such" varies according to the standpoint from which it is viewed. Indeed, a real thing may not present itself as such except as a succession of perceptions.

> These perceptions enter into a synthesis of identification with one another, and it is by, and in this synthesis and the parallel synthesis among the corresponding noemata, that what appears successively constitutes itself, for consciousness, into this real thing which it is, one and identical as opposed to the multiple perceptions and also to the multiple noemata.[6]

In light of this, two problems arise: first, what is the relation of the act and its noema to the real thing perceived through the act; and second, what relations do the noemata as they are synthesized through identification bear to one another. One thing is clear: that the real object is not to be confused with the noema either single or in synthesis.

Not only is the noema distinct from the real object, but it is distinct as well from the act in that it is not an intrinsic part of the act and does not exist within consciousness in the same manner as the act does. The "perceived tree as such," whether it be in memory or in first hand encounter, may remain identically the same regardless of the variety of acts to which it corresponds. Were it an element of the act it would appear and disappear with the act and would be tied up as the act is to the place the act occupies in phenomenal time.

The noema as distinct from the real object as well as the act, is an unreal or ideal entity. It belongs to a sphere of meanings or significations. The unreality of entities that belong to this sphere lies in a certain independence from them of the concrete act by which neomata are actualized. Every noema may correspond in its identical form to an indefinite number of acts. Noemata are found not only in perceptual life, but there is a noema corresponding to every act of memory, imagination, judgment, thinking, and so on. *In all of these it is through the act that the object stands before the subject's mind.*

Husserl's noesis-noema doctrine is not an explanatory theory. It is a descriptive statement of an objectivating mental state; a description of a mental state through which the experiencing subject is confronted with an object. Every mental state of this kind must be accounted for in terms of identity and temporality. Unlike the traditional conception of consciousness in which emphasis is placed upon temporality, the succession of acts, and the variations each act undergoes by its duration. In Husserl's conception of consciousness he points out that the temporal event in the stream of consciousness must have reference to a sense, an ideal unity. Gurwitsch writes:

> Identity is to be acknowledged as a fact irreducible to any other; it turns out to be a fact of consciousness, no less authentic and no less fundamental than temporality is.[7]

We may not render identity of the noema explicit and ascertain its identity through memory or original experience unless we also become aware of the temporality of consciousness. Temporality and identity are co-related.

Each act, as, for example, a categorical intuition, or the act expressed in the expressions "I think," or "I experience," has its corresponding noema, which is an object such and only such that the subject is aware of it and has it in view when he is experiencing the particular act. Consciousness then should be considered as

> ... a correlation or correspondence, or parallelism between the plans of acts, psychical events, noeses, and a second plane which is that of sense (noemata).[8]

The correspondence is not that of one to one relationship, but rather, the same noema may correspond to an indefinite number of acts.

It is this noetic-noematic relationship that is meant by Husserl's concept, intentionality. The formula, "consciousness of something," means:

> ... a conscious act is an act of awareness, presenting the subject who experiences it with a sense (read, "meaning"), an ideal atemporal unity, identical, i.e., identifiable.[9]

Consciousness is to be defined with reference to a sphere of meaning. To experience an act is the same as to actualize the meaning. Every fact of consciousness must be treated in terms of the relation: experiencing subject to thing experienced as it is experienced. No mental state can be accounted for except with regard to the objective sense, of which the experiencing subject becomes aware through his act. Intentionality means the objectivating function of consciousness.

The following rather extended note is inserted with the hope of throwing additional light on this conception by tying it to Dr. Parsons's theory of action.

Examples are multiplying of attempts to predict what our fellow humans will do next by allowing ourselves to say—while getting critical about how we say it—how they have gone about constituting and transforming the worlds of objects with reference to which they act. One gets the distinct impression from such a sensitive index as the intensity of convention quarrels that professional students of human conduct are turning in increasing numbers to the use of the action framework as we understand it; and we may expect the trickle to become a trend once it becomes generally realized that the subjective categories have as little to do with subjectivism as the most pious "objective" behaviorist would wish.

All the mischief starts with the paradigmatic insight of that now famed horseman who, one dark night, rode across a long flat sheet of ice. Upon learning from an inn-keeper that he had ridden across Lake Geneva, the horseman blanched with fright and dropped dead. Whatever Lake Geneva "really was" is besides the point as far as the attempt goes to account for the rider's decision to take up his journey across the ice and to make his own fatal sense of what he had done.

At least three kinds of concerns come out of the attempt to do by this incident all that it deserves. First is the concern for a theory of meaning-relevant behavior, a crude and approximate alternative designation of that which is designated by the term *action*; second, the concern for a theory of the objects of action; and third, the concern for a theory of change.

To begin with, one needs a way of formally conceiving of what was going on with the rider such that the conceptions would be universally applicable. One cannot appreciate the unique way in which the solution of this problem was attempted, nor understand entirely what Parsons has in mind when he says of Murray, Lewin, Freud, and others that they were employing variations of the action frame of reference unless one realizes that in setting to this task Parsons took quite the opposite direction from that of seeking out empirical universals. Further, he was not seeking nor did he intend to settle for a set of analytical constructs such that they enjoyed fictional or "if—then" status. The question he asked was rather a very radical one, and one which a person adhering to the "strict" empiricist tradition of this country would find strange.

Charged up by Weber's suggestion, "*Jede denkende Besinnung auf die letzten Elemente sinnvollen menschlichen Handelns ist zunächst gebunden an die Kategorian 'Zweck' und 'Mittel,'*" Parsons went digging for the mole in the attempt to find out what in fact were the categories that were universal in the sense that any human being in reflecting on an action—that is to say, appraising the meaning of an action—would necessarily have to use. In a word, what categories were apodictic to the representation of action. Their apodicity is the source of the meaning of Parson's statement that one cannot demonstrate the validity of these categories; they say not one thing about how the world looks; rather, they are the givens, so to speak, the invariant terms in which we conceive and speak of the world of activity. In the book, *The Structure of Social Action,* these categories are named as actor, norms, ends, and means. In this sense of their meaning these categories were designated by Parsons as having phenomenological status, and insofar as wider structures evolved in the theory of social systems, these wider structures also had phenomenological status.

Whether these are the terms with reference to which we must necessarily conceive of any meaningful act is questionable. There is considerable evidence from the phenomenological researches of Edmund Husserl that the invariant structures are different from those which Parsons proposed, while the implication can be drawn from Schütz's analysis of Weber's theory of motivationally relevant understanding that the structure of action which Parsons proposes is applicable (with some revision) to the case of teleological action, while failing to meet adequately the test of evidence in the cases of the type of expressional activity found, for example, in relationships of deep intimacy.

One can say, then, that while Parsons had been radical about the problem, he hadn't been radical enough in that he sought these apodictic structures without challenging some very important naturalistic constructions not the least of which are the idealistic conceptions of primal categories and the concomitant correspondence theory of reality. This would mean that there are still ontological elements in the meanings of the structures he proposed—in this case a scientific ontology—which would mean in turn that the break with ethnocentrism had been incomplete.

One very important consequence for a theory of social action emerges from the fact that these concepts may be apodictic, which is to say, have been derived by the procedures of a "dogmatic" science: as invariant structures they become conditions of action with logically the same significance for action as the physical and biological conditions with which we have become acquainted. Along these lines there is a very promising kind of unsettledness in Parsons's thinking. In talking to a seminar in Theory of Social Systems he spoke about the *structures* of action as invariant points of reference around which institutions might "cluster" (e.g., the action structures of a friendship relationship in which deeply intimate feelings were expressed might be such as to exclude the consideration of others entirely, though conditions for example of general mistrust in the society or conditions under which privacy would not generally be experienced as is conceivable in some pre-literate societies would bring with them institutionalized elements as "phases" so to speak of the structures of the actions under view.)

Parsons agreed at that time that structures of action might also mean structures of experience. Such consent has very far reaching implications for the theory of action. One cannot refrain from asking whether, once this door is opened, Parsons would travel the road that Husserl marked out in *Ideas,* where, for example, Husserl analyzes the structures involved in the experience of assumption, with structural differences made between for instance neutral representation and fanciful representation. One is led to point querulously to Scheler's work on shame and sympathy, asking, "And what about that?" Many implications boil up out of such an equivalence. For one thing, it opens the way for a thoroughgoing phenomenological examination of these apodictic structures; for another, it changes the leading metaphor of man as an actor to man as an experiencer, which would substitute for the concept of man as a teleological force the concept of man as a "see-er" (the animal symbolicum in the phenomenological sense rather than in Cassirer's neo-Kantian sense); and would go far toward putting the concept of meaningful behavior on a thoroughly rational footing.

One can surmise how such a concern might have been arrived at. It is my opinion that it came about after the change was made from conceiving of an action system in terms of means-ends chains, to the actor-situation schema. It seems to me that this would have been so because the actor-situation schema brings to full clarity the indivisibility of the relationship between modes of orientation and the objects of action. In fact, it is almost startling to find how closely this schema approximates Husserl's description of the structures of experience. The acts indicated by the modes of orientation can be equated in meaning with Husserl's concept of quality or noesis without distorting anything other than the classification of modes of orientation that Parsons tentatively employs. The concept, situation of action, designates objects of action which Husserl refers to as the matter of the act, the noema, or intended object, while the fact that these objects represent for Parsons an "order of nature" can without difficulty be referred to Husserl's meaning essence which, as that which is intended in just the way it is intended, means an object which is real for action with reference to some conceptual scheme (e.g., the mountain as the material representation of an obstacle for the military strategist, or the chalk diagram as the visual representation of an equilateral triangle).

The importance of a "breakthrough" to a full phenomenological position can hardly be overestimated as far as the ideal of achieving a fully rational theory of social action is concerned. Once achieved the problem of mathematical representation might be achieved at any time, since at this point it would be entirely a matter of effort. Evidence that this statement is something more than sincerely spoken eyewash is found in the general analytical proposition that Scheler was able to generate in his study of shame.

It may pay us to examine the actor-situation scheme a little more closely for not only does much by way of future promise rest on it, but the clarity of our representation of a social system and the problems of change are dependent upon what we have to say in the theory of action.

We can take a running start by noting again that the modes-of-orientation-situation-of-objects formulation seems to be identical to Husserl's theory of the noesis-noema structures. For example, the term "modes of orientation" designates the acts of judgment, assertion, question, joy, anger, fantasizing, etc. But we have also the situation of objects—those things toward which anger is directed, those things asserted, assumed, judged, seen and so on. Now the thing that presses for examination is the observer's conception of object, that is, the object of action. Here we have a question which is so obvious that one rarely finds a person engaged in research asking it, while all told no more than a dozen social scientists have attempted to push the problem beyond the not nearly so obvious obviousness of the division of objects as concrete and abstract, real and ideal—beyond the ghost of solipsism that lurks just the other side of such a challenge—and beyond the snares of an idealistic ontology—to that rational ground where James's promise of a radical empiricism is indeed fulfilled.

The point that Husserl proposes is that the object which the actor has in view—*that is, the object attended to in a particular way*—the intentional object, is in fact the object of his action and the only object of his action if we would remain in the realm of concrete matters. It is precisely at the point that we would insist on an ontology that covers all like a benevolent cloak that we come up with such a high order abstraction as a concrete object. We do talk of concrete objects meaning by that objects which are "unmindedly" given; presented to us in their hard, sensorily accessible ways, but we may miss the fact that sensations are the conditions but not the contents of a perception. There is the story of the greedy movie-goer to make the point. This gent thought he saw something on the floor near his seat, and while appearing to watch the screen in order to not attract the attention of the party sitting next to him, bent slowly, arm outstretched until he reached it. He sat up suddenly snapping and shaking his fingers. "Somebody spits like a quarter." By which we mean then that the term "concrete object" is itself a meaningful concept which designates an object appraised within a naturalistic attitude. If physics had remained within such an attitude it would still be wrangling over Einstein's use of Reimannian geometry, since anyone employing the naturalistic attitude can see even with half an eye that two parallel lines can never meet.

Rather than concreteness referring to the quality of an object out there in all its fullness—the "cake"—concreteness is the quality of an experience in which meaning intentions can be fulfilled by acts of perceptual presentation. Can one still run into a door without meaning to? Of course. Then what do we mean by objectivity? Objectivity refers to the fact that an intended object can be intended in the same way more than once and regardless of the mode of awareness. Within the naturalistic constructions an empirical proposition is a reflection of nature's uniformities, whereas a rational examination of this formulation reveals the sheer impossibility of relying on it by other than an act of faith, so that we must hold instead that an empirical proposition is itself the statement of a uniformity presented in the form of a restricted frame of possibilities of experience that the observer by acting according to the rules represented by the scientific attitude and setting up the conditions which the proposition prescribes will in fact encounter.

An examination of the object of the actor's action as Parsons intends it does not differ in any respect from Husserl's formulation, though there is some evidence from Parsons's methodological beginnings that he could not underwrite Husserl's view that all the objects of the world, regardless of what attitude is employed are nothing else than intentional objects, or noemata, and that the world in fact consists of nothing else than these noesis-noema structures.

In his paper "Actor, Situation and Normative Pattern" we find Parsons insisting that the objects toward which the actor acts are objects which are meaningfully relevant to his action, and that the situation of objects is a situation of action. But the problem arises at this point, what can situation of objects mean? Certainly it cannot be a summative thing, a mosaic of meaningful objects waiting for fulfillment. It is also apparent from our preceding discussion that we cannot talk of the intrinsic significance of an object in the sense that an automobile recommends itself as a means of conveyance because when all prejudices are put to the side it is really and in fact nothing else than an automobile.

The concept of the "order of nature" is the clue, for it is precisely within a theory of being, the actor's theory of being, that an order of nature has meaning, and it is with reference to this "frame of reference" that the meaning essence of the object, Husserl's third structure, is defined. Peculiarly enough, it is when we ask, where did the "frame of reference" come from that we recognize the frame of reference as nothing else than the designation of the actor *in a role or cognitive style*. What in effect the framework does for the actor is to define a finite province of meaning within which any given object acquires its particular significance for action.

Within a role, the apodictic dimensions of which, according to Schütz, are a way of "bracketing" the world, a way of relating an identified self to an identified other, a way of experiencing the self, a way of experiencing time, a form of "spontaneity," and a given mode of "attention to life" and serve to circumscribe the horizons of meaning—as we find, for example, when the subject is faced with a miscellaneous array of objects and when asked to consider them as if he were a student, selects paper, pencil, and books, while selecting another set when asked to consider them as a proud papa would—the various arrays of intended objects are experienced by the actor in accordance with the noesis structures, simple and complex, that comprise his various modes of orientation. Suppose we pay some attention to them.

The "actor within a role" may be teleologically oriented, which is to say that with reference to a given frame, the end as a future state of affairs "transcends" so to speak, the time space considerations with which the objects are bound, thereby breaking the relevant objects into means and conditions. To the extent that we have conduct devised in advance and based upon a preconceived project we are speaking of action as it is proposed in the structure of the Unit Act. An intention to realize the project transforms the forethought into an aim and the project into a purpose. If an intention to realization is lacking, the projected action becomes something very much like a daydream. If the intention is present we speak of purposive action or performance. One can have covert as well as overt performances, as we noted before in our discussion of Action. The breakdown could proceed further, but this much would seem to be sufficient temporarily at least to deal with the concept of teleologically oriented action. We wish to call attention to two elements in the structure of this mode of orientation: first, a particular way in which time is experienced—that is, the peculiar way in which the material of a teleological action is related to the actor's conception of Past, Present, and Future; and second, the intention to the realization of a project.

This mode of orientation is to be compared structurally with a mode of orientation such as we find in grieving or suffering, where the time dimension is lopped off as far as a meaningful future is concerned, and where there is no project involved and no intention to realize one. Similarly, other structures like the form of sociality, the form of spontaneity, attention to life, the mode of experiencing the self, the "bracketing of the world," change markedly in their values, as do the noesis-noema structures as to complexity, rate and direction of change, and logics of transformation.

Now it is within these modes of orientation that we find the act-object—the noesis-noema structures—of judgment, assertion, valuation, anger, joy, and so on, and the things judged, asserted, valued, etc. Thus the two "modes of orientation," cognitive and affective, insofar as these terms refer to noesis-noema structures, complex though these structures may be, are structurally distinct from the modes of orientation in that sense that we have spoken of teleological and expressional modes. The difference is found in the fact that teleological and expressional modes refer to the presence in the structure of experience of elements that we have referred to the frame of reference or role, whereas cognitive and affectual structures find their place *within* these dimensions.

Some further remarks about cognitive and affective as designators. The invariant structures as we saw are meaning intention or act, intentional object, and meaning essence, or that which is intended in the object just as it is found in view, the content of which is dependent as we remarked before upon the accompanying frame. (Husserl finds another structure, intensity or clarity with which the intended object presents itself, but we can ignore this structure for present purposes.) These structures are *always* found together—one's description of an action being elliptical to the extent that one fails in an interpretation to specify explicitly or by implication the value of the relevant structure.

Now let Greek characters represent any given value of the meaning intention, e.g., α, β, γ; let upper case Roman characters represent any given value of an intended object, e.g., *A, B, C*; and let lower case Roman characters represent any given value which the frame provides, the meaning essence, e.g., *a, b, c.* Any meaningful action, or, to say it in another and equivalent way, any meaningful expression may be represented as follows: αAa.

The first thing that we would stress is that the value of any given structure can change without changing the values of the other structures, though when such a change occurs, the meaning of the expression changes. Thus, we can hold the object and the essence constant, while varying the noesis, as we find in the following sequence of expressions: There are men on Mars; That there are men on Mars is questionable; I hope there are men on Mars. With our little graphic gimmick we can exaggerate the different structures of those expressions: αAa, βAa, γAa. Or we can hold the noesis and the essence constant while varying the intended object, as we find in the following sequence: The time has come to speak of many things . . . of ships, of shoes, of sealing wax, etc. α*Aa,* α*Ba,* etc., where the act is that of assertion and the meaning essence is "nonsense." Or we can hold the noesis and the intended object constant while varying the meaning essence, as for example when I say, "I vote for Truman" and mean by it such various things as "I vote for one of the two presidential candidates"; "I vote for Papa"; "I vote against the Republicans"; "I vote by necessity but without hope." α*Aa,* α*Ab,* α*Ac.*

Limiting ourselves to the gross differentiation of structures as such without attempting to pay attention to the structural differences between noeses—differences that we find for example between positive assertions, neutral assertions, value assertions, fanciful assertions, etc.—we find that the game can become rather involved as we proceed to hold various combinations of structures constant while varying the others. Thus, for example, consider what happens when we appraise a sign like Δ. By no means is it simply given that this is a triangle. I can appraise it as an ink mark, in which case we have one value of *A* and *a*. But I can appraise it as the representation of the genus, triangle, or as an equilateral triangle, or of the representation of any object I choose: the head of a man, a topological region, the boundary of an area of the paper, the insignia of some organization, and so on. For each of these possibilities I can vary the act so as to praise, condemn, consider, etc. And if for another example we want to get fancy and take objects constituted in one attitude and appraise them with another, we can do that also, as we find when I consider a Moebius strip with a natural attitude, in which case the premise that I can actually hold a one sided sheet of paper in my hands raises the hackles on my head.

The point of all this is that whatever we mean by affective and cognitive as terms is defined in terms of the structural make-up and the structural transformations of actual experiences. A further point: these transformations proceed according to certain logics or rules. Thus we have the logic of rational discourse; the logic of expressional action; of the action of various pathological states; of free association; and so on. The problems ramify in their complexity if we extend our concerns to the logics of action of the various orders of social relationships.

It is with the view to such considerations as we have cited here that we would insist that the concepts of thinking, willing, and feeling enjoy at present no better than "If … then" status, and that much research is needed into the experience structures which these terms supposedly designate. Once we get behind the barriers that Kant set for us, we find a field that is practically unexplored.

Social Identity

Categorized representations of self and other are designated by the generic term *social identity*. Regardless of where the criteria of the categorization are drawn from, or according to what rules they are applied, all such representations will be known as social identities. Thus, whether we are referring to milkman, Dick Tracy, parent, person, male, female, Negro, leader, our "actor," or the psychologist's representation of the object of his study or judgment, the term applies.

The social identity is an object of social treatment, referable as an object to a self or an other, and phenomenologically appraised by the observer. It is always inductively arrived at by the observer, and in this sense differs from the psychological representations of "personality" which are metaphorical "as … if" constructions. The social identity is seen by the actor as a real object and is experienced directly as a real object. The identity is social in the sense that it is an element of a cognitive style which cognitive style is dialectically relevant to a series of transformations of social relationships occasioned by working acts performed with reference to another actor. As an object, its mode of reality, like any other object, is found with reference to a specific finite province of meaning.

Social identity is used in much the same way that Samuel Strong uses the concept *social type*. In itself this should be enough to caution the reader against equating the concept identity with the concepts of actor, self, ego, and role. While these latter concepts when strictly defined are heuristic devices, referable to the language of syntax for their meaning, the concept of social identity is a directly given object of experience referable for its meaning to the language of things.

The conception of identity as an object is found in accordance with C. S. Peirce's formula:

> Consider what effects that might conceivably have practical bearings you
> conceive the object of your conception to have. Then your conception
> of those effects is the whole of your conception of the object.

Like any object, its meaning as an object is found in the mode of
action taken with reference to it. However, it is constituted for the
observer as a peculiar type of object. It is a *symbolic* object, and always
and only a symbolic object. The reality of the social identity as an object is a non-empirical reality where the rules of action toward it have
meaning in a symbolic rather than a logico-empirical sense, and where
changes in the identity as an object as effected and the meanings of
the changes are apprehended by the actor according to symbolic rather
than logico-empirical considerations.

Suppose we compare the reality of the social identity for action
with the reality of a chair. If one wants to build a chair one selects the
lumber, cuts it, fits the parts and joins them with hammer and nails.
To destroy it one may break it up, burn it. To sit on it, one arranges
a spatial juxtaposition of bearing surfaces—in short, one performs
physical manipulations that finally render the end of the action. The
criteria of "success" are derived from the norms of physical mechanics,
and these criteria yield in turn a number of propositions by which one
recognizes a given order of consequences as indicative of the accomplished end of the action.

The social identity has its relevant orders of manipulative criteria
and operations, albeit one cannot sit on an identity except figuratively.
However, the operations by which it is manipulated as an object, together
with the attendant criteria, exist and, in fact, constitute as operations and
criteria the most common experiences in our lives. Just as there are the
parts of speech and grammatical rules by means of which the manipulations of chairs are indicated, so the language provides the parts of speech
and grammar that indicate the modes of manipulating social identities.
For example, consider the following terms, which are intended in their
literal sense: oppose, attack, defend, insult, validate, invalidate, repress,
excommunicate, hire, fire, impeach, invest, invoke, substantiate, trans-
substantiate, punish, destroy, create, recreate, kill, resurrect, compromise,
coerce, beautify, sanctify, desecrate, buy, sell, will, barter, falsify, integrate,
bestow—to name only a few obvious operations.

The reader will observe from this illustrative list that the rules of manipulation in so far as they give literal meaning to these terms are symbolically meaningful, and are operative in a non-empirical sense with reference to a non-empirical reality. The changes of identity that are implied by such terms are effected and the meanings of such changes are apprehended by the actor according to non-empirical considerations. This is not to say that the meanings of such terms cannot be apprehended by the observer according to empirical procedures. It only means that they are not constituted by the actor according to the guiding rules of scientific actions. That they exhibit their own lawfulness goes without saying. But what this lawfulness consists of still remains to be investigated, and cannot be clear until we know much more than we know at present about the logics of symbolization. An important implication for research emerges at this point: To the extent that identities are relevant to action, to that extent they lend a ritual or magical aspect to the action, the aspect of ritual or magic being dependent upon where the identity is employed in the ends-means structure of the action. Inasmuch as an exchange of identities is an integral procedure of every social communicative process, all communication has a ritual aspect, and since social action always involves communication, every social action should yield its ritual meaning for the agents if this aspect be sought out.

By way of clarifying the meaning of identity we might abandon the action framework temporarily in order to make a note on the number of identities. Cataloging all the identities to be found in the social universe would be an endless task, not only for their great numbers, but because they are continually changing, with new ones being created (literally) and old ones being dropped. At any given time, however, the number is a finite one. If anyone were inclined to the task he might make a miniscule start by consulting the *Dictionary of Occupational Titles*. A strange and fascinating social world is revealed by reading these definitions of occupational identities.[10]

There is a very interesting peculiarity of the social identity as an object of an actor's experience. Among the various statements that the actor makes in defining the identity are those which are intended to account in "because of" and "in order to" terms for the sequences of different signs that the identity seems capable of generating without the direct intervention of any other thing. Such accounts are known as "motivational theories." Apart from their intrinsic interest as accounts of why the identity does what it does, the motivational account that is assigned to it is, as far as the observer is concerned, of crucial importance, for an identity has not been defined for the observer until the definer of the identity has rendered such an accounting. It is in terms of such motivational theories that the actor is able to orient himself to a set of expectations with reference to an identified person. His working acts then serve the function, among others, of "testing" the expectations that the motivational aspect of the assigned identity provides. We put quotation marks around the word "testing" the expectations that the motivational aspect of the assigned identity provides. We put quotation marks around the word "testing" because the ways in which the motivational theories are constructed determine whether the acts serve as "tests" of expectations, or the means for confirming expectations. Compare, for example, the constancy with which identities are held in the family, with the rapidity with which identities change when one is engaged with strangers or competitors.

The motivational account is an intrinsic part of the meaning of this social object. The identity may be defined in terms of attributes—including everything from physical attributes such as height, weight, color, to personal traits of pleasant, dour, dependable, kind, bad, good, etc.—all of them being meaning elements with reference to which a person is said to have been described. We are undecided at this point whether the definition of the identity in terms of traits is to be considered a form of motivational account. Our inclination is to regard the two as the same.

Social persons as objects differ from the objects of the real life of minute to minute unreflective decisions, overt appearances, and the working attitude. When we are in the area of social persons, we do not say that identities exist; rather we say that they are *meant*. The importance of the distinction cannot be overemphasized. It becomes one of our very important problems to trace out how variously they can be meant, and one important facet of their meanings is the assigned sense of existence and reality which the actor "lends" them. The practicing psychoanalysts, perhaps better than most students of human conduct, have come to encounter and to tell us what kinds of variations of meaning may come to be designatory of persons.

The actor in defining the other may invoke many kinds of sources of motivation. That is to say, his designating metaphor, in representing the potentialities of activity with which the actor invests the other person, may point to the most varied kinds of sources of activity. Consider some examples of models that may be used: the animal, the organism, the rational human, the God-seeker, the sin-seeker, the complicated rat, the "real person," etc. Every model answers the question as to the source of motivation, with one locating it in the forces of the environment, another "in" the person, another in the purpose, another in the act, another in the instrumentalities of action, and of course, in any combination of these. The sources are to be listed after empirical examination. The scheme need not be, and we would expect that it rarely is, scientifically systematic, though it will be systematic in accordance with the peculiar logic of its usage by the actor who employs it. Regardless of the ways in which they are constructed, identities furnish the premises for the treatment of the other person Not only then are the identities the source so to speak of the norms which govern social actions but the terms of the motivational account point to the paths which lead directly to the operative values of a social system. We can hypothesize that as a social system changes, the motivational theories will change also.

Representing as it does the terms in which the other person is identified by the actor, the motivational scheme furnishes the paths which lead the observer to the operative values of the particular social arrangement in which the actor as an identified self is engaged. The notion need not be strange if we recall (1) that the identity is nothing else than a scheme employed by the actor for interpreting the signs generated by the other persons—a scheme whereby the question of the other person's intentions is answered; (2) that the scheme furnishes a motivational account, the terms of which are related by the copulas of "because of" and "in order to"; and (3) the actor's completed interpretive expressions will employ these copulas in such a way that the relevant values will be contained expressly or implicitly in the expression. A correlated notion: the clearer it is that the actor has assigned ontological status to the identity, the clearer will the value elements of the arrangement emerge.

Some fugitive notions:

(1) If the observer is to render the phrase "the actor's expectancies of performances" in rationally testable terms, he needs to set as his aim

the ability to show how such "expectations" are derivable, *according to the logic that the actor employs,* from the terms of the motivational scheme that the actor uses.

(2) The identity is not to be confused with the epithet. For example, if the actor identifies a person as a cop, and adds, "He's a dirty sonofabitch," we have one identity involved not two. We need constantly to bear in mind in arriving at the identity, the difference between that which is being characterized and the terms used in effecting the characterization. If we bear in mind the discounting rule, "Why, in the actor's view, does the other act as he does?" we shall avoid confusing a term which serves, for example, as a designator, as intensifier, etc., with a term which means the object as it is meant in itself. Thus one motivational element of the cop as cop *may* be found in the fact that he is regarded as a sonofabitch. This is to say that a given term does not bear its grammatical significance on its face value. The key is always, how has the actor intended the term? Thus, for example, the student who knocks on the door looking for the course assistant in order to register a complaint about his midterm grade, may be regarded by the assistant as a student-with-a-complaint. The fact that the assistant then tells the course instructor, "How about seeing so and so; the sonofabitch has a kick," does not involve a changed identity, but at best may add another facet of meaning to the identity, e.g., nuisance, threat, etc.

(3) Like any other object, the identity has its "inner" and "outer" horizons within a given finite province of meaning.

(4) We shall need to examine the meanings of the terms of the identity for their expressional and specific referent character. This should help us in making clear the fact that the identity like any other object enjoys a unified meaning, that is to say, is real in a particular way within a particular mode of apprehension. For example, the occupational description that we pick out at random from the *Dictionary of Occupational Titles* describes a "Painter, Depilatory" as follows: A laborer, by-products operations. Removes sheep pelt from trucks and spreads it out on drain table, hair side down; dips brush in depilatory solution, and spreads it evenly over flesh side of pelt; folds pelt along backbone line, wool side out, and hangs pelt on rafter hook. The specific referent meanings of these terms, and hence the peculiar reality of the identity here being referred to would come out of the context of the cognitive

style of the personnel manager or foreman of a wool processing plant. But these same terms can be given expressional meanings without changing a letter, and with the result that altogether a different identity would result, as for example, were one to consider this description as having been rendered by a member of the anti-vivisection society; or to make the expressional meanings more involved, were the description to have been rendered by a poet, who by heaping in the references of the terms was symbolizing specialization in industry but meant by each of the terms *lack of specialization* when men were "whole men," thus portraying, in all, the ironical identity of the natural man who had lost his birthright. And so on. Any actor's characterization of an identity can not be accepted at its face value as "obviously" meaning X and only X. We just saw how the identical terms could refer to three different identities, with each claiming concreteness according to the cognitive style which provided the conditions of its meaning. The use of expressional and specific referent symbols needs to be watched, for they provide us the materials for diagnosis of a social system that are important in the same way that pulse and blood pressure are important to a physician attempting the diagnosis of an illness.

Identity Constancy and Identity Transformation

We have emphasized, perhaps to the point of the reader's fatigue, that identities as meaningful objects do not exist; they are meant. This means, within the plan outlined here, that we as observers are not allowed to frame our questions with regard to the phenomenon of identity constancy by asking what there is about the "real person" himself that remains constant, but rather must ask, early-gestalt-wise, what are the conditions under which the person's interpreter regards the person as the same. To put it another way, identity constancy is a "function" of what conditions of the interpreter's experience? This point is crucial if we are to avoid on the one hand the dilemmas that a scientific ontology of persons leads to, or the sterilities of subjectivism that the act-psychologists of the late nineteenth century became embroiled with.

We must look to the actor's ontological scheme if we are to make sense of identity constancy. When we do this, we find that identity constancy is nothing else than the phenomenon of the actor's having reified a cluster of life's possibilities as these possibilities have reference the terms of the identity to the other person. By reification we mean the conceptual representation of the possibilities of experience according to some principle of classification. That the classifications may be exhaustive or not, open or closed, internally consistent or not, built up according to rules of scientific method or not, needs to be determined by investigation. We expect to find that the most common and fondestly entertained categorizations of experience will have nothing to do with the alien and alienating rules by which we regulate our lives when we seek to get scientific about it all.

We need now to define what we mean by "constancy." Granted any success, we shall have by implication the general meaning then of the term *identity change.*

Before proceeding with our discussion of identity changes, we need to be clear about one insight that so far, at least, appears to stand up to close scrutiny. That is, constancy of meaning can occur and does occur despite the most marked hyletic changes in the object under appraisal, and conversely, one can have marked changes in identities even though the hyletic elements remain constant. One of our very crucial problems is that of determining the conditions under which constancy or change or meaning occurs under hyletic variations.

Our term *constancy* refers to the *practical* lack of change over a time span of n-length in the significances of the identity's terms for an actor, within a given finite province of meaning. By "practical" we refer to the exigencies of investigation as well as the effectiveness of any statement of prediction in which an identity's meanings are involved as conditions or predictors. Ideally, the fact of constancy cannot be assumed; it must be empirically demonstrated. Where this condition proves difficult to handle, we shall need to assume constancy but will need then to earmark what significances we are assuming to be unchanged. To make statements then about the "same identity" we need to talk in terms of the coordinates of (1) time and (2) sameness of meaning. Hence, if we refer to Identity2 and say it represents Identity1 after transformation, we need to show how the meanings of I2 are "derivable" from I1, for otherwise obviously we are not talking of transformations of an identity, but merely the sequential appearance of two different identities.

To talk of identity transformations, then, we need to be able to relate a sequence of identities in terms of some "principle of continuity." By "principle of continuity" we refer to a set of considerations which we shall list in a moment which are used *by the observer in ordering the specific content of these considerations as this content is obtained through investigation.* When we say, for example, that one consideration is a co-ordinate system which furnishes the dimensions along which variation of identity elements can occur, the notion as it stands is, figuratively speaking, an "empty vessel" (in reality, nothing else than a reminder of something that needs accounting for) to be "filled" by the empirical material to be elicited from investigative procedures.

What are these considerations? They are: (1) a set of criteria by which an identity is defined and recognized by the actor as meant in itself and different from some other identity. Where the criteria for two identities mean the same for each, we are dealing with the same object, and there is no rational basis for discussing how one can be changed into the other. (2) A common definitive meaning of the two identi-ties whereby comparability is possible. (3) A coordinate system which furnishes us with the dimensions along which variation can occur. (4) The basic rules or logic which limits the possible transformation that can occur—regarding, for example, rate and direction. (5) Procedural rules, or rules governing the specific tactics of transformation; rules, for example, binding on the "decision" to effect a change. And finally, (6) the tactics or "operations" by which the transformation is effected.

This is quite a load, so suppose we try an example to lighten the atmosphere. First, however, a quick note. Instead of referring to these six "considerations" as a "principle of continuity," let's supplant it with the term, "transformation scheme" and then get even fancier about our terminology by making the difference between an "alpha transforma-tion scheme" which has to do with the changes in identified others, and the "beta transformation scheme," which applies to changes in the identified self. The alpha transformation scheme, or better, *an* alpha transformation scheme refers to the considerations bearing on the changes in the identified other when the identified self remains the same and when the meanings relevant to the transformations occur within a given finite province of meaning. Later in the paper we shall take up the rationale behind our insistence on a difference between the alpha and the beta schemes.

One further point: The alpha transformation scheme has reference to the changes of the identities found in the form of sociality. The form of sociality it will be remembered is one of the six terms by which we define an actor in a role. Thus, an alpha transformation scheme is said to be employed *by an actor; it is not employed by a person.* The concept of the alpha transformation scheme is a construction which we use to aid us in explaining the variations in the treatment that one person affords another, with this explanation being rendered through the conception that the treatment person A affords person B has its premises in the way in which person A "defines" person B. The "definition" is found in the vocabulary of motives that the person A uses. The conception states that the successive definitions occur according to some principle of regularity. Our construction is designed to represent these changes and to aid us in describing them.

The example: the following is an example of a formally closed alpha transformation scheme. (For convenience, we'll use the symbol αT to mean "alpha transformation scheme.") During the war I was attached to the Gulfport Field Station Hospital. While reflecting on the relationships between doctors and patients, I was struck by the fact that once you came under the treatment of an Army doctor, there was relatively little "slack" as far as variations in the positions you could occupy as far as the Army doctor was concerned. From the point of view of the doctor, which is to say, where the identified self of the doctor was held constant, an αT operated with the identity of sick soldier at the point of beginning, from which four alternative identities fanned out. The Army physician saw sick soldier to cured soldier; sick soldier to malingerer; sick soldier to Army dischargee; and sick soldier to very sick soldier. The latter four identities were logically derivable from the Army regulations bearing on the treatment of sick soldiers. The common element that makes comparison possible consisted of the criteria by which a person was identified as an Army participant; that is, the criteria by which a person was "eligible" as a meant object in the Army doctor's finite province of meaning in which a body of rules and sanctions were regarded as "proper" to the treatment of a member of the "system"—the soldier. Thus, if you were listed at Field

Headquarters, or if it could be confirmed that you were listed at some Field Headquarters, you were allowed into the game; if not, you were counted a "civilian," which meant that you were advised to seek the help of a town physician, unless you were a "Field Employee" in which case a different αT applied to you.

The identity "sick soldier" was defined by the criteria of "symptoms" based on the results of medical examination and accorded significance in accordance with the logic of medical prophylaxis and cure, with both criteria and logic being tempered by the Army rule of "keeping them on the job." (It is at this point that we get a glimpse of the wider "system" for which the criteria had significance and for which the manner of application of criteria had consequences. We are tempted to follow up this train to trace out the "operational significance" of the term "responsibility" which got such a big play as a term of treatment.)

The identity of "cured soldier" was defined by the criteria of "symptoms" or "lack of symptoms" based on the results of medical examination and accorded significance in accordance with the logic of medical prophylaxis and cure. One element of meaning made the difference between sick and cured soldier. Being regarded as a sick soldier meant one was accorded medical attention. Being regarded as a cured soldier meant that one was "discharged back to duty," that is, the doctor made a file of the case, and forwarded the file to the Office of Hospital Records.

One was accounted a malingerer by the doctor if (a) one's symptoms could not be ordered according to the logic of medical cure, but (b) could be ordered according to the logic of personal responsibility for meeting "obligations to the war effort." Peculiarity enough, doctors found it a very difficult identity to assign; line officers found it easy. For the doctor, the identity of "malingerer" was rarely clear cut, incorporating as it did the meaning of possible medical misjudgment.

Unlike the identities of cured soldier and malingerer, whose meanings had their counterparts in the common experiences of the doctor in the normal course of civilian life, the identity of dischargee was a creature born of the Army. The criteria of definition consisted of one's symptoms, ordered according to the logic of medical cure, plus one additional criterion which was based on the following question: Was the medical condition such as to impair the person's ability to effectively carry out general Army duties. To define a man as a dischargee, meant that the doctor attested the man's unfitness for continued service in the Army, and by signing the appropriate documents, set in motion the "machinery" by which the dischargee was "processed" and formally "alienated" from the service.

The identity of the "very sick soldier" was defined by the criteria of symptoms medically appraised, plus the answer to the question of whether the local station hospital had the facilities or was empowered to handle the defined illness. Obviously, this identity is an amorphous one and represents a great many specific identities. All were alike, however, in that once defined this way, the doctor arranged to have the person transferred to a General Hospital.

Within the cognitive style, or role of Army Physician, where the physician was identifiable by the observer as an Army doctor, these then were the various identity positions which he recognized; they make up some of the components of the transformation scheme. But there are other components.

What about the coordinate system which we promised would furnish us with the dimensions along which variation could occur? Unfortunately for the reader, we'll need a running start before we get up to the "go" line of this example. First, we need to underline a point made before: the notion of the coordinate system is the observer's. But the specific references of the coordinate system, that which is meant by the actor's coordinate system, must be arrived at empirically. Otherwise, one runs the risk of assuming a rational actor, and we wish to avoid this assumption, and any assumption regarding the "rational" or "irrational" character of the dimensions of variability that the actor has reference to in dealing with a succession of identities. That we as observers treat the coordinates rationally does not affect the fact that the coordinates may be irrational in make-up. The syntax applicable to the transformations of the figures of the dream is certainly unlike the syntax which governs the statements that Freud makes about dream syntax. Similarly, our task as observers is to treat in accordance with rational norms, the "dimensions" which the actor employs, whatever they may be and however they may be constituted; our job in a word is limited to "analytical description."

What are some examples of a "coordinate system?" One that comes immediately to mind is the two dimensional surface of plane geometry. The directions of transformation of such an ideal object as a triangle, for example, are fixed by the dimensions of length and breadth. In the Horatio Alger stories we find a transformation scheme employed by the author with reference to the changes of "position" through which the author puts his hero. The dimensions here are age, wealth, and moral integrity. The sociologist may treat identities defined with reference to the axes of age, religious affiliation, and occupation, and call his resultant identity a "status." The psychiatrist, may employ dimensions "derived" from the constructs representative of personality structure. A family member will employ a dimensional scheme with reference to the possible "positions" of his wife, his son, his parents (Remember, we are talking at this point only of "dimensions" and not about how they are related. That is, we are not talking yet about the rules by which they are "organized.") The points at which we start looking for the dimensions are found in the criteria of identity definition. We needn't be too surprised if we find that age is a definitive criterion of one identity position, while it drops out of use entirely in an identity further up the line. The transformation schemes of fantasy are filled with such double takes. A knowledge of the rules of fantasy, however, should put us back on the track of completing the task of nailing the contexts of comparability and variation. For example, I may engage in a fantasy in which I am identified as a Don Juan while the successive objects of my fantasy are an inaccessible woman, who through appropriate logic and fantasy gets changed into a "hot piece." Now we know that the dimensions which make up the coordinate schemes of fantasy are not given from the outside nor do they serve as a point at which the actor gets engaged with others for their verification through working acts, so that whatever is found in the dimensions is put there by the actor in the form of a set of terms replete with their "immanent" meanings. We might expect to find then that the dimensions of fantasy consist of the dialectics of language alone, so that "inaccessible" in being defined to begin with by its contrast with the "hot lay" has provided at the very point of its introduction into the fantasy for its "reasonable" alternative meaning. The problem of dimensions is at once both complicated and intriguing. Between the writings of Freud and Kenneth Burke we should make some progress with it with the promise of far reaching pay-offs as far as the problem of the structures of experience is concerned: Freud because he has underlined the blooded kinds of meanings that can accrue to Webster's anemic terms, and Kenneth Burke because he alone among semanticists, to the best of my present knowledge, has turned full attention to that crucial semantical phenomenon of implication. (See his book, *Grammar of Motives.*)

The coordinates employed by the Army doctors were not drawn from the "self-contained" meanings of fantasy, but rather were thoroughly socialized, with a very definite set of empirical consequences attending their usage. These coordinates were the fact of illness, the source of responsibility for illness, and the future utility of the other for the Army. Incidentally, if we take these three dimensions and lay off along each one a crude kind of unit of measurement, we wind up with a device which yields us an index of position which represents each of the identities that were "possible" for the doctor. For "the fact of illness" we might have "established" and "not established;" for the "source of responsibility" the units "self controlled" and "beyond self control" or "natural illness" or "act of God;" and for "future utility for the Army" we might have "good as new," "useful at low efficiencies" and "junk." The units are good, of course, only insofar as they represent the units that the Army doctor employed. However, even knowing that this is the case, our picture of the doctor's brand of "geometry" would be incomplete because we have no way of knowing how the coordinates are to be related to each other. That is to say, we may have the terms of the doctor's geometry, but we lack the rules which tell us how the terms are to be combined. Like the other terms of the transformation scheme, the rules are not to be assumed, but must be arrived at through investigation.

We are proposing that investigation should uncover two sets of rules: (1) the basic rules of the game, which represent how the subject "allows" himself to combine, oppose, contrast, contradict, imply, terms, as well as formulate expressions of the terms according to mood—e.g., imperative, conditional, optative, hypothetical, etc., and which furnish the means by which the observer can construct the subject's effective "truth table." One need only compare the discourse of intimate or hostile conversation with that of scientific discussion to grasp the notion that there are many different modes of discourse, and that the meanings involved in each are governed by a logic peculiar to each mode. Von Domarus shows in *Language and Thought in Schizophrenia*, for example, how the logic of schizophrenic discourse differs from the logic of scientific discourse. Piaget's materials are suggestive of similar differences in the logics employed by children. By way of making a crude separation of goat from sheep logics, we would like to differentiate the logic of rational discourse from the logics of social participation, meaning by the first term the two, three, or n-term logics which professional logicians have so astutely described, and meaning by the second the as yet barely investigated rules governing the meaningful construction of such expressions as commands, requests, questions, exhortation, and so on.

We propose that the way into the problem will be found by a phenomenological description of the semantic properties of specific referent and expressional symbols. Comparing, for example, the symbolism involved in such an article as "Auditory Discriminations in the Cat" with the symbolism involved in advertisements and in such articles as "Is Red-Fascism Rampant" should yield a quick, albeit limited and tentative pay-off. Investigations of the language of children, the language of the dream, professional argots, the language of lovers, the language of telegrams, of greetings, of denunciation, of rite, of poetry, of the graphic arts fairly clamor for investigation.

The transformation scheme is made up not only of the basic rules, or logic, but (2) of procedural rules. Procedural rules are what we ordinarily refer to as the norms of activity. We might as easily conceive of them as instructions for activity.[11] The term refers to everything by way of norms from the technical directions for wiring a radio to the most absolute kind of prohibitive instructions such as are found in the Ten Commandments. The rules governing the ways in which a number of boards are to be treated in order to render them into a bookcase differ from the procedural rules for solving an arithmetical problem which in turn differ from the rules binding on the task of effecting a change of identity. To the extent that identity transformations have public significance, such as one finds in the case of the Army doctor, or such as one finds in trials, employment procedures, ceremonies of investiture, introductions, etc.—to that extent one can look at the various "how-to-do-it" manuals, e.g., the *Bible* to *Army General Orders* to *Rules of Evidence* to *1001 Ways to Get Rich,* for a first, albeit highly idealized approximation of the norms that are operative. However, many transformation rules binding on identity transformations have private significance (though this does not mean they are idiosyncratic to the solitary individual and hence are not employed by anyone else. The rules employed by the paranoid, for example, have private significance, are widely employed, though privately, and are without what Znaniecki might call "social validity"—that is, they do not enjoy public support). It goes without saying that a person can be said by the observer to have acted according to a given set of norms although the actor might have been entirely unaware of what these norms were, and is unable to talk about them as objects of discourse. This only means that the observer must set up beforehand what he is going to consider as evidence that norms of a given type have been employed. In the sense that this evidence is furnished by the acting person, the person does "tell" the observer about these norms.

Incidentally, we need to underline the fact that nothing is meant in the concept of the transformation scheme that implies that the term is to be used only in those cases where the actor employs purposeful calculation in effecting an identity switch. Regardless of whether the actor is oriented to the switch of an identity as the intention of his activity, or whether the switch occurs as an effective though unanticipated consequence of his activity, the transformation scheme applies. One has a transformation scheme wherever an actor is engaged in a social action. One can have a transformation scheme, then, in which alternative identities are *not* provided for. It is one of our tasks to state the characteristics of relationships in which this is the case.

Returning to our example of the Army doctor, we shall have to welsh on our promise to show the logic involved in the doctor's transformation scheme. We could say that the familiar two-term logic taught in Philosophy 2 applied, were it not for the fact that for the doctor such an elementary principle as the principle that A does not equal not-A did not hold. Rather than there being a body of criteria whereby A was defined such that we were provided by the principle of exclusion with the class not-A, we had instead a more liberal kind of arrangement in which reasonable procedure allowed that that which was accounted as *A,* sick soldier for example, was arrived at through a process of progressive encompassment. It was as if the term *sick soldier,* rather than being simply the designator of the criteria which it meant as a term, was instead a thing meant in itself and such that a proper knowledge of it provided the premises for selecting the criteria of admission. Not the smell of the rose, but the smell of the word was what counted. There was a moral fitness to calling a man a sick soldier; it was not a take-it-or-leave-it designation, for which, for example, might have been substituted the term *X-person.* As evidence, we can trace one complication in the fact that an occasional soldier who was sick took it upon himself to write to his parents and to his congressman complaining about the treatment that he was being afforded. Occasionally there was a repercussion in the form of a letter of inquiry with reactions by the doctors that bespoke anything but a take-it-or-leave-it concern for the letter. It is this reaction that we have in mind when we say that the term *sick soldier* had an element of moral propriety among its various other meanings.

In a word, then, the term *sick soldier* was an expressional rather than a specific referent identity designation. It is to be compared in make-up with the identity of Military Occupational Specialty Number as this identity was entertained by the Headquarters Personnel Section, and where moral elements were so sloughed off that the essential criteria could be summarized with the macabre designation of "bodies." (A paper currently in preparation deals with the social personality of the "Statistic" in our society, where social personality means an identity that enjoys public social validity.)[12]

The procedural rules are easier to illustrate from our example than the basic rules. They consist of a combination of technical and moral precepts; the technical precepts being related to the question of successful treatment of illness, as well as the directions which mesh with bureaucratic requirements; and moral precepts which are relevant to the proprieties implied by the meaning of soldier as a "human being." (Admittedly, this rough statement doesn't tell us what we've found; it tells us what to look for, but for the present we must leave the rest to implication.)

The final element of the transformation scheme is the treatment tactics. We can call them the "operations" or "the work" but with this reminder: the all of what is meant by tactics under no circumstances, is to be regarded as no more than that which is manifested in overt conduct. We do not say, for example, that the transformations of geometrical figures is effected by the scribbling of the geometrician, though we do say that the transformations cannot be *communicated* without the production of at least a modicum of sign material. Similarly, we cannot say that the overt behavior of the individual is all that is meant by transformation operations. The tactic is an intention or meaningful performance, whether expressed overtly or not, the consequence of which, as far as the actor is concerned, is the hypothesizing, definition, verification, addition, denial, change, etc., of a meaning or meanings of the object being treated. The tactic is to be defined in terms of the noesis-noema structures. Consequences are to be measured in terms of the changes of rate, course, or terms of treatment. Thus, for example, the doctor in treating the sick soldier seeks the signs of disease, prescribes drugs and rest, examines, reassures, and within the terms of treatment builds up an order of expectations with regard to "the effect of medical care." That is to say, the treatment of "disease," implies the anticipation that signs of "no disease" will be found. The identity of cured soldier is defined by the evaluation of the signs of "no disease."

An alpha transformation scheme is to be regarded as "open" or "closed" depending on the extent to which the "slack," represented by the extent to which the anticipations which are meant by the terms of an identity, is provided for in the logic of the scheme. In some schemes, for example, the actor can't lose: if events go one way, his scheme provides an explanation for them; if they go the opposite way, the scheme still provides an explanation for them. For example, one finds a heads-I-win-tails-you-lose arrangement in much of the current discussion about Russia and the U.N. If Russia vetoes a U.N. proposal this is proof and understandable as such that Russia is truculent and wants to pick a fight. If Russia agrees to a UN proposal this is proof that Russia is truculent and wants to pick a fight. Why? Because Russia is sly, tricky, playing the game according to its own rules, and out to advance its own ambitions at any cost. The man who says, "If my wife doesn't have beans for supper tonight I'm going to raise hell and if she does have beans, I won't eat them." Operates with a similar "can't lose" arrangement. Another example: In the Parsons-Stouffer Wednesday evening seminar, Dr. Stouffer described a "situation of influence" in which a group of professional statisticians, after finding the statistical services of the Bureau of Vital Statistics of the government in need of repair, undertook a carefully laid out plan to oust the head of this department. Nothing so much was suggested by the maneuvers of the statisticians as the tactics of a tightly played game of chess in which every effort was made to anticipate and to map beforehand what the consequences of a given move were likely to be. Of particular interest is the fact that the plans of the "If this, then that" character were based on studied appraisals of those who, *to begin with, were cast in the role of opponents.* Of the multitude of possible identities that they might have been assigned, one particular range was chosen: that is, the range of office holders within a bureaucratic structure who were dedicated to the perpetuation of the holdings, who made the difference between bona-fide insiders, and interlopers, who could be pressured, and when pressured would respond by moves to preserve their positions as far as it was possible, making only those decisions to change or compromise that were required in the light of the rationally encountered necessities, imposed by the combination of rival quantums of power and certain very specific rules of the game. (Remember, we are not concerned with the "accuracy" of the statisticians' appraisal but only with the considerations regarding the other persons that they selected as relevant to a plan to influence these opponents if, in the view of the statisticians, their own plans to achieve their own ends were to be realized.) The possibilities of action to the opponents had as an elementary ground the basic rules of the game—general rules that such identities, by definition, knew. In chess, they would be the rules which prescribed how one could move the pieces (the pawn may move unidirectionally, one space at a time, except for the first time it moves, etc.) Thus, assassination was a welcome possibility, but within the basic rules, it was prohibited.

Now the trick was to so define the identity of the opponent that one could extract from a knowledge of the model, those specific tactical decisions that the other would make, decisions limited not only by the basic rules of the game, but bound as well by the materials that the identity would, *within the rules of its definition,* take into consideration, in the manner in which this material would be considered (i.e., according to the logic of rationally calculated appraisal and choice of alternatives.)

Several facts of particular significance to the point under consideration here now emerge. (1) The deliberate, rational, hypothetical procedures that the statisticians used in defining their opponents; (2) the definition of the motivational scheme operative for the opponents as actors who by definition would be capable of keeping up with the game and weighing what they saw in rational terms. (The similarity to the rationale of the confidence game needs to be noted. In this type of game, one must assume an actor bright enough and stable enough to "see through" his situation so as to recognize the direction of his advantage, make for it, and stick with it.) and (3) the fact of having *meant* these persons in the way they were meant, *these meanings furnish the premises of the statistician's treatment of them.* Within the limits imposed by the hypothetical character of the regard with which the opponents were defined (the terms of their make-up being a function of "sufficient" knowledge), the system was, so to speak, logically closed. The statisticians could not lose out on an interpretation of anything that came up, though they might withal have lost the game, in which case the blow might have been softened, perhaps, by their having known "why."

It is perhaps a peculiarity of the "theories" which accompany activity within formal arrangements of status, that they are of this "heads-I-win-tails-you-lose" character. It may be this very factor that can be held responsible for the fact that the Harvard Business School boys have been able to emphasize with a sense of discovery that "workers have families." The formal status scheme of the typical manufacturing enterprise provides the identity terms for the unproductive worker of lazy, inept, incompetent, uninterested, etc., and the transformation scheme of the management personnel provides the alternatives of improved producer, probationary worker, or dischargee. The terms proposed by the Harvard Business School bring in a new alternative identity: the worker with psychiatric disturbances. It will be interesting to see what revisions in formal structure are occasioned by the change in the terms of treatment, and to see what new tactics of treatment business managers introduce in their attempts to strike a measure between rationalized profitable operation and personalized regard. One might expect something like the emergence of "efficient psychiatry." The trend in some quarters to employ an "industrial chaplain" might be just this sort of thing. In its general form the problem is that of tracing the "response" of a formal status system to new, and in some ways "incongruous" or incompatible "immanent dynamisms" that the "worker-with-family-troubles" introduces. There are further problems of reestablishing the "heads-I-win" scheme of interpretation as well as the question of what it looks like after the transformation has been "completed." One can count on its being reestablished because of the lack within the scheme of the agnostic attitude toward persons exemplified in scientific experimentation, within which attitude the heads-I-win scheme breaks down.

This much will have to do temporarily for the alpha transformation scheme. The discussion of identity transformations cannot be completed without a discussion of the changes that occur with the identified self, the beta transformation scheme. There are some tricky meanings involved, however, in the concept of the identified self, and we can best deal with the subject by first going back to the concept of the "form of sociality" with the view of making some necessary distinctions without which our confusions are apt to be so severe as to wind up even beyond the help of humor.

If we are to be at all pious about our methodology, it is necessary to take up the question of how the scientific observer is related to his data. In throwing out the correspondence theory of reality, we have in effect set for ourselves the question of what is involved when the observer elects to "see sociologically."

The scientific observer is an actor in the same logical sense that the subject of investigation is represented as an actor. Like the subject of investigation, the scientific observer is to be represented in terms of a cognitive style, and where, presumably, the scientist sees "through the eyes of the scientist," he sees through the cognitive style of scientific theorizing and investigation. At a previous point in the paper, we noted some of the features of this cognitive style. Here we want to point out how his "view" differs from that of the actor, a point that needs to be made clear if we are to realize and follow through the realization of the difference between the identity as a methodological device and the identity as a directly experienced object of experience.

To aid us we shall employ a symbolic representation of our concepts. The symbols, it goes without saying, *prove nothing*. They are useful here in that through presenting a visual difference, they underline a meaningful difference between terms.

Let S mean "self." Self means the subject of an action; that which is meant in the first term of the expression, "I talk to John."

Let:

= mean "means" or "be equivalent or identical in meaning to"

o mean "of the other"

a mean "of the actor"

ob mean "of the observer," where observer designates a mode of viewing and *not* a person. It designates a cognitive style of reflection. It is to be contrasted in meaning with

p mean "of the participant," which designates the cognitive style which accompanies unreflective engagement in working acts. We need to underline that *ob* and *p* are different cognitive styles. For any given actor they can appear only in action and never at the same time. Both can be referred to the same person or to different persons.

σ mean "in or employing the cognitive style of scientific theory and investigation."

γ mean "in or employing any given cognitive style"

> mean "includes in the terms of its meaning"

A mean "actor," with subscripts meant as differentiators. It can mean as well, "the animal symbolicum"

I mean "Investigator"

α*T* mean "alpha transformation scheme"

β*T* mean "beta transformation scheme"

x mean "related to," or "related through tactics of treatment to," or "whose meaning has consequences for the treatment of." The sign | | as for example, | *iS* | means "remains constant in meaning." Where this is the case, the expression **x***io* is to be read, "the tactics of treatment have consequences for the meaning of the identified other."

i mean identity, or identified

( ) mean "of the actor" who is designated by a subscript, e.g. ( )A_1

: mean "such that"

∃ mean "there exists," where "exists" has ontological meaning

⊓ mean "there is meant"

Further symbols will be added as we need them.

When we talk of the actor's form of sociality we mean the following:

(1) ⊓*Iσ* for whom ⊓ *Aγ*: *Aγ* > (*iSa* **x** *io*)*A*

or

(2) ⊓*Iσ* for whom ⊓ *Aγ* : *Aγ* > (*iSa* **x** *is*)*A*

The alpha transformation scheme refers to the systematic changes of *is* and *io* where | *iSa* | for *Aγ*.

Now if we read the expression *is* we get "identified self;" and if we read the expression *iSa* we get "identified self of the actor." And if we read the last terms of expression (2) we get "the identified self of the actor whose meaning has consequences for the treatment and hence the meaning of the identified self of the actor." What kind of cabalistic double talk is this?

The words may be the same, but the meanings are different, and the difference between the small *s* and the large *S* are intended to underline the fact that such is the case. The sign *is* means "identified self" where we mean that the actor treats himself as an object of his action. We hesitate to say "treats some *aspect* of himself" because this implies that behind the aspect is the really-real-whole-full-blown-self, and this kind of meaning we are taking particular pains to avoid. Rather, the identified self, as a term, may designate a whole array of different identities though in one important respect they are alike: they all have reference to the actor; they represent the actor. Thus the *is* and the *io* are alike in that both are objects of action, *intended objects* of action, regardless of whether the action be that of judgment, praise, evaluation, aggression, love, etc.

Now we said that one could not talk of an identified other or of an identified self as objects of action, unless one specified the other term in the expression of the "form of sociality," namely the "identified Self of the actor," symbolized as *iSa*. Unlike the *is*, *iSa* is *not* an object of the subject's action. It is meant to designate rather that the subject experiences his own action as self-originated; and *when he pauses for reflection over what was done* he attributes the action to an *is* as the originator. Mead refers to *iSa* as the "I."

Does this mean that the "I" represents the "essential" actors: *the source of motivation?* Mead answered this by locating the essential source in the neuropsychic predisposition; an organization of neuro-psychic "attitudes" founded in the "blood and nerve fiber" of the "organism." But to take this course is to break with the attempt to account for action in its own terms and from the point of view of the actor. Instead, the effect is to concretize the biological organism, and engage thereby the metaphysics of materialistic or idealistic positivism. One uses a preconceived ontological scheme as a substitute for the laborious process of and problems of scientific description. The process is permissible, of course, as long as one does not lose sight of the fact that the terms of an ontology merely serve to divert a portion of the stream from the point where the dam is being built. As a matter of scientific principle, however, such terms must be accessible at any time to the test of rational meanings and evidence. The fuzziness of the motivation concepts, where a concrete biological organism is envisaged as the "vessel" of the motive is quite apparent and need not be challenged here again for its rational character. So all the talk about an "essential" actor can be challenged, and in light of what we have offered as an unsuitable consequence of such a view, all talk of an "essential" actor, the *real* personality, is here rejected.

There are alternatives. One such alternative is that of the "transcendental mind." That is, the *I* may be conceived of as the unengaged Viewer—found in the various vocabularies of motives which posit the mind (or its equivalents—ego, self, real person) *and* Nature. The Viewer manifests itself through action while remaining aloof and inaccessible to the game of investigation. But this solution is not possible because we would insist that only that can be accounted as relevant or real to action (regardless of how it is relevant or real) which *is* subject to the rules of inquiry. Otherwise one courts proprieties of belief instead of rational skepticism.

There are many more alternatives, but only one, we are convinced, will withstand rational appraisal and the tests of observation: the *I* in the language of things is a term used by an observer to designate a subject's actions. The concept of "subject of action" designates not the vessel which "contains" sources or impellents or motives (in the causal sense) of action, but designates only where the observer must look to observe conduct.

We regard it as a serious error in the task of building a universally applicable science of conduct to look for an essential source or beginning of action. Action and not the "concrete individual" is the given, and needs no demonstration of how it is possible. What is possible, and what is needed, as far as the motivation problem is concerned is (1) investigation into the structures of the various types of action—e.g., dreams, fantasy, wishes, prayer, judgment, apology, investigation, doubt, etc.; (2) the scientific description of action sequences; (3) the "discovery" of those ordering principles by which such phenomena as sequences, integration, etc., may be logically explained—that is, the recital of those conditions under which the phenomena in question will appear. It appears to us, at this point at least, that current strategies in the treatment of the motivation problem will undergo radical and fruitful revision to the extent that three problems are thoroughly investigated: (1) the problem of language; (2) the problem of social logics (that is, the host of differently systematized rules for manipulating meanings); and (3) the problem of the various modes of understanding.

The sources of motivation of the other person, incidentally, are not found within the other, but "within the actor." They are entirely imputed by the actor to the other.[12] That the actor may regard them as self evident does not influence, one way or the other, the fact that the observer places the motivations in quotation marks—not because they are to be tested as to their accuracy, but to call attention to them as the terms of the actor's treatment of the other who is regarded by the actor as motivated in the manner that the actor imputes to him. The meaning of these motivation theories is to be found in the fact that the actor treats the other on the basis of the belief that the other acts under the order of "impellents" that the actor assigns to the other. The observer does not look for the "truth" of the actor's motivation theories, unless he be of a mind to insist that the actor abandon his own "prejudiced" purposes, and act only according to the purposes of science. Every social relationship will have its peculiar order of motives that the actors assign to each other. One crucially important task of the observer is to find out what these motivation theories are that the actors employ. The social sciences today are indeed chasing the will-of-the-wisp of subjectivism when they seek to define for themselves what it is that really impels the actor. In their minute-to-minute contacts, actors are constantly "asking" of each other, and "answering" the question of why they act as they do. The apparently universal character of motives is an empirical universality, not a formal universality. As social structures change, as social realities change, motives will change. As far as the motivation problem is concerned, scientists can make only one assumption of universal applicability: namely, that man everywhere, under any and all circumstances, is a "seeing" animal. But the analytical scheme remains.

"Self" with the big *S* means action; self with the small *s* means an intended object. Now the question is: why do we use the adjective "identified" as a modifier of action; i.e., identified Self means identified action? What are we attempting to point up in this expression? Just this: the actor's action with reference to the identified other takes place on the assumption by the actor of how he is given to the other. The other, by his actions, furnishes the actor with the material by which the actor discerns the intentions of the other, these intentions being the material by which the actor's assumptions with regard to his own self giveness are confirmed, threatened, etc. The intentions of the other are never given "in themselves;" one cannot talk of de facto intentions of the other. They are always imputed to the other by the actor on the basis of whatever signs the actor "chooses" to employ. Going a step further, if we recall expressions (1) and (2), we find that *iSa* is rendered as a meaning element in the construct of the actor *that the observer uses.* Thus, *iSa* is a construction *of the observer.* The giveness of the actor's self which the intentions of the actor's other, as these intentions are discerned by the actor, serve to confirm or upset, are always hypothetical for the observer. They are rendered in the following prepositional form: "Assuming the animal symbolicum, if the elements of the cognitive style have the values *a, b, c,* etc., such that the form of sociality includes an *iSa* of library guard, then the actions referable to the actor with respect to an identified other, book borrower, will always be such as to effect, at the least, a test of the actor's self regard. Metaphorically speaking, the dialectic of the process is such that it is as if the actor says: "By your actions you tell me who I am, and by my actions, I'll tell you who you are." This dialectical process occurs regardless of whether communication occurs between two persons or a person and an inanimate object. Which is to say, that the library guard is a library guard because he treats another person as a book-borrower; or the geologist is a geologist because he treats a mountain as a rock formation. Or, to put it in a way that should circumvent the misunderstanding that arises from the use of the term "is," *the stability of the actor's giveness as an identified self is directly dependent on whether it continues to be possible for the actor to treat the object according to the terms of the actor's definition of the object.* On the premise that continuity of action is possible only if an object of action is involved (the reader is referred to the discussion of the noesis-noema structures, pp. 117–124; 132–145), we mean by the phrase "continues to be possible for the actor" the host of possible devices by which the anticipated possibilities that are proposed by the terms of the definition of the object are squared with the phenomenal presentations which are actually encountered, that is, the host of devices—we shall note in a moment what they look like specifically—by which the actor continues to make sense of the actually encountered phenomenal presentations—the ways in which the subject keeps the object on the track, or better, the ways in which he keeps track of the object. (We would like to emphasize that this formulation does not mean the same and is not intended to mean the same as the formulation which runs to the effect of the difference between what the actor expects to happen and what "actually" happens. This second formulation is a derived case of the first one. It is a special case in that the formulation implies by the term "actually" the experiencing of phenomenal presentations which actor and observer "idealize" or conceptualize according to the same rules. Hence what the observer sees as an "actual event" is regarded as seen by the actor as an event in the same way. The effect of a more general formulation is to point out the problematical character of the "interpretive devices" used by the actor. Where this is overlooked, we are apt to indulge in false ironies as we find, for example, when the observer names an event according to logico-empirical procedures and makes the difference between men's aspirations and their "actual" successes, only to encounter some bird who sees every defeat as an opportunity, or who sees himself defeated but feels that he had it coming to him as a trick of Fate.)

We are trying to point up the problematical character of the devices which are accessible to the subject and which he employs in dealing with events in such a way that they are seen or not seen as violations of expectations. The observer may see that the actor's resources in defining the situation are such that no matter which way events go they "make sense," or that the actor can or *will* make sense of them; or the opposite, whichever way events go they never fulfill requirements or never can. The observer may know *on the basis of logico-empirical naming* that a subject with a high aspiration level is riding for a fall. But to say on *this* basis that expectations and events are at variance with each other is to risk stepping out of the frame in which action is depicted from the actor's view, while becoming embroiled in exactly the kind of "rationalization" that proves to be so intriguing when we take notice of the devices that the subject uses. That violations of expectations, even the violations that death so "universally" proposes, occur is not to be accounted for on the basis of the scientifically ontological character of events, but rather must be accounted for on the basis of the ways in which the event is "named" such that the terms of the naming when set in dialectical contrast to those provided by the definition of the situation result in the experience of violated expectations. We would insist on this formulation as a matter of methodological principle, even while realizing that for many practical purposes we can assume that observer and subject name events according to logico-empirical precepts. The procedure is legitimate insofar as we are aware that in employing such a procedure we are availing ourselves of an interpretive principle common to many members within the social order in which we live. If we are not careful we may find ourselves assuming as given the very facet of the problem of order which we need to investigate. The risk is not indeterminacy but the determinacy of ethnocentrism.

The devices come out with dramatic clarity whenever the actor encounters a breach of "normal" expectations. The tactics employed in such contexts will be of particular concern to us in our experimental work. Here, however, we need to point out that while incongruity brings the tactics to the fore, we need to assume that in the "normal course of things" these interpretive stretchings are a constant element of the actor's actions. What are some of these devices? They are encountered "in the literature" under the designation "functions of cognition." Actually, they are neither functions nor are they limited in the evidence of their use to "cognition." They are rather terms used by the observer to designate the ways in which the actor effects certain configurations of meaning. Thus, there is the "device" of *naming,* which consists of categorically designating meanings in terms of an essentializing principle. Another device is *defining,* which consists of assigning an order of significance to a phenomenal presentation, regardless of whether the presentation is presented from "inside" or "outside." There is the device of *selection,* a device which has been commonly observed and has been cited again and again in figure-ground problems. Faced with a host of stimuli, all of which presumably hammer with equal emphasis for admission, the actor nevertheless seeks and entertains certain ones and takes no account of the others. *Discounting* refers to the device whereby in conversation, for example, the listener supplies the modifiers that the speaker, if he is ever to finish speaking must omit. The listener also cancels, extends, or shortens the modifiers, or adds or telescopes huge blocks of modifiers. Children discount differently from adults. For children, a cue is a whole or none affair. Catatonic schizophrenics discount themselves into physical and even physiological inactivity. The concept has its biological coordinates. *Standardization* is a device whereby a present meaning is fixed by a past universal concept. Thus, specific experience is possible only to the extent that the significances of naïve presentations can be generalized. *Bureaucratization* is the consequence of fixing a present meaning by giving it a position in a scheme of meanings. Thus, conceptualization is impossible without recurring contexts. *Time organizing* is the device whereby the past is arranged, the present is located, and the future possibilities are arranged in manageable terms. *Reality designation:* The mind is a linguistic product, composed of concepts which designate certain relationships as meaningful. These relationships are not realities, but interpretations of reality. Hence, different frameworks of interpretation will lead to different conclusions as to what reality is. In an action frame of reference a thing is said to be real insofar and only insofar as the actor feels that he is able to fit it into his ongoing activity. Insofar as a concept is meaningful, it is designatory of a reality; and the intentions or operations designated by the concept indicate whether the reality is of an empirical or non-empirical character. It is only this consequential reality that the actor deals in. The question is not whether a thing is real or not but how is it real? In what reality class does it belong? It is an important function of the cognitive style to tell the observer how a thing is real for the actor.

A further note on the constancy of the identified Self. For any given *iSa* one should find a characteristic pattern of interpretive devices. Insofar as "breaks" are found in the usual flow of interpretive devices, one should look for and expect to find changes in the meanings which comprise the *iSa*. Or to put it another way, if one is aware that a person has changed his way of seeing things, one may confidently expect to find a changed identity. To say of a person that he is a different person is to mean the same thing as "he sees things differently." One must not be thrown off by the fact that the labels remain the same. Only the most dramatically evident changes of identity involve a change of label. Labels and meanings are tied inseparably, which means that even though the label remains the same, the meanings attached to it can change. The alias, for example, is more than a name, for it signifies to bearer and apprehender alike a new mode of treatment. The meaning of the identity for action is found at just this point. The identity is real for bearer and apprehender, not on the basis of the behavior that accompanies it, but on the basis of the treatment that is called forth toward it. The change in identity takes place within the dialectical process of treatment. Herein lies the significance of identities to the process of communication.

In our discussion of *iSa* we have defined the term, made note of the fact that it can change or remain stable, and we told what its stability depended on. By implication we have some limited insights into what can effect changes of *iSa*. It should be no trick to trace the changes of identities that occur, and to trace with these changes the consequences for further activity. In the priority of tasks implied by the logic of our program, such investigations demand immediate investigation. We shall entertain the notion that the changes that occur, occur in accordance with principles of regularity, and these principles we shall refer to as "beta transformation schemes." At this point in our thinking, however, we must mark the concept of the beta transformation scheme as a room, included in the house, but as yet unfurnished. While the problem of tracing the conditions under which a change of *iSa* will be effected promises solution, the problem of a accounting for changes from one specified *iSa* to another promises to be complicated in the extreme.

* * *

The observer is an actor as well and is to be represented in terms of a cognitive style. His specific form of sociality differs from that of the actor in the following way:

(3) $\sqcap I\sigma : I\sigma > (|iSob| \times ia)I$

where $ia = \sqcap A\gamma : A\gamma > (iSa = p$ or $ob \times io$ or $is)A$

That is to say, *ia* is a sociological dummy which must be constructed along the lines of the animal symbolicum and cognitive style which mean together, actor. This is to be compared with expressions (1) and (2) where *io* and *is* while it is also the actor's construction is not necessarily considered hypothetically by the actor, and is constructed according to principles that must be determined by investigation. This is what we meant above when we said that the purposes of the observer are constant. *ia* for the observer is a methodological tool, and never goes beyond this status as long as the observer remains within the finite province of meaning of scientific inquiry. For any A, and including I, *io, ia,* and *is* are to be regarded as having any kind of objective status. What this status is, what principles enter into its constitution, what its sources of motivation are, are entirely problematical. Where the actor uses the scheme we have outlined, however, *ia* always means A. In other words, for the scientific observer *ia* should be written $\sqcap ia$; and $\sqcap ia = \sqcap io = \sqcap A\gamma$. For the actor, however, it is most usual that the identity of the other or self means $\exists io$ or $\exists is$. This is a pragmatic rather than a formal truth. Formally put, the formulation would read: $\sqcap I\sigma$ for whom $\sqcap A\sim\sigma : A\sim \sigma = \sqcap f : f > \exists io$ (where $\sim$ = not and f = finite province of meaning).

Where must the observer look in order to find the materials with which to construct *iSa* and *io*? And what procedure must he use in order to encounter them?

Suppose the observer makes the request of the subject: "Tell me something about yourself." (Incidentally, our science must continue to limp as far as the reliability of our formulations are concerned, which depend upon data evoked by such a complex request until we know more than we do at present about the logic of social requests.) We do know, however, that the actor, in answering answers through the minimum form of sociality, *iSa* x *is,* while the observer listens through the form of sociality of *iSob* x *iA* > (*iSa* x *is*). It is his *is* that the actor's statements depict. The observer, however, is not "locked" within the action in the way that the actor is. For him the actions of description, no less than the phenomenal attributes of the described object are accessible to him as data. If, to the observer, the actor's statements convey the phenomenal object representative of the actor's "self" to the actor, the actor's actions in the course of conveying this object are the materials from which the observer constructs the *iSa.* Not only is it the case that the two may not be the same, but it is also the case that the meaning of the phenomenal *is* for the agent's actions, his *iSa,* can never be seen merely by reflecting on the phenomenal character of *is.* This meaning can be found only when the relationship of *is* to *iSa* is established "from the inside"—from the point of view of *iSa.* In the observer's view of the actor, the observer sees one social object: *iSa.* This he achieves through the relationship *iSob* x *iA.* The *is* of the actor must be brought into view only after the observer makes the transition from *iSob* x *iA* to |*iSob*| x *iSa.*

Two points need to be stressed. First, this transition is *not* the transition from detached appraisal to sympathetic introspection. Second, the concept of "seeing things from the actor's point of view," even where the rules of procedure provide for sympathetic introspection, does not mean that the observer is "taking the role of the other." Insofar as this notion of "taking the role of the other" is literally intended it is nonsense. The "transition" refers entirely to the rules of analytical procedure. It means that the observer, after dealing with the Actor as a theoretical object within the cognitive style of scientific appraisal, brings under consideration another and different scientific object, namely, the model representative of the self-identified Actor. Like the representation of the Actor, this model consists of a series of analytical propositions based on the assumptions represented in the propositions which designate the Actor. Seeing things from the point of view of the *iSa* means proceeding hypothetico-deductivewise from the propositions which represent *iSa* to interpret the significances of the terms which the subject provides as descriptive of *is* or *io*. The meanings of *is* for the agent's actions, *iSa,* are than seen as hypotheses which await testing by further communicative effort. There is no more subjectivism about such procedure than there is when the physicist adopts the point of view of the model representing the behavior of free falling bodies within the assumptions of physical mechanics within the rules of scientific procedure. If it is said that the physicist is a "stranger" to his objects, it can be said in the same sense that one person is a "stranger" to another. Just as it is nonsense to say that the physicist can put himself in the place of the object he sees and see things as the object sees them, so it is nonsense to say that the social scientist can do this with his objects. The notion of sympathetic introspection, a very useful one, can be distorted in meaning to the point where it becomes so much romantic fol-de-rol if the point is lost sight of that like the procedure we have described it designates a form of hypothesis and observation, though in certain important respects it differs from this procedure. In the procedure we have outlined one arrives at the formulation of a hypothesis in the following manner: There is meant an Actor employing a given cognitive style such that according to the assumptions of the cognitive style if *X* is the way things are seen, *Y* is what *is* signifies. If it is established that the specified cognitive style is given such that *X* is the ways things are seen, then the hypothesis is drawn deductively from the model that *Y* is what *is* signifies. Experiment then serves to confirm or deny the factual character of the hypothesis.

According to the procedures of sympathetic introspection the formulation runs: There is meant an Actor employing a given cognitive style such that the Actor is represented by the premises of action of the investigator's cognitive style. According to the assumptions of the identified self of the investigator ("If he were I"), if *X* is the way the investigator sees things, *Y* is what *is* signifies. If the investigator, upon examination of his experience, establishes that *X* is the way things are seen by the investigator, then the hypothesis is drawn on the basis of the principle, "What holds for me holds for him," that *Y* is what *is* signifies for the Actor. Experiment then serves to confirm or deny the factual character of the hypothesis.

The usefulness of the device is seen in its very limitations. The investigator attains economy of effort by assuming that the investigator's premises of action are the premises of action of the Actor, and if X is the way things are seen by the investigator, then X is the way things are seen by the Actor. Under certain conditions such assumptions can be made with practical certainty, e.g., highly rational activity, and the assumption of sufficient knowledge. By the same sign the big limitation of the procedure is that for most working acts the investigator's premises will not be the same as the actor's.

Having mentioned several times that the identity is a social object of direct experience for the actor, it might be well to set at rest the reader's misgivings with regard to the meaning of a "directly experienced" object. The meaning is simply made, and stems from the phenomenological difference between the identity apprehended through working acts and the identity apprehended through scientific theorizing. It is with reference to experiencing an object through working acts that we use the term, *direct* experience. An object of direct experience is one given to the apprehender as something existing in and of itself; a thing apart from the viewer and different from the viewer as the viewer sees it; it is not a product of his postulation; it cannot be changed simply because the viewer so wills it; it is external to him; in a word it is given to the apprehender without his intervention, as he sees it. Also involved is an order of intentionality on the actor's part in which he seeks to accomplish some practical purpose; in a word, he intends to "reform" the world of the natural attitude at least to the extent that his purposes with regard to the object are accomplished.

If the identity as an object is directly given in the world of working acts, it is also given "directly" in the world of objects of the dream and of fantasy. In the dream the "givenness" of the object is self proposed, "encountered," different from and external to the self. Unlike the givenness of working acts, however, the rules governing the action of dreams make no provision for the intervention of the actor. "He takes what he gets and likes it." Though he participates with the object, it is phenomenally constituted according to the logic of its presentation.

In fantasy, quite the opposite is the case. The object *is* whatever the fantasier "decrees" it to be. If a given line of fantasy action isn't fitting, one may "wipe it out" and start over again with a more amenable object. It is given then by the actor according to whatever rules of the game he happens at any particular time to play by.

All this is to be compared with the object of theoretical science, which like the fantastic object, can be anything the theoretician chooses *within a set of socially sanctioned and rational rules of action.*

When we talk of the identities which the actor employs, we are talking of those objects *meant* by him according to whatever rules of action he employs. It becomes a sizeable and important task to show how the objects of one finite province of meaning are related to the objects of another finite province of meaning, as for example, when one fantasizes a love object and in the next minute actually encounters the love object now redefined with the newly incorporated materials of the fantasy.

Communication

Except that the term "interaction" seems to set men off to the task of tracing stimulus-response patterns in the vain hope of giving that term practical meaning, we would use it in place of communication. And excepting entirely the meaning of S-R patterns, the two terms will be used synonymously. Communication (or interaction) can take place between an actor and a chair, between the actor and himself, or between two or more actors. In one respect the process is exactly the same for all three cases: communication refers to the process wherein the actor treats an array of signs (we say treat rather than responds in order to underline the fact that the process is *always* an active one; the concept of the actor as a passive perceiver upon whose sense receptors the "stimuli" of the "environment" clamor for admission is to our way of seeing misleading, if, indeed, it is not entirely neutral to the task of interpreting the phenomena of behavior); and in treating these signs generates further arrays of signs for treatment. At this same level, communication with another person, social communication, differs from communication with a chair (as for example when the actor interprets signs of position, construction, etc., as a thing on which to sit, so he sits or makes the statement that it can be sat on) in only one respect: by virtue of his treatment of the signs generated by the "presence" of the other, the actor generates an array of signs which the other in turn treats, and thereby in turn generates another array which are unique to every exchange, are far less predictable and constant than the signs of "material" objects, do not depend upon the effort of the actor for their *realization* as signs, are constantly changing or being replaced by others without the intervention of the actor, and always afford the actor more than he "asks" for. (It is also true that from the observer's view, the actor always gives more than he intends to.)

The vehicle of communication is the working act. The working act serves the exceedingly important function (there are other functions also) of an instrument by which the hypotheses (in the form of expectations) that are provided by his conceptions are tested. Every working act is an experiment in miniature; man is forever testing, accepting, and revising his universe.

From the actor's point of view social communication takes place between an identified self and an identified other. From an observer's point of view communication takes place between actors where actors means the animal symbolicum employing a cognitive style. The concept of communication has nothing whatsoever to do with the concept of concrete person, except that one cannot say that communication occurs between "concrete persons." For the scientist "concrete person" is a reification of the possibilities he entertains as "fulfillable" that an object, empirically constructed in terms of the criteria of n-attributes will answer his questions or submit to observation. For the scientist, "concrete person" occupies exactly the same logical status as *io.* In exactly the same way as io, the "concrete person" for the scientist is real in a universe of things which are real by virtue of their meanings rather than by their ontological, indubitably "out-thereness" character.

What does the process of communication look like from the viewpoint of the actor? To begin with, there are at least two types of signs that are available to the actor for his interpretation. There is first the ready made outcome of the other's communicating acts, as, for example, a signpost. The term *culture* will be used to refer to products of communication. Second, the actor may attend in simultaneity to the communicating actions as they proceed, found, for example, in two persons engrossed in conversation. In this latter type the signs are conveyed piecemeal, portion by portion, and within a framework of space and time. While the one actor conveys his thought through this sequential order of actions, the interpreter follows with interpreting actions.

Now the communicator does not experience only what he actually utters. A complicated mechanism of retentions and anticipations serve to connect one element of his speech with whatever preceded and what will follow until the unity of what he wants to convey has been grasped. All these experiences belong to the communicator's inner duree. On the other hand there are the occurrences of his speaking brought about by him in the space and time of the outer world; he witnesses his own gestures, his own sounds as events occurring within the space time framework of the outer world. The communicator experiences the ongoing process of communicating as a working in his vivid present.

The listener experiences his interpreting actions in his own vivid present, although this interpreting is not working; it is purposive, project oriented, through covert action. Like a working action it is a performance, for it embodies an intention to realization. The listener experiences the occurrences of the other's action as events occurring in outer time and space, while at the same time he experiences his interpretive actions as a series of retentions and anticipations happening in his inner time and connected by the intention to understand the other's "message" as a meaningful unit.

The communicator's speech, while it goes on, is an element common to his as well as the listener's vivid present. Both vivid presents occur simultaneously. A new time dimension is therefore established, namely, that of a common vivid present. Both can say later, "We experienced this occurrence together."

Some further remarks. In addition to the signs provided by speech, there are the bodily movements which, as an "expressional field," are accessible to interpretation as signs of the communicator's thought. This expressional field may vary considerably, reaching its maximum in the face-to-face relationship. The community of space permits the partner to apprehend the other's bodily expressions, not merely as events in the outer world, but as factors in the communicating process itself, even though, as in the case of reflexes, they do not originate in the working acts of the communicator.

Each type of social relationship has its particular type of time perspective, though each type is derived from the vivid present. There is the quasi-present in which the actor interprets the outcome of the other's communicating acts. There is the peculiar time dimension in which the actor is connected with contemporaries he has never met, or with successors, or predecessors. There is historical time in which the actor experiences the actual present as the outcome of past events. And so on. All of them originate in the intersection of duree and cosmic time.

Style, Tactics, and Strategies of Communication

The officer who reprimands the enlisted man by telling him that he doesn't like the enlisted man's attitude often means that it was not what the enlisted man said that evoked disapproval but the way the enlisted man said it. It is this manner of delivery, "the way in which the enlisted man says it to the officer," that we are referring to in the concept of style. Like the other components that we spoke of before—those of cognitive style—style is present in every communicative process.

Kenneth Burke has pointed out that to say a person has a style is to mean that that person has a way of "ingratiating" himself with others. He points out, however, that Matthew Arnold's style, while it served to "ingratiate" him with those that were like him, if used in calming a noisy drunk would prove to be something less than effective. So, while we would apply style as a component of every actor's communicative endeavor, we would allow for the consequences of style for communication. We might then differentiate between an "effective" style and an "ineffective" style. Insofar as a style furthers the intentions of the agent, we might say that the style is effective. Where the style is not effective, the agent will experience the fact in that the action does not go "according to plan;" it changes direction, the agent "loses control" of it, and the terms of communication may consequently be at such variance with each other that the course of action, as far as the agent is concerned, becomes unpredictable.

In certain types of highly formalized actions, style will be norma-tively prescribed, as for example, in the meeting of buck private and commanding officer. In other types of formalized activity, style and strategy will be so normatively prescribed as to show little variance in their combined presentations. Church services show this congruence. In other actions it may not be possible to predict what style will be used to accompany a strategy. Relationships of deep intimacy are of such a character. Those for whom success in their endeavors depends upon insuring the effectiveness of their communicative activities with others will develop a considered philosophy of style. A few examples: salesmen, dating athletes, diplomats, authors, discussion leaders, policemen, field investigators, therapeutic psychologists, and confidence men.

Style is a cue in the communicative process. All that is meant by "expressional aspects" of behavior—tone, tics, posture, physical gesture, inflection, etc.—is meant by style. Our great need is for a vocabulary of style. It is referred to at present by such terms as awe, fear, joy, sobri-ety, abandon, etc. The term refers to the constant play of expressions that accompany and make up a definitive aspect of conduct. During verbalization its physical auditory coordinates are pitch, intensity, and loudness. Visually it is encountered in those gestures which do not *mean* or signify in accordance with the rules of ordinary language—e.g., the tic, the wave of the hand, bodily posture, etc. It has its physiological criteria in blood pressure, pulse, rate and texture of salivation, changes in blood chemistry, endocrine activity, etc.

Elements of style may or may not refer to an object. An element of style is always an element of noesis, but it is, so to speak, "free" to wander about within the action, now as an integral part of the tactic, now as a forced accompaniment, and now as a thing "divided," one part of which accompanies the tactic while another manifests itself almost as a contrapuntal character, divorced from, but affording perspective to the intentionalities apparently involved in the "main action."

Style expresses somatic communications; it consists of the language of the "body"—as Cassirer puts it, the "language of emotions" as dif-ferentiated from the "language of propositions." Style is an operating principle of the self-identified actor. As such it represents not a reading of the universe, but self expression without regard to the universe. It is found in its "pure form" and can be seen without the intervention of tactics in the birth cry, acute panic states, and severe catatonic schizophrenia.

Tactics and Strategies: A acts towards B as if the signs that B provides are not haphazardly given. When we say that A understands B we mean *only this*: that A detects an orderliness in these signs both with regard to sequence and meanings. The orderliness is assigned to B's activities by A. The "validity" of A's conception of the signs generated by B are given in accordance with some regulative principle established for A when his return action evokes a counter action that somehow "fits" A's anticipations.

Understanding means a mode of treatment of B by A that operates, as far as A sees it, under constant confirmation of A's anticipations of treatment from B. Understanding is not referred for its "truth" or "falsity" to what the other "really" intended; it is not referred to an "external" body of criteria, and Icheiser in discussing the image of the other man in such terms has fallen into serious error. Each person reads the signs in his own way and in his own time using criteria that are always and only intrinsic to his cognitive style as it is constituted at any given point.

It is the progressions of signs produced by B and interpreted by A that we are referring to when we speak of tactics and strategies. On the basis of observing the "order of action" and of observing the orderly presentation of cues, the observer arrives at a "reconstructed" plan which he imputes to the agent. He calls this "plan" a strategy, referring to the fact that the communicator in organizing his cues for presentation *in effect* leads the communicant, *through* the acceptance of meanings, *to* an end state of action, whether that end be the purchase of a commodity or an acknowledgment that he has been *understood*, and including, as far as the observer sees things, unanticipated end states. (Any given point in a train of action may be considered an end state. The designation depends upon the purposes of the observer. To fail to bear this in mind results in the search for the "natural" or "obvious" beginning and end of an "act.")

If strategy be considered to designate the communicative "plan" as it appears to the "auditor," then tactics refer to the substrategies which operate in extended series.

The tactic and the strategy arise from the fact that the agent cannot present his "stream of thought" at one instant. Communication, as we noted before, is a temporal process. If one will reflect on his own experience, he will find that the succession of thought as it occurs "internally" undergoes a selective ordering process in which form it is presented "piece by piece" to the other fellow. All the elements of cognitive style will affect the "plan" and style of presentation. Strategy, then, refers to the total organization of the content and temporal position of cues which make up a course of action.

The strategy is not necessarily organized consciously. As a matter of fact, so much of communication is repetitive in purpose and circumstance that most strategies drop out of awareness, so that it is only when a regularity is interrupted, as in preparing a term paper, meeting a strange person, talking with a superior, that one gives conscious consideration to such a matter as arrangement.

Nor is the actor necessarily aware of the significance of the strategy that the observer finds. As in the case of the cognitive style, it is the observer's responsibility to reconstruct the strategy in accordance with his own interpretive criteria. I should like to extend this point.

The observer, by his awareness of the components of the agent's actions, may legitimately speak of effective tactics and effective consequences, meaning thereby to differentiate between the course of actions and their consequences as they appear to him and as they appear to the actor. Insofar as the actor is not interested in predicting his own behavior—in that his bias differs from the investigator's bias—he will deal with a different range of "significant" symbols than will the interpreter. He will not only take different cues into account but will assign them different meanings than will the observer. If a member of the Klu Klux Klan be asked after a meeting, "Why did you burn the cross?" the answers that are received must be discounted in their meaning with reference to explanation in a reflective context, and compared with "explanation" as it appears in the symbols elicited during the burning. The Kluxer's reflections are not to be considered explanatory material of the action, but are rather extensions of the original action in the sense that they are the action of burning considered now by the Kluxer as the object about which he is talking. No matter how close to the performance the observer gets with his questionnaire, there is still the gap between the two contexts. He might administer the questions while the Klan member is applying the torch. It would make no difference. The observer, therefore, is left alone in his world, and is on his own responsibility to record as much data as possible, after which he can make anything he chooses of it.

A given tactic or strategy can be employed in any number of different styles. In debating, for example, one may "devaluate the currency" of his opponents' arguments, though whether he does it with a whisper or a shout is another matter. Style and tactics are so commonly combined in communication that there may be a tendency to overlook the fact that the two are separable and must not be confounded. They need not always go together, however. For infants and panic states one is struck by the fact that the communicative effort is all style. It is in the course of the socializing processes that style becomes diversified, then later combined rigidly with crude tactics, then differentiated further as far as the two are concerned, until in the adult the two are so articulated that we have the picture of the two being fitted together in all sorts of combinations.

The following are tactics commonly found in ordinary conversation. A word of warning. We do not cite them out of an intention to debunk them, nor will the reader have understood their significance for the problems of communication if he thinks of them as debunking devices. No counter reality is being proposed, hence no ironies whatsoever are involved. They are discounting devices in the sense defined above, whereby one revalues the material in its naïve appearance so as to see things as the *actor* sees them—the *actor* not the person.

Voting for an essence. A tactic whereby when one is faced with a number of features of an action, a personality, an object, a social relationship, a proposition—one feature is selected to stand for the definitive characteristic. One person says of another, "I thought all along that **x** was such and such, but after he did *that,* I saw what he *really* was."

Casuistic stretching. This is a technique whereby the actor stretches the meaning of a term, thereby extending a frame to the point where it incorporates material that would otherwise challenge the frame's integrity. Tool Owners, Incorporated, an organization that was formed during the wave of strikes after the war, would have called every person with money in the bank a "Tool Owner," thereby making all of us capitalists, thereby banishing the distinction in interests between workers and management.

Devaluating the currency. The economist speaks of devaluating the currency, by which he means that the standard value behind the means of exchange is lessened, thereby lessening the purchasing power of the units of currency. In communication the same process applies. One may lessen the "purchasing power" of an argument, an activity, an identity, a plan, an orientation, by morally challenging the backing. Often the act of challenge is enough to impugn the currency.

Ringeleveo with symbols. It is common to stake out property rights to a symbol and label it "ours." It is also common for the opposition to steal the symbol claiming rightful ownership. Counter stealing may then take place. Moral indignation is a concomitant frequently associated with this tactic, and exhibited by the opposition in the face of the theft. In academic circles the fight rages over the caretaker rights to "fruitful work" and "Science." In the marketplace, lines are drawn over the rights to oversee the "common good."

Ingesting the opposition. Ingesting the opposition is accomplished when it is shown that room is already provided or can be provided in the frame for the meanings cited by the opposition. This is a common tactic with salesmen, personnel men, arbiters, and public relations men. Casuistic stretching is one tactic employed within this strategy. It is a strategy common to all who take seriously what they feel to be their responsibility in upholding the integrity of an orthodox orientation. Priests, for example.

Consulting the dictionary. This is the practice of fixing the meaning of an action by referring the action to a set of meaning-conferring criteria that are external to the context of the action. One is thus able to say, "You said thus and thus, but what you really meant was such and such." Or, "You treat the other guy badly because you think he is a Jew and Jews have all the money, but it says here in this book on prejudice that Jews don't have all the money. You lose the argument because you're prejudiced." The unconscious is such a dictionary.

Do not handle the merchandise unless you intend to buy. Another way of saying that one has no right to employ a technique or voice an opinion or use a particular vocabulary unless he will take the responsibility of using them in a certain way, or of rendering the remainder of the cluster of opinions, or will take a prescribed set of consequences for using the vocabulary.

Being driven into a corner. This tactic is especially effective with men of strong moral sensibilities. It is the tactic whereby if one challenges the principles of a frame (always an orthodox frame) one's action may be so defined to him by the keepers of the frame that one is forced from challenging a little to challenge a lot.

Transcendence. Where the terms of one perspective show a poor fit with the reality requirements of another, the terms may be renamed at another level where, by withdrawing from the specific, a common basis of agreement may be found. In the course of some field work in a small Texas town, I had occasion to interview a leading real estate dealer who was also a staunch Baptist. After a pause in our conversation he commented on my name and asked me what my religion might be. I told him I was Jewish. He said in return that he was Baptist. Sensing possible hostility, I observed that we were all children of God. I was attempting a transcendence. Upwards. (However, he wouldn't play. He observed after a thoughtful pause, "There are still differences." Transcendence upward and transcendence downward. Upward means in the direction of higher value; downward in the direction of lesser value. Transcendence upward was a prevalent tactic during the war in the propagandistic attempts to achieve unity of diverse occupational, ethnic, and class interests.

We shall expect to find that various cognitive styles have their appropriate tactics. We may even find that certain tactics are pathognomonic of particular cognitive styles. At the least, we expect to find that changes in cognitive styles will be accompanied by changes in the appropriateness of tactics. Hence, we have at least one set of considerations here by which it should be possible to induce incongruity, Tactics that are appropriate to cognitive styles means also that tactics will be appropriate to types of social relationships. This leads us to the consideration of our next topic, Group.

Group

Within a theory of communication the term *Group* means an aggregate of cognitive styles which are definitive of finite provinces of meaning which, while they may or may not be the same, are communicatively related to each other by working acts. Physical proximity is not a necessary and certainly is not a sufficient condition for the definition. It is a condition found in certain types of groups. A gathering of persons related to each other only by physical proximity might be called an aggregation. There is still another term that refers to the common social features of a gathering—the logical concept of "class," as when one says, "All the people assembled here are students." But to say, "This is a group of students" means that the working acts of the actors take place in a world of "student relevant things." That is to say, the acts are predicated on cognitive styles in which the meanings of "student" (regardless of whether the term is the actor's or the observer's) are the relevant meanings that are being used in the two identities of self and "other" found in the concept *form of sociality*.

Because our definition of group differs somewhat from the definitions of group encountered in the common sense of social science, further light on what is meant by the term may be obtained by considering what is meant in light of this definition by the following three statements: (1) The statement that at any given time an actor participates in more than one system of action—or its corollary, that an actor at any given time is a member of many different groups. (2) The statement, There exists a one member group." And (3) the statement, "There exists an actor."

(1) Sociologists are fond of pointing out the "interconnectedness" of action within a social system. Let the coal miners go on strike in West Virginia and racial tension mounts in Detroit. Thus, it is pointed out, it is exceedingly rare in a "highly integrated society" to find an autonomous action system. The actions in one system send their reverberations into many others. Therefore, it is said, the isolation of an action system is only analytically possible; that empirically each man is a part of the whole; no voice is wholly lost.

Now our intention is to increase the practicality of this insight by placing limits upon its application. Not to place such limits is to run the risk of confounding action as it is depicted from the actor's point of view and action as it is depicted from the view of an outsider on the *assumption* of the actor's point of view. The first is logically prior to the second.

We can make the difference between the two views by noting that the problems in the first view are those of stating the conditions under which certain premises of action will be employed by the actor. The problems of the second view are those of stating the conditions under which a given order of consequences will result from an actor's action. The premises of the action constitute a set of these conditions. The paradigm of the problem in the first view is this: Under what conditions will actors "see" things in a particular way, and how, by virtue of seeing things as they do, is this related to some order of the actor's conduct? This formulation is to be compared with the paradigm of the problem in the second view, which is: Under what conditions will a given order of consequences eventuate from a given course of conduct?

For the first view the social relationship is problematical, while the consequences of social relationship *R1* for other social relationships, *R2* are of no moment except as these consequences are part of the actor's "definition of the situation." For the second view, the social relationship is assumed, while the consequences of social relationship *R1* for social relationship *R2* is precisely what is being sought, while the actor's view of the consequences are compared with the consequences as they are presented for the observer by his "wider knowledge," i.e., his appraisal of events within a scientific theory of reciprocal "cause and effect."

In the first view the observer is concerned with depicting the regularities of action on the basis of a hypothetical representation which he calls an actor. This representation consists of a series of propositions which propose for the observer the actor's world of possibilities which are named, organized, and treated by actors according to an order of "insights" peculiar to the actor at any given point in his travels. It may be that the actor is so depicted that he considers possible future consequences of his conduct, or it may be that he is depicted as paying them no heed; it may be that the actor evaluates his past conduct and retains certain notions about past conduct which he "uses" to regulate future decisions, or he may have none of this. Withal, the crucial thing is that the actor is depicted as conceiving of a world of things which he affects or which affect him, and the study of action in terms of premises is concerned with formulating statements which describe the regularities of action in which the actor will engage on the basis of the way in which the world "presents itself" to him, and *only* on this basis. That the observer, faced with this task, represents the actor engaged with other actors makes no difference as far as these problems are concerned, for the very definition of the actor provides for a mode of engagement with other actors, i.e., the concept of the form of sociality. The peculiarity of the formulation is that it provides for an aggregate of actors who view *others* as events. The problem then is: granted that a regularity of action occurs, under what conditions of regard that actors entertain for each other does a given regularity appear. This roughly is what is meant by the representation of a group in terms of the premises of action.

Now it happens that the methodological rules of the game of scientific interpretation that the observer plays are such that where he plays with formal theory he can hold certain sectors of theory in abeyance (i.e., he makes certain assumptions, such as the constancy of the actor's view, the constancy of action, communication is a fact, understanding works, etc.) and putting these aside proceeds to elaborate a vocabulary and grammar of theoretical and empirical considerations which designate and relate certain phenomena in their own right. He refers to the principles which define the relevant limits of analytic and synthetic statements he makes as "level" or "universe" of discourse. Such principles are found in his statements of assumption and purpose.

At the level of discourse limited by (a) the purpose of scientific description, and (b) those assumptions designated by the term "going concern" (we noted a few above) the phenomena which are treated in their own right are those of de facto action and the effects of de facto action. From which we get the rational meaning of the following illustrative statements of this level: the functional effect of an open market system in the allotment of living quarters is a mobile labor force; bad money chases out good money; if the coal miners go on strike, racial tensions will mount in Detroit; the classical Chinese kinship system is incompatible with the requirements of Western industrial capitalism.

In light of all this, the statement that at any given time an actor participates in more than one system of action is neither true nor false when it is proposed at the level of action depicted in terms of the premises of action: rather, the statement is nonsense. Within the "flow" of the actor's experience, at any given time he is acting with reference to one and only one system of action, and at any given time he is acting as a participant in one and only one group. That is to say, it is the task of the observer to identify the actor by an order of statements that are sufficient to the task of accounting for all the actions taken with reference to the objects of a given finite province of meaning.

This rule, incidentally, provides us with a means for avoiding the representation of the actor as a mosaic of roles and avoids the otherwise practical necessity of representing a group in ideal-typical terms.

What about the statement that at any given time an actor is a member of many different groups? This is often represented in textbooks by the common area of several intersecting circles. It is found in Dewey's "segmental" representation of the "public mind," while J. F. Brown makes much ado of simultaneous "membership characters"—a person being a union member, a husband, American citizen, etc. all at the same time. Again we must allow a certain measure of accuracy to the insight, while realizing what the limits of the insight are for the student of social actions.

The statement is true in one and only one specific sense; namely in the sense that the actions of a particular person may, after analysis, be classified according to criteria that define a logical class of things—students, husbands, Americans, etc. The peculiar contribution of this insight consists of the fact that empirically the actions of a person have never been exhaustively depicted when one and only one classification was employed, although theoretically a one class person is "possible."

But, the question goes, if the actions of a person may be classified according to logical class membership, why can we not go beyond this and say that though a person in wartime acts as a worker producing arms, is there not at the same time a body of norms that are motivationally relevant to his arms production but yet govern the actions for all those who would call themselves patriots. In this sense does he not enjoy membership character in more than one group at a time—in this case the group of workers and the group of Americans.

Both at the level of functional consequences and the premises of action, the answer is as we see it unequivocally no. The reason for such an answer will be apparent if we compare again the meanings of the terms person and actor. Person is a residual concept which designates the referent of many kinds of action. Its meaning does not extend beyond this point, namely that the investigator uses it to designate a party to his interviews who is not illusory. Persons, then, do not act; nor is a group made up of persons. *Actors* act, and a group is made up of *actors*.

Now an actor is not a "concrete individual"; an actor is a series of propositions which incorporate and relate the six concepts of cognitive style. Actor is an intended object for an observer employing the finite province of meaning of scientific inquiry. As such it does not have, nor need it have, status as an object in the world of our daily working acts.

Further, these propositions, as we said in the rule above, must be sufficient to all the relevant actions taken with reference to a given finite province of meaning. What we are saying in effect, then, when we say that the worker on the job is governed by the norms of patriotic effort is that we are dealing with a group of actors the meanings of whose jobs extend beyond the common utilitarian meanings of job appraisal. The operation of such patriotic norms is entirely a feature of the worker's "job attitude." If some workers are oriented in this way while others are not, this refers only to the organizational features of the group, and not to the fact that some members act as though they were "nothing but arms producers." The phenomena appear as features of the actor's particular mode of attention to life, his epoche, his form of sociality, his specific form of time perspective, his mode of self awareness, and his form of spontaneity.

All right then, what of the view of functional consequences? A worker's production on the production line certainly affects his own marital relationship, does it not? Again we must dismiss the formulation, and for the reason that it is impossible to speak of the functional consequences of one action system for another *unless two different orders of actors are being referred to*. Otherwise, we are speaking only about the consequences of actions within a system for that same system.

(2) Suppose we now consider the second statement: "There exists a one member group." While we used the first statement to point up

some implications of defining a group as an aggregate of cognitive styles, this second statement can be used to throw additional light on our usage of the concept, "aggregate."

Such a statement emerges from the following chain of reasoning. A social action is one in which the actor takes into account the behavior of others in orienting his own action. An action is said to be social when on the basis of it the observer is able to detect an empirical order of consequences for the actor's relations to other actors. Now the conditions of this definition are met in the case of the actor who, in soliloquy, alters his relations with another actor without coming into face-to-face contact with the other actor.

If the reasoning stopped here there could be no criticism of the statement. But the reasoning proceeds to jump the track. Why indeed, it goes, if the presence of the other actor is not required, and the actor can act socially without the other actor, and every social action is group action, then lo! The smallest group we have is that which comprises an identified self related in some way to the image of another actor.

The fallacy is an obvious one and stems from confounding (1) the relationship that exists between the identified self and the identity of the other, which refers to the form of sociality, one of the concepts by which the actor is defined, with (2) the relationship that exists between two actors. That is, the other actor is lost sight of entirely, with the result that group member becomes synonymous with group.

Recalling the symbolism we employed in a previous part of this paper, when we say that in a social action the actor "takes the role of the other" we mean $(iSa \times io)A_1$. This represents the form of sociality which is one of the six concepts which represent A_1. The formulation is $\sqcap A\gamma : A\gamma > (iSa \times io)A_1$. When we say that the actor takes the other into account in orienting his action we mean that the actor deals in terms of two orders of considerations: (1) those interpretive principles that are provided the actor by the motivational scheme he entertains as representative of the other; and (2) the signs that are generated by or referred to the other as another actor. The social action may be predicated on the motivational scheme which represents *io,* but it is only and always expressed through working acts. Thus $A\gamma_1$ communicatively related to $A\gamma_2$, $A\gamma_1$ c $A\gamma_2$, is the smallest group. The error in saying,

"There exists a one-member group," lies in saying iSa **x** $io = A\gamma_1$ c $A\gamma_2$. The action within the relationship iSa **x** io is a social action insofar as it results in a series of consequences for $A\gamma_1$ c $A\gamma_2$. The relationship, iSa **x** io, is possible, however, only for a group member. But the observer has not accounted for the group involved until he has completed the relationship to read:

$$⊓(A\gamma_1 \text{ c } A\gamma_2) : [A\gamma_1 > (iSa \text{ } \mathbf{x} \text{ } io)A_1] \text{ c } [A\gamma_2 > (iSa \text{ } \mathbf{x} \text{ } io)A_2]$$

$A\gamma_1$ and $A\gamma_2$ must always be referrable to persons (as this term has been defined as an empirical construct before.)

(3) What is meant by the statement "There exists an actor"? We have repeated almost *ad nauseum* that "actor" does not mean "concrete person." In fact, one should make the case that the term "concrete person" is entirely misleading in the finite province of meaning of the scientific attitude in which the scientist lives. It is a concept employed in the finite province of meaning of the natural attitude, where the modes of treating the signs of the presence of the other are such as to render the hypothesis of the tangible objectivity of another self irrefutable. As the child knows, what else can that gesticulating figure on the porch *be* than his mother. But for the scientist the reality of "a person" is the reality of a unity of meaning, with tangibility being one feature of this unity of meaning, though it is by no means the sufficient criterion of its reality. In other words, "person," like "actor," designates for the scientist an *ideal object*. As an ideal object it is refutable; its meaning can be challenged and changed. The only things that are irrefutable are the signs which pure intuition (as this term is defined by Husserl) presents.

This being the case, one can apply the term *actor* to refer to a corporation as well as to the "indivisible person." Both are identical in the logic by which they are constructed as unities of meaning. Both are intended objects within the finite province of meaning of the scientific attitude. This is what F. H. Allport, in many respects the least of the sinners, failed to see in pointing to persons as the only real social entities, the corporation being "nothing but an institution." It is also the source of error of those who would allow that "there is such a thing as an individual mind" while talk of a group mind only invites their wrath. Within the scientific attitude the rules by which they are constituted as existent entities apply in exactly the same manner to one as to the other. It is only within the natural attitude that the question is possible: But you can see a person; who ever saw a corporation? The thing to remember is that the fact that a person is "seen" arises, not as a property of the peculiar ontological character of "the person," but is a property arising out of the epoche of the actor in the natural attitude. But the scientist deals in a world of theoretical scientific objects where the only claim to reality that a concept can make must rest entirely on the test of utility. Compared to the world of the natural attitude, the scientist's world is indeed a strange and misshapen one, a veritable Alice in Wonderland world, where if a "man" is of no use to the game in progress he is ruthlessly bumped off; where a table is not a thing to eat on but is a whirling dance of sub-microscopic particles. Viewed through the eyes of the natural attitude the objects of the scientific world are fantastic in a way that puts to shame the wildest offerings of the comic books. It is no wonder that Bernard Shaw, having lived in this world of scientific objects, and realizing the incongruities of the objects of the two worlds, could say in a public interview on the occasion of his 91st birthday, that death is the most incongruous of worldly possibilities, and no rational man should tolerate it for a minute.

The actor-person, and the actor-corporation are logically identical in that they represent the end products of the same process of idealization peculiar to the scientific mode of action, according to which the phenomena of the world are peculiarly transformed according to the purposes of science. Phenomenolgcially speaking, they are different as unities of meaning. And we must look to a phenomenological analysis of their constitution if we are to detect what these differences are. The problem is an intriguing one, indeed. At this point, we shall simply make one difference between them. The actor-person designates a single subject who acts as the other in the social relationship that the investigator establishes to carry out his interviews; and an exhaustive representation of the actor-person is possible without relating the subject socially to any other actor than the investigator. The actor-corporation, on the other hand, designates a plurality of interview subjects related socially as others to each other as well as to the investigator, and the representation of which cannot be completed without taking the relationships to "others" into account. In this sense they are constituted differently not because of what they are, but because by the rules of the game the investigator is unable to conceive of actor-person and actor-corporation in any other than this elementary way.

In representing a group as A_1 c A_2 then, it is possible to substitute for A_1 and A_2, customer and corporation, husband and wife, Army and soldier, management and labor, government and business, etc.

A note on the significance of the concept of "working acts" for the theory of groups. Let us assume two empirical persons, X and Y. Let us suppose that we have an intimate knowledge of X such that we know that he is "in" and "out" of a group 100 times a day as he gives up working on the pile of insurance forms on his desk in order to indulge in a daydream about his coming vacation. Now, is this the direction we follow in portraying group structure? That is to say, will we have eyes out for the frequency with which alternate states of attention to life come into evidence for the multitude of actors that make up "the office?" The answer is no. X is a group member, not on the basis of the portrayal of his mode of "internal activity," *but rather is a group member on the basis of the treatment that is paid to him by Y.* This principle needs to be underlined and rehearsed until it is known and used as a matter of course. It is to be compared with the attempt to define a group as a synthesis of individual egos. The "synthesis" is effected within this principle *in the working act.* If *Y treats X* as a group member, then *X is* a group member. This principle is universally applicable, and admits of no qualification or exception. It is a profound error of Icheiser's to have formulated the principle to read that if Y treats X as a group member, X's status as a group member must still be decided with reference to the wider knowledge of the scientific observer, or, even worse, can be decided only in the light of further evidence as it emerges in the historical process. Another form of this value loaded subjectivism consists of saying, as many writers on prejudice say, that if Y treats X as a Jew, Y may be mistaken after all because X may be in fact a member of the Unitarian Church. And in most cases such a pronouncement is delivered without a trace of humor and labeled a "phenomenon" of "suggestion." Such a view, with its implicit irony, is of use as a social tactic where one is interested in passing judgment on one's fellows. In effect it invites the actor to stop being absurd and start acting like a scientist. One might with as much justification be surprised that children speak grammatical English at such an early age. The point is that the premises of any action are always sufficient to the action. And it is the premises of action to which we must look for the data of group structure. The actor rarely doubts the objectivity of the meanings in which he deals. It is precisely for this reason that the observer, if he is to deal objectively with the data available to him, must remain focused *on what the actor makes of the signs.* If we once realize that objectivity is a property of the intentionality of consciousness then we need no longer be bothered about whether we have read X's mind correctly, nor need the false duality of subjective and objective data plague us. We never deal in subjective data. All that is meant by subjective is that the observer as an actor makes statements or engages in conduct that another actor makes absolutely no sense of. *The objective character of a statement is found in what the other actor makes of the statement.* There is no intervening judge, and least of all does the appeal to *the real truth* stand as anything but a way of making friends and influencing people.

The principle: If *Y treats X* as a group member, then *X is* a group member. An illustration: Let us suppose that the office manager looks up from what he is doing and notices an office worker paring his nails. One might say that the office worker is not part of the office service at this point since he is engrossed in a personal reverie. But this would make an analysis of group structure dependent upon the analysis of individual "ego-structures" rather than upon the interpretation of naively available material. Let's say that the office manager acts toward the office worker as if personal reverie "on the job" is something to be expected on the job as a matter of course; he looks up and makes no movement toward the office worker, plus the other criteria that would define "matter of course." One could hypothesize at this point that the integrity of the group is not impaired by the reveries of the members, but rather that such a manner of viewing on the part of the office manager is a feature of the structure of office relations. If the office manager be asked by the observer, "Is he being paid to indulge in reverie while the office papers go unattended?" and the office manager answers, "It's very boring work, those insurance forms," then we have isolated an interpretive tactic, an element of office ideology by which the actions of the "others" are invested with reasonableness; are understood; a tactic by which group membership is retained and the system continues to operate without reorganization. It is one of a multitude of acts of understanding which comprise the dynamic background of the phenomenon of regularity in social relationships.

We are in a position now to expand on what we meant when we gave a general definition of group at the beginning of this section. The following considerations need to be underlined: (1) The term *group* does not refer to persons; it refers to Actors. (2) It does not mean an empirical reality; a group does not "exist": it is an analytical construct, and is thereby a scheme of interpretation; a group is meant. (3) As a term it is a designator of certain interpretive rules of procedure. If we propose the synthetic proposition: At a certain time and place, if the policeman blows his whistle, the motorist will stop, we mean, when we say this, that activity is to be interpreted within a theory of groups; that two actors are assumed such that Actor A is represented by (a) a form of sociality in which he is given as a "policeman" and treats an identified other represented by the term, with what it means for the policeman, of *motorist*; (b) that he is to be represented by an epoche defined according to the principles of traffic control; (c) that the relationship of duree and standard time is such that the passage of time is measured and accounted as real by the actor in terms of the relationship between the number of cars that pass him and the number of cars that remain halted at the intersection and so on for the other elements of cognitive style. The "motorist" as the other Actor is defined with reference to the same categories; and communicative tactics that take place are such as to include a specific array of presentations which each realizes in accordance with the place of such meanings within the finite provinces of meaning that accompany the relevant cognitive styles. We can refer to the whole model as a "traffic situation," which means nothing more than specifications we cite regarding the cognitive styles and communication, the empirical references of which are the empirically idealized presentations which the observer makes when he brings into scientific view two empirically constructed persons which he calls "policeman" and "motorist": person in uniform; person driving an auto.

Seen within a theory of groups, the synthetic proposition, "At a certain time and place, if the policeman blows his whistle, the motorist will stop," emerges as only *one* of the many synthetic propositions that are generated by our manipulations of the relevant values of the rules of procedure represented by the terms of our analytical model. Take, for example, the analytical proposition: the stability of the actor's givenness as an identified self is directly dependent on whether it continues to be possible for the actor to treat the object according to the terms of the actor's definition of the object. This proposition does not tell us a single thing about what the world looks like. It is rather a shorthand designation of a set of complicated instructions which tell us what possibilities of experience will be fulfilled for us as observers if we do as the instructions say. The instructions say: consider the empirically idealized policeman. If you interview him and find out that as a cop he views the persons passing in the autos as motorists, and treats them as if all persons driving autos are motivated by the devilish intention of breaking the law; and if when you ask the policeman about who these people are in the cars, he tells you the equivalent of, "They're a bunch of crazy lunatics who have no respect for law and order unless you hold a club over their heads"; and if the transformation scheme that he uses is such that whatever the motorist does, the policeman can't lose in his interpretation—everything they do serves to confirm his hypotheses about them and himself. Thus, if the motorist glowers at the policeman he doesn't like being held back. Okay, we'll put a little heat on that egg. While if the motorist smiles at the policeman, he's sucking around for a favor and wants to get away with something. And if you assume that the other elements of the cognitive style of the Actor as policeman remain practically unchanged during his treatment of the motorists, then insofar as objects of his treatment of them will confirm him in his regard for himself as someone doing his proper duty as a cop. That is to say, if you ask him the equivalent of, "Who are you?" "Why do you blow your whistle?" "Why don't you sit down and take it easy?" "What are you getting at?" "What do you do for a living?" etc., he will tell you that he is a policeman, that he is a member of the police force, that he is responsible to a whole array of identified other persons who he refers to as "the Sergeant," the Captain, the Mayor, and that "citizens" are supposed to obey the law, meaning himself as a "representative of the law." If you ask him now, "Is your wife a citizen?" and he says, "Of course," and you ask, "Is she supposed to obey you," he will say, "Sure, but what the hell does that have to do with me being a cop?" meaning by this that if she were to drive up in a car and run past the crossing aisle, he would start to yell, "And where the hell do you think *you're* going," until he "recognized" her as his wife, upon which recognition he would say, instead, "For Pete's sake, Gladys, stay behind the line or you'll get me in Dutch with McCarthy," and this is something he could formulate and mean in the sense it is meant by him only if he is re-given, so to speak, as a husband. Or, he could have said, "And where the hell do you think *you're* going," meaning by this, perhaps, "Picture me as a cop, honey, treating you like you were anyone on my beat," but not meaning, "And where the hell do you think *you're* going, citizen-who-is-supposed-to-obey-the-law?"

But now suppose that in this world of unharnessed possibilities, we had asked, "Is your wife a citizen?" and the cop had answered, "Of course," and we asked, "Is she supposed to obey you?" and he said, "Of course, she's no better than anybody else," whereupon who should drive up but his wife, and what does he say but, "There's my wife. Where the hell does she think *she's* going? Hey, Gladys, where the hell do you think *you're* going?" and means every word of it as just what was meant for the citizens-who-are-supposed-to-obey-the-law, then we would have to hypothesize that whatever else wife-Gladys might mean for him as an identity of wife, within the cognitive style of cop she means citizen-who-is-supposed-to-obey-the-laws. And if he treats the citizens-who-are-supposed-to-obey-the-law but don't in surly fashion and gives them tickets and advice in public, then if his wife means no more than citizens-who-are-supposed-to, etc., but don't, he will give her tickets and advice in public. One might feel offended at this and ask, "But what's the point in her being his wife," to which the answer is, "Ask Gladys." "But," the critic will howl, "the cop used a form of personal address: he said, 'Hey, Gladys." The model stands adamant. It says that under the assumptions as they stand, "Hey, Gladys" can have meant the same as and no more than the impersonal form of address implied in the "And" of "And where the hell, etc." "Bunk," says the critic, "no real cop could act that way." Maybe not, but we're not interested in real cops; we're talking about formally conceived cops. And formally conceived cops act just as we say they do and no other way. That's why we don't bet on formal cops; we couldn't lose on such a bet. But we can lose if the person we refer to by the empirical construct of cop doesn't say what he's supposed to. This is what we mean when we say that a synthetic proposition is no better than the consistency of the logic by which it is derived. Everything, and we mean just that, the whole business—epoche, form of sociality, mode of self awareness, time orientation, noesis-noema structures—stands or falls on its ability to win on the bets which experiment decides.

Spelling out further what was implied in our general definition of group—cognitive styles, each with its finite province of meaning, where these finite provinces of meaning did not necessarily have to be the same—we have a *social group* when the communicative efforts of the actors, which is to say, when the conduct of the actors results in some order of consequences for the cognitive style of at least one of the actors. This is the same as saying that the action of *A* has consequences for the premises of action of actor *B*. "Premises of action" refers to an order of analytic propositions made by the observer to represent the elements of the cognitive style of the actor The formulation of the "motivation" problem would run as follows: There are two orders of motivational statements; (1) the actor does such and such "because of"; and (2) the actor does such and such "in order to." The first order statement will run, The actor does such and such because he is engaged in such and such a form of sociality, because he employs such and such an epoche, because of a time orientation of such and such a nature, etc. When these elements are conceptually represented for the actor, the formulation says in effect that a concept "motivates" an intention. The second order statement runs to the effect that the actor does or says something in order to do or say something else. The second order formulation then refers to the principle of continuity in a train of conduct.

The principle of continuity then may refer to the actor's intention to realize a project or the intention to carry out a line of conduct for its own sake and without reference to the attainment of a goal. By "premises of action" we mean, then, the propositions formulated by the observer based on the values of the elements of cognitive style, and intended to furnish a rational and explicit account of the action of the agent as well as the course that the action will take. The statements are called premises inasmuch as they are exactly that. A prediction of behavior must be capable of being ordered to syllogistic form. It goes without saying that an actor performs no such intellectual endeavor in undertaking a course of action. "Premises" has no reference to the participant's view; it has reference only to the observer's practices.

Although many problems are unsettled, and many others still remain to be treated, we have covered sufficient ground now to be able to state the problem of the thesis. To recall once more; the term *social group* designates an aggregate of cognitive styles where the conduct of the actors results in some order of consequences for the cognitive style of at least one of the actors. Now we find as a matter of statistical description that actions and consequences occur with sufficient regularity to enable us to describe these regularities with the use of such terms as influence, power, force, and so on, each of which is a summary designation of a social relationship. Thus, for example, suppose we offer the following definitions:

1. We shall speak of a relationship of Influence when, regardless of how actor A regards B, the premises of actor A eventuate in a course of action by A which effects a change in some element of actor B's cognitive style.

2. We shall speak of a relationship of Power when actor A is so regarded by actor B that A's treatment effects a change in some element or elements of B's cognitive style, the changes being of such a character as to limit B's alternatives of action to those or that one which A desires.

3. We shall speak of a relationship of Force when regardless of how B regards A, the premises of action of actor A eventuate in a course of action by A the effect of which is to limit B's alternatives of action without A intending a change of B's cognitive style and regardless of B's cognitive style.

4. We shall speak of a relationship of Advice when actor B's regard for A is such that the premises of actor A eventuate in a course of action by A the effect of which is to change B's cognitive style in such a way as to eventuate for B in the realization of alternatives of action.

The number of such analytically descriptive statements is entirely a function of how much time and effort we want to spend turning the crank. We cite these few as paradigms of a relationship as it is conceived in our scheme.

Our concern in the thesis is for the conditions under which a relationship is possible. It is our aim to be able to so represent two actors that we shall be able to translate a descriptive statement of a relationship as it is exemplified in our examples into a hypothesis. In effect we are seeking to give a descriptive statement of a relationship its theoretical premises. We shall be satisfied when every descriptive statement of a relationship can be stated as a hypothesis which is drawn from an analytical mode. We shall only be satisfied ultimately with this, but we shall settle in the thesis for less—much less. The long-winded conceptual paraphernalia that we have elaborated in this prospectus is designed to aid us in this task.

Part II

Specific Problems

Statement of Thesis Problems

When we say that we hope to be able to translate a descriptive statement of a social relationship into hypothetical form, we mean that our task is that of studying the conditions under which the action which is represented in the term "relationship" occurs.

The first and fundamental question concerns the relationship of the observer to the data. We are choosing to settle the question of relativity involved here with two assumptions. (1) We are assuming the methodological position of Felix Kaufmann as this position is found in his book *Methodology of the Social Sciences*. (2) Since the observer is to be conceived of as an actor, and inasmuch as we have rejected the idealistic thesis of a correspondence theory of reality, the question is: How do we insure the constancy of the observer's position? We are doing this by the assumption:

$$\sqcap I\sigma : I\sigma > (|iSob| \ \mathbf{x} \ ia)I$$

where σ refers to the cognitive style of scientific endeavor as it is described in Alfred Schütz's essay, "On Multiple Realities" (*Philosophy and Phenomenological Research*, June 1945, pp. 563–571), and $|iSob|$ means an identified Self which remains constant, where constancy of Self is possible if there is constancy of the Investigator's purposes

205

which are to represent, observe, interpret, and predict the activities of potential subjects of interview and observation. The further question of the extent to which the observer by his modes of operations influences the data being studied will be handled by experimental design and the "corrective formulae" that are implicit in the rules of interview procedure.

The descriptive statement that we shall be concerned with is statement 2 on page 203. The statement reads:

> We shall speak of a relationship of Power when actor A is so regarded by actor B that A's treatment of B effects a change in some element or elements of B's cognitive style, the changes being of such a character as to limit B's alternatives of action to those or that one which A desires.

Suppose we translate this statement into hypothetical form, and use the modifier (x) to indicate the problematic materials that make up the concerns of the thesis. The statement reads:

> Assuming $I\sigma$, let there be meant a dyadic group made up of $A\gamma(x)$ c $B\gamma(x)$. When A is regarded by B (x)-wise, A's treatment of B will be interpreted in such a way (x) by B as to encompass a change (x) in an element or elements (x) of B's cognitive style, the change being of such a character (x) as to limit B's alternatives of action (x) to those or that one which A desires (x).

The problematical materials designated in this statement can be incorporated into the statement of our general problem: the nature of experience structures and their transformations, where the term *experience structures* refers to (a) the elements of cognitive style and (b) the noesis-noema structures in terms of which conduct is represented.

This general problem breaks down into the following specific concerns: (1) the relations that obtain at the empirical and analytical levels between the elements of cognitive style; (2) nature of the transformations of cognitive style which occur during communication; (3) the conditions under which these transformations occur; (4) the principles of regularity which describe the kinds of transformations; (5) the relations of cognitive style to conduct (noesis-noema structures); (6) the organizational characteristics of noesis-noema relations, e.g., compare the structural organization of a narrative expression with a narrative ironical expression; (7) the noesis-noema structures and their transformations that are typical to various types of combinations of cognitive styles; and (8) the principles of regularity which describe noesis-noema transformations.

Limitations of time will make it impossible to set for ourselves the task of paying the same amount of attention to all of these concerns. We shall limit ourselves as far as extensive treatment is concerned to points 5 through 8. In order to do this, it will be necessary to be able to assume the character of the cognitive styles that are involved. These will be "given by the experimental design." Allowing that such an assumption can be made (we shall see in a minute what the grounds for it will be), the specific problem materials indicated in the statement can be read in the following proposition: (Where (G) means "Given by the experimental design")

Assuming $I\sigma$, let there be a dyadic group $A\gamma(G)$ c $B\gamma(G)$. When A is regarded by B (x)-wise, A's treatment (G) or B will be interpreted in such a way (x) by B as to motivate a change (x) in an element or elements (x) of B's cognitive style (G) the change being of such a character (x) as to limit B's alternatives (x) to those or that one which A desires (G).

The problematical character of actor A will be reduced by making him a stooge in the affair.

To help us in "slowing up the process" of B's interpretive activity, we shall use the device of cutting B off by facing him with incongruous material. The effort of the thesis will be directed to examining the meanings and efforts that make up the grounds and tactics that B employs in meeting this treatment. The observer will be witness to the following type of scene. Two persons, A the stooge, and B the experimental subject, will be engaged in some activity. At some theoretically strategic point in the activity, A will make a request of B which B will find incongruous. Further activity will depend upon B making a "decision," in the course of which he will treat the incongruity in some way or ways. B's decision will be such as to eventuate or not eventuate in the fulfillment of A's request.

The task of observation and post-experimental interview will be to gather information on such points as the following: (1) the specific make-up of *B*'s cognitive style. (2) The fact that the treatment did or did not take. (3) The identity that *B* assigned to *A*, and how, if anything, it changed. (4) The meanings that were involved, and the ways in which they were related to each other in effecting the experience of incongruity. (5) The tactics of interpretation that *B* employed. (6) The alternatives that *B* actually faced, compared to the alternatives that he could theoretically have faced. (7) The factors that effected the selection of an alternative. Were they such as to limit them, to propose them, to block them off entirely from view? What were the meaning-terms of these factors such that the preference of one alternative over another "made a difference" to the actor? We expect the questions to become increasingly precise once the actual gathering of material gets under way.

The experimental work of the thesis is divided into two programs. The first program which might be regarded as a pre-experimental program, is concerned with two problems. (1) If we want to say for the experimental program proper that the cognitive style of actor *B* is given, we need some way of knowing with some degree of practical certainty that the conditions that we would like to have present—that is, the elements of *B*'s cognitive style—are as we have depicted them in the actual experimental design. For example, under one set of given conditions we need to have a subject employing a cognitive style in which the form of spontaneity is that of teleological conduct, whereas in another case we want the form of spontaneity to be that of expressional conduct. While we shall have checks provided in the form of interview questions in the post experimental period to determine what the subject's form of spontaneity was, the actual experimental matters will be considerably clarified if we are able to know what the cognitive style of the subject "is" at the point that he starts getting the treatment. Thus it is our hope that we shall be able to state the given conditions in terms of rules of experimental procedure. For example, at this point in our conception of the thesis, we intend to use two sets of given conditions; two types of cognitive styles. Suppose we designate them temporarily in terms of the form of spontaneity and the norms of activity that are attendant upon the identities assigned in the form of sociality. We have then (a) teleological institutional; and (b) expressional noninstitutional. Now if, in the experimental program proper, we wish to ask, "What kinds of noesis-noema structures do we find in a set-up where actor *B* is given according to the cognitive style, teleological institutional?" We want to be able to say that the cognitive style of actor *A* is given according to the following procedures: "A phone call was made to the Remington Typewriter Corporation. The representative in charge of sales was told that we were interested in buying a typewriter, that we needed it right away, that we liked model *X* particularly, that we were prepared to pay cash, but that the purchasing agent was a busy man and wanted to speak to a salesman who knew his business. We assumed that the "representative-in-charge-of-sales" thereby understood that he had a prospective customer in tow, that immediate action was called for, that the customer wanted to talk turkey about a specific machine, and that whether the sale was successful or not depended a lot on the salesman playing to make the sale." Whether the representative indeed understood it this way, and whether the salesman does indeed employ the cognitive style that we assume in our representation of him as Actor *B* must remain to be decided on the basis of what we learn from observation and interview. But to get the game started, to get it started with some degree of control over the conditions that we wish to establish, and to keep it under way with something like the feeling that we shall not need a dozen pairs of eyes to keep track of what is going on, such as we would need if we had no way of knowing how to represent the subject, is our intent. To aid us in making such assumptions, the first task of the pre-experimental program will be that of finding out to what extent we can assume that the victim which our procedures have brought to the scene of the crime has the "right attitude." An auxiliary value of this effort and an important one, will be that of obtaining specific empirical references for the analytical categories of cognitive style; and consideration of this material should serve to deepen our understanding of the relationships between the analytical categories. For example, it is not clear to us at this point how a change in time perspective is related to changes of the identified other. Where changes in the identified other take place within a closed transformation scheme, such as we find in formal social organization, it appears that the time perspective remains the same, assuming, of course, that the identified self remains constant. But what of the case where the transformation scheme is an open one, as we find, for example, in the chance meetings of parties who are unknown to each other, and where even such a relatively stable categorization as "stranger" is not employed—as we find, for example, in such public encounters as those found in the course of a subway ride, where the other riders are anonymous to the actor, even while they are not strange for him, and even while he entertains certain notions of vague familiarity and friendliness. One finds in an encounter of this sort that the time perspective is defined with reference to the movements of the train with its sequence of stops as this sequence represents for the actor the approaches to the destination of the actor. What the other riders do is irrelevant to the way in which the time perspective operates. However, let the rider next to the actor make a request of the actor and the anonymity of the other disappears and with it disappears the old time perspective to be replaced with a time perspective which includes the future which is peculiar to a relationship of mutual engagement with another in a common enterprise, whether the enterprise be conversation or the fulfillment of a request for information, etc. The information we collect in this pre-experimental period should help us in clarifying some of these questions and thereby help us in tightening the analytical model.

(2) There is a second important task of the pre-experimental program. The reader will recall that the experimental situations are to be so rigged that at a certain point in the exchange A makes a request of B such that B has to "stop, think, and make a decision," on the basis of which decision the action then proceeds. We intend to so design the experiment that the exchange is broken into by A introducing incongruous materials. That is, A introduces materials that we hope to be able to count on beforehand will be found incongruous by B. (Actually, the game is such that we cannot lose whichever way it goes. If the material is incongruous we want to find out why it was, how the victim saw it, what measures he used to make sense of it, and what these measures imply for the question of "modes of understanding." And if the material flops, we want to know why it flopped, how the victim saw it, what measures he employed such that it flopped, and what these measures imply for the question of "modes of understanding.") Nevertheless, it is desirable that we be able to count on the subject experiencing an incongruity, given the conditions under which we say he should experience it, and this is desirable on several counts. First, for the reason of economy of investigative effort. Having predicted that the subject would experience incongruity, and we find such is the case, we are able to take up the postexperimental interview

with some feeling that the possibilities that might account for the experience are limited, and hence the hope that the fact of incongruity can be quickly established, its conditions verified, and thus we can turn to the important questions which deal with the ways in which the subject made sense of what was going on. The most important significance of the experience, perhaps, is the fact that it serves as an indelible marker of a whole train of events for the subject, and hence might make references to it and the events surrounding it easily accessible to questions. This is particularly true if one considers that incongruity as it arises out of a breach of expectations can be expected to draw the subject's attention, even for a brief moment, to incongruity as an object of action.

A second reason for playing with the phenomenon of incongruity has to do with the desirability in theory building of being able to constantly "reverse the field," so that at one time one looks to the analytical model to supply the conditions under which a phenomenon will be encountered, and at another time, plays the game backward by taking the phenomenon and feeding it as an empirical datum into the analytical machine to see what provisions, if any, the machine has made for it. We would hope thereby to be able to state at what points the theory is vague, what the theory covers and what it does not cover, etc. Now at this point in our efforts, we can make only a bare handful of statements about how a person does understand. Attaching the question directly would mean an almost interminable collection of case material. However, we can attack the problem by putting a "knower" into a position where he does not understand, or at least where understanding becomes problematical. If, in such a case, we are able to state the conditions under which understanding falters, then without yet knowing how the "processes" of understanding will finally be described, we have at least some systematically encountered hints of what may be necessary to a determinate description.

The second task of the pre-experimental program, then, is to find out under what conditions incongruity can be induced. Knowing these conditions, we shall be able in the experimental program proper to induce incongruity systematically so as to be able to focus entirely on the "devices" by which incongruity is handled—that is to say, the devices whereby a "normal flow of expectations" is again instituted. It is at the point of "resolution" that we hope to find the material that bears on the question of how it is possible for one person to understand another. Tentatively, we are betting that incongruity can be induced under the following conditions: Assuming the cognitive style of the working attitude of everyday life, where the actor retains a standard against which the new material is "measured," incongruity should result from a switch in the rules of the game, from a switch of time perspective, from a switch in identities, from a switch in the interpretations of the actor's intentions as they are reflected back to him by the other, in a switch of attention to life, in a switch in style—to enumerate just a few. To the extent that the values of the elements of cognitive style are specific to a given finite province of meaning—e.g., the actor acting as a geometrician, as a typewriter salesman, as a masher, etc.—to that extent the conditions of incongruity can be stated in specific terms, i.e., the switch in the identified other from customer to any other identity which is not dialectically relevant to customer—e.g., an identity that the actor cannot contrast, oppose, equate, compare, etc., with customer.

Having done a lot of talking about "incongruity" and the "conditions of incongruity" we might spare the reader unnecessary despair by telling what we mean by the term. Webster does a good beginning job for us. He says the term means "not compatible," "not conforming to," "being at variance with," "lacking propriety," "having inconsistent or inharmonious parts, qualities." If we can fill out Webster's hints by designating *what* is not compatible with *what*, we'll have a fairly decent substantive definition. Suppose we designate the whats as $What_1$ and $What_2$. (We'll see in a minute how the distinction can be useful.) By $What_1$ in the general case we mean always and only the reified possibilities of experience, or, the conceptual representation of an item of experience, where the meanings generated by the conception, or, the anticipated further treatment of the item stems from the item's place in the finite province of meaning *being employed by the actor*. The $What_1$ then has these three elements in its meaning: (1) consistency and (2) continuity of (3) expectations. By the term $What_2$ is meant any conceptualized phenomenally presented experience. The incompatibility is found in the fact that the presentation ($What_2$) only *partially* fulfills the meanings proposed by $What_1$. Among other conditions under which incongruity is impossible as an experience, e.g., in the absence of the memory functions of recall and retention, there are two conditions under which it is impossible: (1) if the meanings of What$_2$ bear no dialectical relationship to those of What$_1$. In such a case, What$_2$ as an intended object has meaning within a different finite province of meaning from that of What$_1$, which is to say that the actor has switched cognitive styles. (2) If the What$_2$ fulfills the meanings proposed by What$_1$. In such a case we have a unity of meaning, or a determinate meaning, which is to say that the subject has grasped a significance of the object under appraisal regardless of whether the object that has been grasped is that which was intended by the other person, and regardless of the degree of clarity with which the meanings have been grasped. Clarity of meaning, and incongruity of meaning are not to be confounded.

Withal, then, we have the general rule: Only insofar as two experiences are in fact compatible in at least one respect can they be incompatible in other respects.

The paradigmatic expression of the experience of incongruity is: "Wait a second! *This* isn't supposed to happen. What's *this* all about?"

If we are successful in working through the two tasks of the pre-experimental program, we shall be ready to take up the experimental program proper. The experimental design will be based on a plan of systematically inducing incongruity for actor *B* where actor *B* is represented in terms of two different sets of conditions. We shall refer to these two sets of conditions as Case 1, and Case 2.

The conditions represented by *Case 1* are:

1. Form of spontaneity: The working acts of conduct devised in advance, based upon a preconceived project where there "supervenes" an intention to realize the project.
2. Epoche: The epoche is that of the "natural attitude"—that is, where the actor suspends the doubt that the world and its objects would be otherwise than as it appears to him. The bracketing is based on specific, and publicly relevant criteria.
3. Time perspective: Made up of a systematically ordered system of retentions and anticipations, with these ordered systematically to accord with the intention to fulfill the project. There is a meaningful ordered Past, Present, and Future.

4. Self awareness: A "partial" self is involved, the self being of a public character. It is given according to universalistic criteria.
5. Mode of attention to life: That of full "wide-awakeness;" alertness, with attentional direction oriented to "external" objects of action.
6. Form of sociality: Closed alpha transformation scheme with more than one *io,* and where $|iSa|$. The *io*'s are defined in specific referent terms. The motivational scheme representative of the *io*'s have public and social validity; *io*'s are institutionalized identities.

The conditions represented by *Case 2* are:

1. Form of spontaneity: The working acts of conduct which is not devised in advance, but rather is experience directly as it manifests itself. Conduct undertaken for its own sake. No project involved and no intention to realize a project.
2. Epoche: The epoche is that of the natural attitude, and involves a bracketing based on diffuse, privately relevant criteria.
3. Time perspective: The time perspective is "truncated" both with reference to a Past and Future. Activity is meaningful for the relatively immediate "here and now" with no systematic ordering of retentions and anticipations.
4. Self awareness: A whole self is involved, the self being that of a private character. It is given according to particularistic criteria.
5. Mode of attention to life: That of full "wide-awakeness," alertness, with attentional direction oriented to the "external" objects of action.
6. Form of sociality: Closed alpha transformation scheme of one identity where $|iSa|$. *io* is defined in expressional terms. The motivational scheme representative of *io* has private social validity; *io* is a mixture of institutionalized and noninstitutionalized elements.

We shall be using adult persons for Cases 1 and 2. In order to deepen the comparative material, we intend at this point in our conception of the thesis problems, to set up two additional cases, each of which will be comparable in several respects to cases 1 and 2, but will be applicable to children between the ages of 5 and 7.

Suppose we name each of the conditions under which incongruity can be induced as an "Incongruity Type." We can then set up a rough kind of table which tells us at a glance what it is that we hope to hold constant, what it is that we hope to use to induce variation, and what the variation is that we are intent on studying. (See table 1.)

The blank squares in the table represent the material that we hope to fill in on the basis of the actual experimental work. This material can be represented by the following topics:

1. The meant objects of treatment in the exchange, together with the ways in which they are meant.
2. The tactics and style of treatment of these objects.
3. The significances of the objects for: (a) *B*'s treatment of the identified other, and (b) the related objects in the finite province of meaning of *B*'s cognitive style.
4. The communicative expressions of the exchange: (a) the meanings that are employed; (b) the semantic properties of the meanings; (c) the organizational characteristics of the noesis-noema structures; (d) the nature of the continuities of noesis-noema structures.
5. The logics which govern the combination, differentiation, opposition, contrast, contradiction, etc. of the terms of social intercourse.

Table 1.

	Incongruity Type 1	Incongruity Type 2	Incongruity Type 3	Incongruity Type 4	Etc.
Adults: Case 1					
Case 2					
Children: Case 3					
Case 4					

In summary: the objects, devices, and logics that are relevant to the ways in which *B* treats the incongruous material. It is from an analysis of such material that we hope to be able to throw some light on the specific concerns of five to eight aspects of our general problem as these are listed at the beginning of the section on page 206. And it is from an understanding of such concerns that we hope to be able to translate our descriptive statement of a "power" relationship into the form of a testable hypothesis.

We shall not have time to work through all the possible incongruity types. The thesis will consist of the pre-experimental program, plus the systematic findings that result from inducing as many incongruity types as time allows. We plan to have completed as much work as might constitute an acceptable thesis by the end of the Spring semester of 1949.

Notes to Seeing Sociologically

1. *Editor's note:* There is one page missing from the original manuscript at this point. It appears that Garfinkel was going to describe some worksite contingencies and their importance. The following lines fall at the bottom of the manuscript page, and then the sentence and page break off: "Thus, for example, suppose we have a subject busily engaged at a work bench. Our model proposes"; this leaves us with an incomplete sentence that continues on the missing page.

2. Marvin Farber, *The Foundation of Phenomenolgy* (Cambridge: Harvard University Press, 1943), pp. 222–243.

3. Farber, p. 223.

4. Farber, chapters 8–14, pp. 222–488.

5. Aron Gurwitsch, "Intentionality of Consciousness," *Philosophical "Essays in Memory of Edmund Husserl* (Cambridge: Harvard University Press, 1940), p. 75.

6. Gurwitsch, p. 75.

7. Gurwitsch, p. 77.

8. Gurwitsch, p. 81

9. Gurwitsch, p. 82

10. *Editor's note: The Dictionary of Occupational Titles* is a book often mentioned by Garfinkel. It contains short descriptions of thousands of occupations. These descriptions are written as if they explain the actual work involved in the occupations. But, of course, they do not. This is Garfinkel's point.

11. *Editor's note:* This idea of instructions for activity—instructed action—will become very important in Garfinkel's later work as an alternative for the problematic idea of rules. It is interesting that it appears already in this manuscript.

12. *Editor's note:* Among other things, this might refer to the paper on "Intra and Inter Racial Homicide," which was published in 1949. That paper presented an analysis of the way racial identities were used in court to decide culpability in homicide cases: i.e., to generate homicide statistics.

References

Allport, Floyd Henry. 1924. *Social Psychology.* Boston: Houghton Mifflin.
———. 1955. *Theories of Perception and the Concept of Structure.* New York: Wiley.

Burke, Kenneth. 1941. *The Philosophy of Literary Form: Studies in Symbolic Action.* Baton Rouge: Louisiana State University Press.
———. 1945. *A Grammar of Motives.* New York: Prentice-Hall.

Carnap, Rudolf. 1934. *The Unity of Science.* Translated and introduced by M. Black. London: K. Paul/Trench/Trubner & Co.
———. 1935. *Philosophy and Logical Syntax.* London: K. Paul/Trench/Trubner & Co.

Cassirer, Ernst. 1921. *Idee und Gestalt.* Berlin: B. Cassirer.
———. 1923. *Philosophie der Symbolischen Formen.* Berlin: B. Cassirer.
———. 1944. *An Essay on Man: An Introduction to the Philosophy of Human Culture.* New Haven: Yale University Press.
———. 1946. *Language and Myth.* Translated by Susanne K. Langer. New York: Harper.

Chomsky, Noam. 1964. *Current Issues in Linguistic Theory.* The Hague: Mouton.

Dewey, John. 1925. *Experience and Nature.* Chicago/London: Open Court Publishing Co.
———. 1930. *Human Nature and Conduct: An Introduction to Social Psychology.* New York: Modern Library.
———. 1934. *Education and the Social Order.* New York: League for Industrial Democracy.
———. 1939. *Theory of Valuation.* Chicago: University of Chicago Press.
———. 1948. *Reconstruction in Philosophy.* Boston: Beacon Press.

The Dictionary of Occupational Titles, 2nd ed. 1949. United States Employment Service. Washington, D.C.: U.S. Government Printing Office.

Domarus, Alexander von. 1947. Grundriss der Inneren Medizin. Berlin: Springer.

Durkheim, Emile. [1893]1933. *The Division of Labor in Society.* Chicago: Free Press.

———. 1895. *The Rules of the Sociological Method.* New York: Free Press.

———. 1897. *Socialism and Saint-Simon.* Edited by Alvin Gouldner. Lima, Ohio: Antioch Press.

———. 1897. *Suicide: A Study of Society.* New York: Free Press.

———. 1912. *The Elementary Forms of the Religious Life.* Chicago: Free Press.

———. [1913–1914]1955. *Pragmatism and Sociology.* Cambridge, U.K.: Cambridge University Press.

———. 1960. *Montesquieu and Rousseau.* Ann Arbor: University of Michigan.

Einstein, Albert. 1920. *Relativity: The Special and the General Theory, a Popular Exposition.* London: Methuen.

———. 1922. *The Meaning of Relativity.* London: Methuen.

———. 1933. *On the Method of Theoretical Physics.* Oxford: Clarendon Press.

Elias, Norbert. [1987]1992. *Time: An Essay.* Oxford: Blackwell.

Evans-Pritchard, Edward Evan. 1937. *Witchcraft, Oracles and Magic Among the Azande.* Oxford: Clarendon Press.

Farber, M. (ed.). 1943. *The Foundations of Phenomenology.* Cambridge, Mass.: Harvard University Press.

Garfinkel, Harold. 1941. "Color Trouble." In Edward J. O'Brien (ed.), *The Best Short Stories of 1941: The Yearbook of the American Short Story.* Boston: Houghton Mifflin.

———. 1949. "Research Note on Inter- and Intra-Racial Homicide." *Social Forces,* 27: 370–381.

———. 1952. "The Perception of the Other: A Study in Social Order." Unpublished Ph.D. dissertation, Harvard University.

———. 1956a. "Conditions of Successful Degradation Ceremonies." *American Journal of Sociology,* 61: 240–244.

———. 1956b. "Some Sociological Concepts and Methods for Psychiatrists." *Psychiatric Research Reports,* 6: 240–244.

———. 1959. "Aspects of the Problem of Commonsense Knowledge of Social Structures." *Transactions of the Fourth World Congress of Sociology,* 4: 51–65.

———. 1963. "A Conception of and Experiments with 'Trust' as a Condition of Stable Concerted Actions." In O. J. Harvey (ed.), *Motivation and Social Interaction* (pp. 187–238). New York: Ronald Press.

———. 1964. "Studies of the Routine Grounds of Everyday Activities." *Social Problems,* 11: 225–250.

———. 1967a. *Studies in Ethnomethodology.* Englewood Cliffs, N.J.: Prentice-Hall.

———. 1967b. "Practical Sociological Reasoning: Some Features in the Work of the Los Angeles Suicide Prevention Center." In E. S. Schneidman (ed.), *Essays in Self-Destruction* (pp. 171–187). New York: International Science Press.

———. 1968. Transcription of discussion in R. J. Hill and K. S. Crittenden (eds.), *Proceedings of the Purdue Symposium on Ethnomethodology.* Institute Monograph Series, No. 1, Institute for the Study of Social Change, Purdue University.

———. 1988. "Evidence for Locally Produced Naturally Accountable Phenomena of Order*, Logic, Reason, Meaning, Method, etc. in and as of the Essential Haecceity of Immortal Ordinary Society." *Sociological Theory,* 6(1): 103–109.

Garfinkel, Harold, Michael Lynch, and Eric Livingston. 1981. "The Work of a Discovering Science Construed with Materials from the Optically Discovered Pulsar." *Philosophy of the Social Sciences,* 11: 131–158.

Garfinkel, Harold, and Harvey Sacks. 1970. "On Formal Structures of Practical Actions." In J. C. McKinney and E. A. Tiryakian (eds.), *Theoretical Sociology* (pp. 338–366). New York: Appleton-Century-Crofts.

Gerth, Hans, and C. Wright Mills. 1953. *Character and Social Structure: The Psychology of Social Institutions.* New York: Harcourt, Brace.

Giddens, Anthony. 1971. *Capitalism and Modern Social Theory.* Cambridge, U.K.: Cambridge University Press.

———. 1984. *The Constitution of Society: Outline of the Theory of Structuration.* Cambridge, U.K.: Polity Press.

Goffman, Erving. 1959. *The Presentation of Self in Everyday Life.* New York: Doubleday Anchor.

———. 1961. *Asylums.* New York: Doubleday Anchor.

———. 1974. *Frame Analysis: An Essay on the Organization of Experience.* New York : Harper & Row, 1974.

———. 1983. "The Presidential Address: The Interaction Order." *American Sociological Review,* 48(1): 1–17.

Richard Grathoff (ed.). 1989. *Philosophers in Exile: The Correspondence of Alfred Schutz and Aron Gurwitsch, 1939–1959.* Translated by J. Claude Evans; foreword by Maurice Natanson. Bloomington: Indiana University Press.

Gurwitsch, Aron. 1940. "Intentionality of Consciousness." *Philosophical Essays in Memory of Edmund Husserl.* Cambridge, Mass.: Harvard University Press.

———. 1964. *Field of Consciousness.* Pittsburgh: Duquesne University Press.

———. 1966. *Studies in Phenomenology and Psychology.* Evanston, Ill.: Northwestern University Press.

———. 1974. *Phenomenology and the Theory of Science.* Edited by Lester Embree. Evanston, Ill.: Northwestern University Press.

———. 1985. *Marginal Consciousness.* Edited by Lester Embree. Athens, Ohio: Ohio University Press.

Hanfmann, Eugenia, and Jacob Kasanin. 1942. *Conceptual Thinking in Schizophrenia.* New York: Nervous and Mental Disease Monographs.

Husserl, Edmund. 1931. *Ideas: General Introduction to Pure Phenomenology.* New York: Macmillan.

———. [1942]1965. *Cartesian Meditations.* The Hague: Martinus Nijhoff.

———. 1943. "Expression and Meaning." In M. Farber (ed.), *The Foundations of Phenomenology* (pp. 222–243). Cambridge, Mass.: Harvard University Press.

James, William. 1897. *The Will to Believe, and Other Essays in Popular Philosophy.* New York: Longmans, Green, and Co.

———. 1902. *The Varieties of Religious Experience: A Study in Human Nature.* New York: Longmans, Green, and Co.

———. 1905. *The Principles of Psychology.* New York: H. Holt and Company.

———. 1907. *Pragmatism: A New Name for Some Old Ways of Thinking: Popular Lectures on Philosophy.* Cambridge, Mass.: Harvard University Press.

———. 1908. *The Energies of Men.* New York: Moffat, Yard and Company.

———. 1909a. *The Meaning of Truth, a Sequel to "Pragmatism."* New York: Longmans, Green, and Co.

———. 1909b. *Pluralistic Universe: Hibbert Lectures to Manchester College on the Present Situation in Philosophy.* New York: Longmans, Green, and Co.

———. 1912. *Essays in Radical Empiricism.* New York: Longmans, Green, and Co.

Kant, Immanuel. 1857. *The Prolegomena for Any Future Metaphysic of Morals.* Chicago: Free Press.

———. [1781]2003. *Critique of Pure Reason.* Mineola, N.Y.: Dover Publications.

———. [1788]2004. *Critique of Practical Reason.* Mineola, N.Y.: Dover Publications.

Kaufmann, Felix. 1944. *Methodology of the Social Sciences.* London: Oxford University Press.

Kuhn, Manford H., and C. Addison Hickman. 1956. *Individuals, Groups, and Economic Behavior.* New York: Dryden Press.

Marx, Karl. [1844]1956. *The Holy Family.* Moscow: Foreign Languages Publishing House.

———. [1867]1992. *Capital.* London: Penguin.

Mead, George Herbert. 1903. *The Definition of the Psychical.* Chicago: University of Chicago Press.

———. 1917. *Creative Intelligence.* New York: H. Holt and Company.

———. 1932. *The Philosophy of the Present.* Edited by Arthur E. Murphy, with prefatory remarks by John Dewey. Chicago/London: Open Court Publishing Co.

———.1934. *Mind, Self and Society: From the Standpoint of a Social Behaviorist.* Edited, with an introduction, by Charles W. Morris. Chicago: University of Chicago Press.

———. 1938. *The Philosophy of the Act.* Edited, with an introduction, by Charles W. Morris, in collaboration with John M. Brewster, Albert M. Dunham, [and] David L. Miller. Chicago: University of Chicago Press.

———. 1982. *The Individual and the Social Self: Unpublished Work of George Herbert Mead.* Edited, with an introduction, by David L. Miller. Chicago: University of Chicago Press.

Mendlovitz, Saul, H. 1975. *On the Creation of a Just World Order.* New York: Free Press.

Mills, C[harles] Wright. 1940. "Situated Actions and Vocabularies of Motives." *American Journal of Sociology,* 5: 904–913.

———. 1951. *White Collar: The American Middle Classes.* New York: Oxford University Press.

———. 1956. *The Power Elite.* New York: Oxford University Press.

Parsons, Talcott. 1937. *The Structure of Social Action.* Chicago: Free Press.

———. 1949. *Essays in Sociological Theory, Pure and Applied.* Glencoe, Ill.: Free Press.

———. 1953. *Working Papers in the Theory of Action.* Glencoe, Ill.: Free Press.

———. 1960. Structure and Process in Modern Societies. Glencoe, Ill.: Free Press.

Parsons, Talcott, and Robert F. Bales, in collaboration with James Olds [and others]. 1955. *Family, Socialization and Interaction Process.* Glencoe, Ill.: Free Press.

Peirce, Charles Sanders. 1923. *Chance, Love, and Logic.* New York: Harcourt, Brace.

———. 1972. *Charles S. Peirce: The Essential Writings.* Edited by Edward C. Moore. New York: Harper & Row.

Piaget, Jean. 1946. *Le Développement de la Notion de Temps chez l'enfant.* Paris: Presses universitaires de France.

———. 1942. *Classes, Relations et Nombres: Essai sur les Groupements de la Logistique et sur la Reversibilité de la Pensée.* Paris: J. Vrin.

———. 1948. *The Moral Judgement of the Child.* Glencoe, Ill.: Free Press.

Piaget, Jean, and Bärbel Inhelder. 1947. *La Représentation de l'espace chez l'enfant.* Paris: Presses universitaires de France.

Quine, William Van Orman. 1940. *Mathematical Logic.* New York: W. W. Norton.

Rawls, Anne Warfield. 1987. "The Interaction Order Sui Generis: Goffman's Contribution to Social Theory." *Sociological Theory,* 5(2): 136–149.

———. 1990. "Emergent Sociality: A Dialectic of Commitment and Order." *Symbolic Interaction,* 13(1): 63–82.

———. 1989. "Language, Self, and Social Order: A Re-evaluation of Goffman and Sacks." *Human Studies,* 12(1): 147–172.

———. 1996a. "Durkheim's Epistemology: The Initial Critique 1915–1924." *Sociological Quarterly,* 38(1): 111–145.

———. 1996b. "Durkheim's Epistemology: The Neglected Argument." *American Journal of Sociology,* 102(2): 430–482.

———. 1997. "Durkheim and Pragmatism: An Old Twist on a New Problem." *Sociological Theory,* 15(1): 5–29.

———. 2000. "Race as an Interaction Order Phenomena: W.E.B. DuBois's 'Double Consciousness' Thesis Revisited." *Sociological Theory,* 18(2): 239–272.

———. 2002. "Introduction" to *Ethnomethodology's Program: Working Out Durkheim's Aphorism,* by Harold Garfinkel. Boulder, Colo.: Rowman and Littlefield.

———. 2003a. "Conflict as a Foundation for Consensus: Contradictions of Capitalism in Durkheim's *Division of Labor in Society.*" *Critical Sociology.*

———. 2003b. "Orders of Interaction and Intelligibility: Intersections Between Goffman and Garfinkel by Way of Durkheim." In Javier Trevino (ed.), *Goffman's Legacy.* Boulder, Colo.: Rowman and Littlefield.

———. 2004a. *Epistemology and Practice: Durkheim's The Elementary Forms.* Cambridge, U.K.: Cambridge University Press.

———. 2004b. "Situated Practice and Modernity: Practice vs Concepts" (in French translation). *The Mauss Review.*

———. 2005. "Garfinkel's Conception of Time." *Time and Society,* 14(2/3): 163–190.

Reisman, David. 1950. *The Lonely Crowd.* Harvard University Press.

Sacks, Harvey. 1992. *Lectures in Conversation,* Vols. I and II. Oxford: Blackwell Press.

Sacks, Harvey, Emmanuel Schegloff, and Gail Jefferson. 1974. "A Simplest Systematics for the Organization of Turn-Taking in Conversation." *Language,* 50(4): 696–735.

Scheler, Max. 1970. *The Nature of Sympathy.* Hamden, Conn.: Archon Books.

Schutz, Alfred. 1945. "On Multiple Realities." *Philosophy and Phenomenological Research* (June): 533–575.

———. 1962. *The Collected Papers I: The Problem of Social Reality.* The Hague: Martinus Nijhoff.

Skinner, B[urrhus] F[rederic]. 1957. *Verbal Behavior.* New York: Appleton-Century-Crofts.

Strauss, Anselm L., and Barney G. Glaser. 1967. *The Discovery of Grounded Theory: Strategies for Qualitative Research.* Chicago: Aldine.

Sykes, Gresham. 1958. *Society of Captives.* Princeton: Princeton University Press.

Szasz, Thomas Stephen. 1970. *The Manufacture of Madness: A Comparative Study of the Inquisition and the Mental Health Movement.* New York: Harper & Row.

Thomas, W[illiam] I[saac]. 1903. *The Relation of the Medicine-Man to the Origin of the Professional Occupations.* Chicago: University of Chicago Press.

———. 1909. *Source Book for Social Origins: Ethnological Materials, Psychological Standpoint, Classified and Annotated Bibliographies for the Interpretation of Savage Society.* Chicago: University of Chicago Press.

———. 1937. *Primitive Behavior: An Introduction to the Social Sciences.* New York/London: McGraw-Hill.

———. 1967. *The Unadjusted Girl: Cases and Standpoint for Behavior Analysis.* Introduction by Michael Parenti. Edited and with a foreword by Benjamin Nelson. New York: Harper & Row.

Thomas, W[illiam] I[saac], and Dorothy Swaine Thomas. 1928. *The Child in America: Behavior Problems and Programs.* New York: A. A. Knopf.

Thomas, W[illiam] I[saac], and Florian Znaniecke. 1958. *The Polish Peasant in Europe and America.* New York: Dover.

Weber, Max. [1904]1930. *The Protestant Ethic and the Spirit of Capitalism.* Translated by Talcott Parsons, with a foreword by R. H. Tawney. New York: Scribner.

————. 1921/1968. *Economy and Society.* Berkeley: University of California Press.

Whorf, Benjamin Lee. 1949. *Four Articles on Metalinguistics.* Washington, D.C.: Department of State, Foreign Service Institute.

————. 1952. *Collected Papers on Metalinguistics.* Washington, D.C.: Department of State, Foreign Service Institute.

————. 1956. *Language, Thought, and Reality: Selected Writings.* Edited and introduced by John B. Carroll. Cambridge, Mass.: Massachusetts Institute of Technology Press.

Wittgenstein, Ludwig. [1933]1958. *Preliminary Studies for the "Philosophical Investigations," Generally Known as the Blue and Brown Books.* Oxford: Blackwell.

————. 1953. *Philosophical Investigations.* Translated by G.E.M. Anscombe. Oxford: Blackwell.

Wright, Bonnie, and Anne Warfield Rawls. 2005. "The Dialectics of Beliefs and Practice: Religious Process as Praxis." *Critical Sociology,* 31(1/2): 187–211.

Znaniecki, Florian. 1919. *Cultural Reality.* Chicago: University of Chicago Press.

————. 1925. *The Laws of Social Psychology.* Chicago: University of Chicago Press.

————. 1936. *Social Actions.* New York: Farrar & Rinehart.

Index

accountable orders, 82, 86
actions, 3, 28, 50, 115, 118
  continuity of, 171
  and culture, 86–87
  definition, 101–7
  details of, 13–14
  functional consequences of, 193–94
  and group membership, 192–93
  identity as location for, 75
  and incongruities, 211
  interconnectedness of, 189
  library guards, 22–24, 27, 77,
    94nn17–18, 110–12
  as location, 74–75
  and meaning-relevant behavior,
    136–37
  modes of, 146
  motivations for, 19–21
  noesis-noema structures, 107, 118,
    132–45
  objects of, 171
  overt and covert, 103–4
  and practices, 94n19
  regularities of, 190–91
  scientific description of, 11–18
  and social identity, 145–51
  structures of, 138
  and style of communication,
    182–88
  subject of action concept, 73,
    168–69
  system of, 192
  theory of, 136–37
  and thesis problems, 205–16
  views of, 4, 19
  within social systems, 189–90
  See also situated actions
"Actor, Situation and Normative
  Pattern" (Parsons), 141
actor-corporation, 196–97
actor-person, 196–97
actors, 16, 27, 113–14
  actor-situation schema, 138–39
  bracketing the world, 124, 126, 141,
    142
  and cognitive style, 193–94, 202–3
  and communication, 39–41, 179–88
  and expectations, 172–73
  and the group as situated order,
    42–52
  as group members, 50–52
  as identified self, 170–71
  and identity, 68, 71, 153
  and mode of attention to life, 112
  and motivation, 19–21, 74–75
  and objects, 140–42
  observers as, 175–79
  power and force of, 53–54
  and reification of self, 72–73
  relationship between two actors,
    79–80, 194
  roles and motives of, 50–52
  and sequential responses, 71–72,
    76–78
  as set of procedural rules, 80–81
  and social identity, 145–51

actors *(continued)*
  and social relationships, 190–91
  and subjectivity, 60–61
  taking the role of the Other, 71–72,
    75–79
  term usage, 107–17
  and traffic controls, 199–202
  and transformation schemes, 154
  views of, 4
  and vivid present, 36–37
  and working acts, 56–57
  See also situated actors
affectual structures, 143–44
aggregation, 189, 191, 194
Alger, Horatio, 157
Allport, F. H., 195
alpha transformation schemes,
    153–54, 162–64
animal symbolicum, 110, 166, 170,
    175, 180
  and actor's universe, 117
  as concept, 107, 108, 110
apodictic structures, 63, 119, 137–38,
    141
army regulations, and labeling of sick
    soldiers, 68–71, 154–56, 158,
    160–61
Arnold, Matthew, 182
attention, modes of, 214
  and actors, 112
  and relationship of objects and
    consciousness, 62–66
  and social practices, 64–65,
    96nn38–39
  vs. consciousness, 59–60
  and working acts, 63–65, 96n39

behaviors
  to confirm identities, 70
  expressional aspects of, 183
  and identities, 70
  meaning-relevant, 136–37
  observable aspects of, 26

beta transformation schemes, 153–54,
    174–75
bias, actors vs. investigators, 185–86
bodily movements, 104, 115–16,
    181–82
Bourdieu, Pierre, 26
bracketing of the world, 124, 126, 141,
    142
Brown, J. F., 192
bureaucratization, 173
Burke, Kenneth, 14, 93n12, 130, 158,
    182
buses, and situated action, 14–15,
    93n13

capitalism, 83
categories, validity of, 137
chairs, interaction with, 35, 36, 37,
    106, 146, 179–80
character, and social structure in
    prisons, 8–9
Chomsky, Noam, 91n5
class
  concept of, 189
  membership in, 192
cognitive styles, 67, 107
  and actors, 193–94, 202–3
  characteristics of, 125
  and composition of group, 43–44
  concepts of, 56, 96n34
  and experiencing self, 110, 115–16
  features of, 110, 112–15
  and observers, 175–79
  and role of physicians, 156
  Schutz's views on, 24–28
  and scientific investigations, 165–66
  and social groups, 202–3
  and social identity, 145
  and sociality, 110, 113–14
  and spontaneity, 114
  and thesis problems, 206–9
  time perspective, 110, 115–16
  vs. situated orders of practice, 24–28

communication, 3, 106, 179–82
  ambiguities in, 32
  and the group, 43–44
  interpretation of, 34–36, 95*n*26
  sequential communication, 7,
    91–92*nn*5–6
  significance of identities to, 174
  and social action, 147
  somatic, 183–84
  style, tactics, and strategies of,
    39–41, 182–88
  theory of, 78–79, 179–82
  use of term, 6–7, 91*n*5
  views of, 29–44, 94–95*nn*22–27
communicative interactions, 13–14,
  29–41, 94–95*nn*22–27
communities of practice, 1, 91*n*1
concepts
  and mode of attention, 64–65,
    96*nn*38–39
  and reality, 62
  and sequential communication, 7
conceptual reduction, 3, 12, 13
conceptual types, 13–14
concrete persons, 48, 57, 180, 195
conduct, term usage, 103–4
consciousness, 135
  Husserl's conception of, 135
  and reflexivity, 34
  relationship to objects, 62–66,
    96*nn*38–40
  and subjectivity and objectivity,
    60–61
  vs. social aspects of modes of
    attention, 59–60
consciousness, modes of, 17, 24, 62,
  112, 124
  and embedding of identities in
    practice, 25
  and observers, 126–27
  and relationship between two
    actors, 79–80
constancy, identity, 151–79

The Constitution of Society (Giddens),
  74
continuity, 119, 153, 171, 202
conversational sequencing, 29–41,
  94–95*nn*22–27
conversations
  accounting practices in, 14–15,
    93*n*12
  tactics found in, 186–88
  and vivid present of actor's working
    acts, 36–37
coordinate systems, 155, 156–58
corporations, 47–48, 195–97
covert actions, 103–4
culture, 36–37, 84, 95*n*25
  as collective symbolism, 84
  and social forms, 85
  and traditional societies, 86–87

data
  empirical, 105, 106, 110
  problematic, 105
  relationship of observer to, 205–6
day dreams, 104, 117
defining device, 173
Dewey, John, 3, 54–55
  critique of, 56, 79–81
  and the public mind, 192
  and the situated actor, 79–81
Dictionary of Occupational Titles, 147,
  150–51
directly experienced objects, 178–79
discounting device, 173
doctors, 159–60
  and labeling of sick soldiers, 68–71,
    160–61
  relationship to patients, 68–71,
    154–56, 158
dreams, 156
duree, 36, 116, 125, 181, 182, 199
Durkheim, Emile, 45, 59, 87
  Division of Labor, 9
  and justice, 88

Durkheim, Emile *(continued)*
and practices, 84–85, 97n46
and social facts, 90
and society, 44

effort, 7
ego-principle, 117–18
empirical data, 105, 106, 110
empirical theorizing, 88–89
enlisted men, 182
epistemology, principles of, 102
epithets, 150
epoche, 110, 112–13, 124, 193, 213, 214
ethnocentrism, 6, 12
Ethnomethodology, 1, 57, 75, 89, 90
exchange process, 30–32, 94n22
expectations, 148, 172–73
experiences
continuity of, 119–20
elements in, 118–19
essentially actual, 103
explanation of, 117–18
and incongruities, 212–13
intentional, 102, 104–6
interpretation of, 103
meaning of, 125–26
organization of, 124
and social identity, 146
structures of, 138–39, 139
temporal, 123–24
experience structures, 206
experiments
experimental design and thesis
problems, 213
experimental method, 34, 95n25
post-experimental interviews,
210–11
pre-experimental program, 208–10,
211
expressional fields, 181–82
Expression and Meaning (Husserl),
132

expressions, symbolic, 104, 105,
106

fantasies, 81, 157–58
force, of groups, 42, 53–54
formal institutions, 46, 47
frame/frame of reference, 136,
141–43, 151, 172
Freud, Sigmund, 130, 156, 158

Garfinkel, Harold, 8, 99–216
avoidance of interaction as term,
6–7
communicative interaction and
conversational sequencing, 29–41
concept of sequential time, 7,
91–92nn5–6
group as situated order, 42–52,
95n30
interest in problem of scientific
description of action, 11–18
and morality of trust, 9
power and force relationships,
53–54
reliance on Schutz, 4–5
on situated action and situated
actors, 18–28, 94nn17–19
use of communication as term, 6–7,
91n5
views on Parson's action frame of
reference, 12–13
views on reflexivity, 17–18
Garfinkel (2002), 21, 48
Giddens, Anthony, 74, 90
The Gift (Mauss), 87
goals, 23, 40–41
Goffman, Erving, 2, 57, 85–86, 95n27
reaction to Garfinkel's dissertation,
3–4
views of order, 88
group, 54–59, 81
definition, 189–90, 199
group synthesis, 51

membership in, 50–52, 60–61, 80, 192–93
one member group, 189, 193–94
power and force of, 53–54
as situated order, 42–52, 95*n*30
and working acts, 197–99
guard identity, 21–24, 94*nn*17–18
Gurwitsch, Aaron, 3, 18, 133, 135

habitus, 26
Hanfmann, Eugenia, 130
Harvard University
  Garfinkel's experience at, 15–16, 18–19
  Weidner Library guard, 21–24, 27, 77, 94*nn*17–18, 110–12
heads-I-win-tails-you-lose arrangement, 162, 164, 165
heuristic devices, 145
homicide, and race, 15, 93*n*14
horizons, 120, 121–22, 124, 130, 150
Husserl, Edmund, 59, 102, 137, 138
  and bodily movements, 115–16
  compared with Parsons's views of objects, 141
  and elements in experiences, 118–19
  noesis-noema structures, 107, 118, 132–45
  and structures of experience, 139
hyletic elements, 120, 152

Icheiser, Gustav, 184
Ideas (Husserl), 138
identity, 133
  behavior to confirm, 70
  cataloging of, 147
  library guard, 21–24, 94*nn*17–18
  as location for action, 75
  meaning of, 77, 147
  and norms, 22–23, 114
  occupational, 147, 150–51
  of opponents, 163–64

as part of situated action, 50
Peirce's views of, 145–46
racial, 78
relationship to temporality, 135–36
significance to communication, 174
and situated practices, 22–24
social identity, 145–51
as social ordering, 55
soldiers, 68–71, 154–56
and state of being in action, 56
identity claims, 60–61
identity constancy, 151–79
identity transformation, 151–79
identity work, 13–14, 21
incongruities, 19, 27, 212–16
individualism, 12, 43, 57, 72, 75
individuals
  focus on, 83–84
  Garfinkel's concern about, 86
  limitations of, 54–55
  and projects, 19
  role in interaction, 89–90
  and subjectivity, 60
  and values, 86
instructed action, 13, 92–93*n*11
intentionality theory, 133, 135
interactionism, 83, 87
interactionists, 46–47
interactions, 7, 36
  accounting practices in, 14–15, 93*n*12
  Garfinkel's avoidance of term, 6–7
  Garfinkel's views of, 55
  indeterminacy in, 95*n*26
  orderliness of, 25, 30–32
  order of, 11
  power and force of, 53–54
  and reflexivity, 17–18, 33–35
  role of individuals in, 88–89
  sequential orders of, 30–32
  and tactics and strategies, 40
  See also communications; communicative interactions

interpretations, and sequential time
for interactions, 36
intersubjectivity, 20
interviews
post-experimental, 210–11
statistical manipulation of, 12
introduction, aims of, 8–9
investigations
bias in, 185–86
considerations for, 153
premises of action, 178
of social order, 6
see also scientific investigations
"is," use of term, 171

James, William, 3, 54–55, 58, 62, 125
consciousness vs. social aspects of
attention modes, 59–60
and radical empiricism, 140
views of order, 85
justice, 85, 88

Kant, Immanuel, 41, 82
Kaufmann, Felix, 205
Kuhn, Thomas Samuel, 120, 121, 122

labeling theory, and sick soldiers,
68–71
language, picture theory of, 96n38
Language and Thought in Schizophrenia
(Van Domarus), 159
library guards, 22–24, 27, 77, 94nn17–
18, 110–14, 170–71
location
action as, 74–75
and object perception, 61
and self, 73
Lonely Crowd, 8–9

manipulation criteria, 146–47
manipulatory areas, 112
Marx, Karl, 59–60, 96n37
Mauss, Marcel, 87

Mead, George Herbert, 3, 54–56,
94n22
and manipulatory area, 112
and motivation problems, 73–75,
97n43
and reification of the self, 72–73
and taking the role of the other,
75–79
meaning-relevant behavior theory, 136
meanings, 57, 106–7
and culture, 86–87
determinate, 213
of directly experienced object,
178–79
focus on, 83
Husserl's views of, 132–33
of identity, 77, 147
imminent dynamism of, 129–30
as interpretation of past
experiences, 103
meaning-situation, 132–33
of objectivity, 140
of reification, 152
role and concept of meaning,
117–32
and social identity, 148
unity of, 213
means-ends chains, 138–39
meditation, 126
mental economy, 131
Methodology of the Social Sciences
(Kaufmann), 205
micro sociology, 57
Mills, C. Wright, 83, 93n12
minority identity, 61
modes-of-orientation-situation-of-
objects, 139–40
morality, 85, 87, 97n46
civil morality of trust, 8–9
and justice, 88
studies of, 8–9
moral reciprocity, 82
motivation, 202

of actors, 19–21, 50–52
and Mead vs. Garfinkel, 73–75,
    97*n*43
motivational schemes, 90, 164
problems with, 104, 169
and situated actors, 79–81
sources of, 169–70
theories of, 113, 148–50, 169
and working acts, 80
mutual exchanges, 77–79
mutual understanding, 30, 81–82

naming device, 172, 173
natural attitude, 47–49, 127–28,
    195–96
noemata, 107, 118, 120, 121, 132–45
noesis-noema structures, 107, 132–45
and style, 183
theory of, 118
and thesis problem, 206–7, 209
non-empirical reality, 146, 147
norms
of activity, 208–9
and behavior as exhibit of, 70
employment of, 160
Garfinkel's meaning of, 22–23
and identities, 114
identities generation of, 70
and identity, 22, 23
and tactics and strategies, 40–41

objectivity, 60–61, 92–93*n*11
Husserl's views of, 132–33
meaning of, 140–41
in research, 16, 93*n*15
objects, 54–59, 61
and actors, 140–42
directly experienced, 178–79
identity as a real objects, 71–72
identity as object vs. symbolic
    object, 66–68
intrinsic structure of, 122
isolated objects, 122

modes-of-orientation-situation-of-
    objects, 139–40
and the neoma, 133–34
observer's conception of, 139–40
as order of nature, 139
persons as ideal object, 195–98
relationship with consciousness,
    62–66, 96*nn*38–40
and social identity, 145–51
symbolic, 55–58, 146
observers
and cognitive style, 175–79
conception of objects, 139–40
and mode of consciousness, 126–27
and objectivity, 60–61
and premises of action, 202–3
relationship to data, 205–6
and subject of action, 73
and tactics of communication, 185
terms used by, 173
of working acts, 16–18
occupational identities, 147, 150–51
office workers and managers, 51–52
"On Multiple Realities" (Schütz), 110,
    125, 205
ontological schemes, 168
ontological status, 71
opponents, identity of, 163–64
ordering systems, 29, 57, 130
emergent order theories, 19, 93*n*16
James's views of, 85
orderliness, 81–82
order of nature concept, 141
orientation, and noesis-noema
    structure, 142–43
the other
identity of, 194
other-oriented character, 85, 88
and social identity, 145–51
taking role of, 71–72, 75–79
overt actions, 103–4

Parsons, Talcott, 3, 59, 83

Parsons, Talcott *(continued)*
  action frame of reference, 12–13
  compared with Husserl's views of
    objects, 141
  and conceptual reduction, 12, 13
  focus on actions, 40
  and norms, 22
  Parson's Plenum, 21
  and social organization, 62–66,
    96nn38–40
  and structures of action, 138
  theory of action, 136–37
Peirce, Charles Sanders, 3, 55, 66–68,
  145–46
perceptions, 134
performance, 104
person
  as concept, 193
  meaning of, 109
  as unity of different roles, 42
personality, 145
Phenomenology, 2, 14, 25, 63, 83
Philosophy of Literary Form (Burke),
  130
physiological reflexes, 103
Piaget, Jean, 159
pieties, 130, 131
power, of groups, 42, 53–54
practices
  and actions, 94n19
  actor as location for, 21
  civil morality of, 8–9
  and cognitive styles vs. situated
    orders of practice, 24–28, 94n19
  focus on, 82–83
  and morality, 86, 97n46
  orders of, 76, 82
  and projects, 27
  reciprocities of, 87
  self-regulating, 84–85
  shared, 92n9
  studies of, 54–55
pragmatism, 2, 92n10

criticism of, 83
  Garfinkel's views of, 54–59
  and morality, 86
  and radical empiricism, 59–60
praxeological validity, 13, 92n10
prejudice, 61
prisons, social character in, 8–9
projects
  Garfinkel's views of, 19, 93n16
  and individuals, 19
  and practices, 27
  recognizability of, 7
  successful completion of, 55
  vs. tactics and strategies, 39–41
psychiatry, l, 164–65
public encounters, 210
public justice, 9

Quine, Willard Van Orman, 130

race
  and homicide cases, 15, 93n14
  racial identities, 78
  and situated actions, 14–15
radical empiricism, 59–60, 62, 140
Rawls, Anne, 1–97
reality
  correspondence theory of, 137, 165
  James's views of, 125
  and mode of attention, 62
  modes of, 65
  non-empirical, 147
  origin of, 60–61
  reality designation, 173
  social construction of, 46–47
  of social identity as an object, 146
reciprocity, 40, 41, 88
referents, 150–51, 158, 159, 161, 193
  of action, 107
  empirical, 110
reflexivity, 17–18, 33–35
reification, 47–50
  meaning of, 152

of the person, 71, 73–75
of person and social action, 57
of person and social roles, 55
of the self, 72–73
Reisman, David, 8–9, 85–86, 88, 94*n*17
relevant possibility, 121
research, 88–89
and adequate scientific
descriptions, 13, 92–93*n*11
assumptions made in, 106
experience structures, 66, 96*n*40
objectivity in, 16, 93*n*15
proposed by Garfinkel, 11, 205–16
See also scientific investigations
"A Research Note on Inter and Intra
Racial Homicide" (Garfinkel), 15
responses, 103
rituals, 84
roles, 42
actor as a mosaic of, 192
of actors, 50–52
actors within, 141–42
and concept of meaning, 117–32
conflicts in, 79
features of, 110, 112–15
Garfinkel's rejection of, 55–56
self as configuration of, 80
self as container for, 75–76
sequential responses vs. taking role
of the other, 71–72
and situated actors, 79–81
"The Routine Grounds of Practical
Action" (Garfinkel), 8
rules, 58, 110–12

Sacks, Harvey, 2, 11
sales representatives, 209–10
Scheler, Max, 138, 139
schizophrenics, 105–6
Schütz, Alfred, 3, 18, 59, 126, 127, 137,
141
and cognitive style, 24–28
and conceptual types, 13–14

focus on projects, 40
"On Multiple Realities", 110, 125,
205
and social organization, 62–66,
96*nn*38–40
scientific attitude, 63–64
and individual behavior, 70
and reification, 47–50
scientific investigations, 102
actor-person vs. actor-corporation,
195–97
and cognitive style, 165–66
and description of action, 11–18
interpretation of actions, 104–5
stating of problem, 127
See also research
scientific sociology, 16, 93*n*15
scientists, and scientific discoveries,
48–49, 95*n*30
selection device, 173
self
and cognitive style, 110, 115–16
formulations of, 55
identified Self, 174–75, 194
and motivation problems, 73–75
as object vs. symbolic object, 67–68
reification of, 72–73
representation of, 170–71
segmental self, 56, 79
sequential responses vs. taking role
of the other, 71–72
and social identity, 145–51
working self, 115, 116
self-awareness, 214
sequential communication, 7,
91–92*nn*5–6
sequential conversations. *See*
conversational sequencing
sequential responses, 71–72, 76–78
Shaw, Bernard, 196
sick soldiers, labeling of, 68–71,
154–56, 158, 160–61
signposts, 35–37, 37, 95*n*25

signs, 30
    and communication, 179–81, 184
    Husserl's views of, 132
situated actions, 18–25, 28, 82,
        94nn17–19
    and bus boarding, 14–15, 93n13
    coordination of, 86
    order of, 75
    power and force of, 53–54
    and tactics and strategies, 40
situated actors, 18–25, 54–59, 79–81,
        94nn17–19
    and the group, 44
    and order of sequences, 7
situated identities, 19–20, 28, 48
    and group membership, 60–61
    and identity work, 21
    and practices, 22–24, 93n18
    and social action, 47
    and social order, 56
    and tactics and strategies, 38
    treating actors as, 27
    See also cognitive styles
situated orders, 82
    group as, 42–52, 95n30
    material vs. conceptual character of,
        25
    vs. cognitive styles, 24–28
situated practices, 3, 28, 91n1
    and actions of library guard, 22–24
    and emergent order theory, 19,
        93n16
    and identity, 22–24, 93n18
    and shared values, 87
    and strategies, 40
Skinner, B.F., 91n5
social actions, 13–14, 55, 96n33
    definition, 194
    details of, 6
    routine grounds of, 8
    structure of, 58
    and transformation schemes, 160
social construction of reality, 46–47

social groups, and cognitive style,
        202–3
social identity, 66–68, 145–51
sociality
    forms of, 110, 113–14, 154, 191,
        193, 214
    representation of, 175–76
    and thesis problems, 208–9
social orders, 6
    creation of, 56–57
    focus on, 83
    and mode of attention, 64–65
    and motivation, 21, 75, 97n43
    and mutual intelligibility, 44–45
    and situated identity, 56
    and tactics and strategies, 40–41
    theory of, 81–82
social organization, 62–66, 96nn38–40
social practices, understanding of, 16,
        93n15
social processes, motivation to engage
        in, 74
social relationships
    and actor's conduct, 190–91
    and cognitive style, 202–3
    and identity as object vs. symbolic
        object, 66–68
    Marx's views of, 59–60, 96n37
social scientists, 75
social systems, 70, 189–90
social types, 145
sociology, teaching of, 14, 15–16
soldiers, labeling of, 68–71, 154–56,
        158, 160–61
somatic communications, 183–84
speech, 38
spontaneity, 213, 214
    form of, 113, 141
    and thesis problems, 208–9
spontaneous life, 102, 103, 104–6
standardization device, 173
statisticians, 164
status systems, responses of, 164–65

Stimulus Response theory, 6–7, 26, 33, 179
strategies, 37–41, 95*n*27, 184–88
Strauss, Anselm, 2
Strong, Samuel, 145
The Structure of Social Action (Parsons), 15, 137
style, 38–39
style of communication, 182–84
subjectivism, 136
subjectivity, 60–61, 96*n*38
subject of action concept, 73, 168–69
supply and demand, 96*n*37
surveys, statistical manipulation of, 12
symbolic actions, 113, 130
Symbolic Interactionism, 57, 91*n*2
symbolic objects, 66–68, 146
symbolism, 147, 159
  and the actors, 108
  culture as collective symbolism, 84
  and social actions, 194–95
  as visual presentation of concepts, 166–70, 174–78
symbols, 92*n*10
  and conversational sequencing, 29
  interpretation of, 31
  meaning of, 29
  and motivation, 20–21
  symbolic expressions, 104–6
  symbolic objects, 55
  symbol treater, 20, 21, 31, 38
sympathetic introspection, 176–78

tactics, 37–41, 95*n*27, 184–88
"taken-for-granted" character, 23–24, 28
temporality, 135–36
temporal ordering, 38
theoretical attitude
  and individual behavior, 70
  and reification, 47–50, 59–60, 96*n*37
thinking, 104
Thomas, W. I., 14

time organizing device, 173
time perspectives, 110, 115–16, 213, 214
traffic controls, 199–202
transformation schemes, 58, 153–54
  and doctors and patients, 156, 158
  of fantasies, 157–58
  of identity, 152–53
  procedural rules of, 159–61
  and social actions, 160
  and treatment tactics, 161–62
treatments
  conditions of, 109–10
  and transformation schemes, 161–62
trust, 9, 30, 88, 94–95*n*23
truth, and subjectivity and objectivity, 61
typifications, 76, 90

unique adequacy, 92–93*n*11
Unit Act, 40, 142
University of North Carolina, Sociology Department, 14
utility, test of, 49
utterances, 45

validity, 30
  of categories, 137
  praxeological, 13, 92*n*10
  and shared practices, 92*n*9
values
  and activities of individuals, 86
  behavior as exhibit of, 70
  shared, 87
  of structures, 143–44
visual images, 120–21
vivid present, 36–37, 181, 182
  and actions, 115
  and actors, 36, 48
  dimensions of, 65, 128
  of working acts, 47
Von Domarus, Alexander, 159

Weber, Max, 137
Whorf, Benjamin, 130
Wittgenstein, Ludwig, 83, 84
work, 11, 12, 92*n*9
working acts, 16–17, 56
   and groups, 45–46, 197–99
   and mode of attention, 63–64,
     96*n*39
   and motivation, 80–81, 148–49
   others treatment of, 78

scientists' interest in, 49, 95*n*30
   and tactics and strategies, 39–41
   as vehicle of communication,
     180–81
   and vivid present, 36–37
   and working self, 116
working consensus, 85

Znieneickei, Florian, 14

About the Author and Editor

Harold Garfinkel is Professor Emeritus of Sociology at UCLA and the author of the classic book *Studies in Ethnomethodology.*

Anne Warfield Rawls, Associate Professor of Sociology at Bentley College, Massachusetts, is the author of *Epistemology and Practice: Durkheim's the Elementary Forms of Religious Life* (Cambridge University Press, 2004).